THE TRINITY:
THE PER

Continuum's Guides for the Perplexed are clear, concise and accessible introductions to thinkers, writers and subjects that students and readers can find especially challenging. Concentrating specifically on what it is that makes the subject difficult to grasp, these books explain and explore key themes and ideas, guiding the reader towards a thorough understanding of demanding material.

GUIDES FOR THE PERPLEXED AVAILABLE FROM CONTINUUM:

THE TRINITY: A GUIDE FOR THE PERPLEXED

PAUL M. COLLINS

continuum

Published by T & T Clark

A Continuum imprint

The Tower Building   80 Maiden Lane
11 York Road   Suite 704
London SE1 7NX   New York NY10038

www.continuumbooks.com

© Paul M. Collins 2008

Paul Collins has asserted his right under the Copyright, Designs and Patents Act, 1988, to be identified as the Author of this work.

British Library Cataloguing-in-Publication Data
A catalogue record for this book is available from the British Library.

ISBN-10: HB: 0–567–03184–5
PB: 0–567–03185–3

ISBN-13: HB: 978–0–567–03184–6
PB: 978–0–567–03185–3

Library of Congress Cataloging-in-Publication Data
A catalog record for this book is available from the Library of Congress.

Typeset by RefineCatch Limited, Bungay, Suffolk
Printed on acid-free paper in Great Britain by MPG Books Ltd, Bodmin, Cornwall

CONTENTS

ACKNOWLEDGEMENTS

The argument developed in the 'Critique of relationality' in Chapter 2 is parallel with the argument I develop in my essay 'Communion: God, Creation and Church' published in Paul M. Collins and Michael Fahey (eds), *Receiving: The Nature and Mission of the Church* (London and New York: T. & T. Clark, 2008). The argument developed in the sections on personhood and perichoresis in Chapter 3; and 'Trinity: Immanent and Economic' in Chapter 4, is partially dependent on material in my book *Trinitarian Theology West and East: Karl Barth, the Cappadocian Fathers and John Zizioulas* (Oxford: Oxford University Press, 2001). The extract from the text of the Athanasian Creed in the Afterword is published with permission: extracts from the Book of Common Prayer, the rights in which are vested in the Crown, are reproduced by permission of the Crown's Patentee, Cambridge University Press.

ABBREVIATIONS

NRSV   *New Revised Standard Version* of the Holy Bible
            (Anglicised Edition) (Oxford: Oxford University
            Press, 1995).
RSV   *Revised Standard Version* of the Holy Bible (London:
            Collins, 1973).
MPG   Migne, J.-P., *Patrologia Graeca* (Paris: Garnier
            Fratres, 1855–66).
MPL   Migne, J.-P., *Patrologia Latina* (Paris: Garnier
            Fratres, 1844–55).

INTRODUCTION

The Christian doctrine of the Triune God has been the touchstone of the modern mainstream ecumenical movement since its inception, and adherence to an orthodoxy expressed in the Nicene Creed is usually required of churches seeking to become a member of a council of churches or a 'Churches Together' body. Yet, in 1989, after six years' work, a study commission of the British Council of Churches published in three volumes *The Forgotten Trinity*.[1] The perceived needs that inspired the setting up of the Commission and the resultant publications rested upon what was understood to be a widespread feeling that the doctrine of the Trinity was irrelevant. This feeling was focused by three imperatives cited in the Introduction to Volume I of the trilogy. They were (a) a fresh examination of the creed of 381 AD following upon its 1600th anniversary (prompted by the Russian Orthodox Church in Britain); (b) the request to follow up questions which emerged from the Faith and Order Commission document *Spirit of God, Spirit of Christ* (1981); and (c) the British Council of Churches itself deciding to focus more upon issues of faith and order.[2] Alongside these imperatives, there was also the recognition that the phenomena of the charismatic movement and its focus on the person of the Holy Spirit, in itself, raised questions about who the God of the Christians is understood to be. The three imperatives, together with the experience of charismatic renewal, provide a useful cluster of issues which this guide will seek in different ways to address, such as the evolution and reception of the creedal statements of the doctrine of the Trinity and the relationship between doctrine and the Christian life and Church. The need to reflect theologically on charismatic renewal, which is experienced in all the mainstream churches, gives a crucial focus to the desire to (re)understand the doctrine of the Trinity in relation to the relevance of Trinitarian reflection in the present day. The issue of the relevance of the doctrine of the Trinity emerged in sharp focus at the time of the Reformation and was compounded by the rationalism of the Enlightenment period, which continues to the present time. The perception that the concept of the Trinity is merely speculative, and possibly a distraction, has shaped the landscape of theological discourse in the West for the past four centuries at least. In my view, the appeal to social Trinitarianism, in particular in Western theological traditions, in the latter part of the twentieth century, has been made in response to the feeling that 'the Trinity' is irrelevant. This guide will chart this appeal to social Trinitarianism in contemporary theological and ecumenical discourse. It will also seek to investigate and explicate features of the doctrinal landscape across the centuries and across the different strands of the Christian tradition. Reflection on the experience of charismatic renewal opens up another core component of the guide, in relation to what has been called the 'world of particulars'.[3] An appeal to the world of particulars may offer a response to the issue of relevance by appealing not so much to speculation about the inner life of the Godhead as to the experience of the Christian life in the present and past.

The doctrine of the Trinity raises many questions, but not least the question of monotheism. If a core tenet of Christian belief is that God is three (as well as one), to what extent is it a monotheistic religion? Such New Testament passages as the baptismal formula at the close of Matthew's Gospel (28.19) as well as the closing salutation of the second letter to the Corinthians (13.13), suggest that there had been an 'early Christian mutation' from the strict monotheism of Judaism.[4] Such a recognition raises serious questions about how to understand and situate the Christian faith and the Christian Church vis-à-vis other world religions. There is a widespread consensus that Christianity should be situated alongside Judaism and Islam as a major monotheistic faith, sharing a common ancestor in that faith: Abraham. However, it might be just as appropriate to situate Christianity alongside 'Hinduism' – not in the sense that there is, as some have argued (wrongly I would suggest) a 'Hindu' trinity: of Brahma, Vishnu and Shiva, but rather in the sense that the belief of Hindus includes the perception that the divine is both differentiated and yet 'one'. Furthermore, such a perception is at least partly rooted in the understanding that the divine can and does become manifest or incarnated in the world. I do not want to suggest that there is detailed comparability between Christianity and

Hinduism. But the shared perception that the divine is differentiated, rather than monolithic, allows that the two faith systems might be situated together. This does not mean that the notion of the Abrahamic faiths is something to be jettisoned, but it does suggest that there may be a variety of ways of understanding and situating faith systems. John of Damascus, through his work *De fide orthodoxa*, gives a clear reminder of the difference between Christianity and Islam. To situate Christianity only in terms of Judaism and Islam could be construed as a forgetting of 'the inconvenient Trinity'.

The response to the doctrine of the Trinity within the Christian tradition has varied widely. On the whole, Christian theologians have continued to reflect on the claims of the councils of Nicaea and Constantinople as core moments in the effecting of the Christian tradition. Schleiermacher, the so-called father of liberal Protestantism, in offering his response to the Enlightenment critique of Christian believing nonetheless retained a notion that the Christian understanding of God is Trinitarian. In *The Christian Faith*, he clearly sets out both the necessity and ambiguity of the 'doctrine of the Trinity'.[5] Karl Barth, in his rejection of liberal Protestantism in preference for 'Neo-Orthodoxy', begins his theological endeavour in a central appeal to 'Nicene' orthodoxy. Despite their radically different approaches to the construction of theology, Barth and Schleiermacher each testify to the central and indefatigable status of the doctrine of the Trinity. However, their writings also testify to profound questions concerning the meaning and nature of language about God. As Claude Welch asked, 'What sort and degree of validity can we attach to these formulae as descriptions of the inner nature of God?'[6] Welch went on to argue that the doctrine can be seen as working at three levels at least: (1) economic, (2) essential and (3) immanent. By these he means that (1) the revelation of God through Christ and the Spirit in the history of salvation is economic; (2) the doctrines of the *homoousion*, co-eternity and co-equality of the three hypostases is essential; and (3) internal relations, such as the generation of the Son and procession of the Spirit, and doctrine of *perichoresis*, this is immanent. I shall return to these categorizations later in Chapter 4, but, for now, they begin to demonstrate the complexity of the questions to be examined in this guide. However, Paul Tillich puts these into perspective:

Trinitarian monotheism is not a matter of the number three. It is a qualitative and not a quantitative characterization of God. It is an attempt to speak of the living God, the God in whom the ultimate and the concrete are united. The number three has no specific significance in itself. [. . .] The trinitarian problem has nothing to do with the trick question how one can be three and three be one. [. . .] The trinitarian problem is the problem of the unity between ultimacy and concreteness in the living God. Trinitarian monotheism is concrete monotheism, the affirmation of the living God.[7]

Thus, the Christian claim that God is both three and one is rooted in the perceived human experience of and encounter with the divine, in the life and ministry of Jesus of Nazareth witnessed in the four Gospels and the Day of Pentecost as set out in the second chapter of the Acts of the Apostles and in the lived experience of the tradition that issues from those two 'events'.

In this guide, I shall endeavour to offer an analysis and interpretation of the interpreters of the doctrine of the Trinity in the Christian tradition. I do this as an adherent to that tradition and, specifically, as a priest in the Church of England. I understand myself to be working within the hermeneutical community of the Church, or churches. It was in that community of faith and interpretation that reflection upon the experience of the life and ministry of Jesus of Nazareth and the Day of Pentecost began. The interpretation of those foundational experiences issued in the writings which were eventually collected together as the New Testament and formed part of the canon of Scripture. The community of faith may be understood as both the author and recipient of Scripture. In that authorship and reception, the Church engages in the interpretation and construction of an 'event of truth', which is the result of the exercise of the will to power. Thus, as a hermeneutical community, the Church continues to shape the hermeneutical tradition of Christianity, as well as being itself shaped by that tradition. The doctrine of the Trinity is a core example of the Church's shaping of the hermeneutics around the 'event of truth' understood in relation to Christ and the Spirit and, in turn, being shaped by that 'event'. The claim of the British Council of Churches in the 1980s that 'the Trinity' was 'forgotten' demonstrates that the doctrine of the Trinity, and the appeal to *koinonia*, became a tool in the power struggle of the modern ecumenical movement.

The theological method which I will use in pursuing the analysis and interpretation of the interpreters of the doctrine of the Trinity will be the so-called 'Anglican' method, as expressed in the work of Richard Hooker, in which Scripture, tradition and reason illuminate each other in the quest to receive the Christian faith afresh in the present generation. To Hooker's triad, I will add Wesley's appeal to experience as well as a recognition of the importance and inescapability of context. The appeal to Scripture and tradition is not made without acknowledgement that the use made of the Bible and patristic sources by systematic theologians has been called to account in recent times; for example, by Michel René Barnes.[8] In treating the different stances of the interpreters of the doctrine of the Trinity, I shall make use of George Lindbeck's categorizations of doctrine as cognitive, experiential-expressive or a combination of these.[9] My own preference in terms of this categorization is that the latter combination of a cognitive with an aesthetic approach to doctrinal statement offers a balanced way of understanding the mechanics of the exercise of the will to power in the construction of an event of truth. I also appeal to Gordon Kaufmann's understanding that such construction is a matter of the (theological) imagination.[10] It is against this methodological background that I also want to make it clear that I espouse the project to interpret an understanding of the Godhead as differentiated in terms of the appeal to relationality, as expressed by John Zizioulas and Colin Gunton among many others. However, I have also sought to take into account the critique of that endeavour. And, in that regard, I have argued that there needs to be a more modest approach to the claims which may emerge from an appeal to 'social Trinitarianism'. There needs to be a clearer commitment to an apophatic approach in the construction of the doctrine of the Trinity, which might be expressed in a 'hermeneutic of relationality' which is satisfied with making interpretative rather than ontological claims. These are the things which the reader can expect to find in this guide. However, having stated my preferences and prejudices, the reader should not expect to find a map of the doctrine of the Trinity, let alone of the Godhead. My intention in writing this guide is not so much to provide answers as to equip the reader in framing good questions of Scripture and tradition and of those who seek to interpret them. This guide is not like other introductions to the doctrine of the Trinity.[11] It assumes a basic working knowledge of the doctrine and scholarly discourse concerning it. However, the structure of core arguments is often summarized in order to facilitate the reader's engagement with more detailed development of those arguments. So, it is not my purpose to propound an overall argument or narrative in order to convince the reader of one model or strand in the tradition over and against another. The material is set out to facilitate further study and research and to enable the reader to make informed decisions in relation to Trinitarian theological reflection.

In the five chapters of this guide, I set out the main areas of concern for those seeking to engage in critical reflection on the doctrine of the Trinity. In the first chapter, I ask the question 'Why Trinity at all?' The chapter responds to this question through an examination of the 'data' of the Scriptural witness, particularly in the New Testament and of the Christian experience of worship and prayer. In particular, I examine the mystical theology of Pseudo-Dionysius and Meister Eckhart and twentieth-century theological reflection on 'mystery'. In Chapter 2, I examine four moments of interpretation of this 'data' in the history of the doctrine. Beginning with the present-day critique of the 'de Régnon paradigm', I proceed in reverse chronological order, to look at the effects of Socinianism from the sixteenth century until the nineteenth century, the background to and issues surrounding the Schism of 1054 and, finally, the exclusion of Arianism and the adoption of the *homoousion* in the fourth century. This chapter concludes with an assessment of Pecknold's interpretation of Augustine's reception of the orthodoxy set out by the Council of Constantinople. Pecknold's appeal to the functionality of the doctrine of the Trinity becomes a key concept for the remainder of the guide. In the third chapter, which is the heart of the book, I set out the core formulations of the 'data' which the tradition has identified for the construction and symbolization of the doctrine. The focus of this chapter is on the terminology used to express the threefoldness and oneness of the Godhead. I also examine the critique of the use of gendered language in the expression of Trinitarian reflection. In Chapter 4, I look at four areas of epistemological concern that emerge from the interpretation and formulation of the 'data'. The first focuses on revelation, the second on the classic understanding that the divine activity is undivided in the world, the third on the relation between the economic and immanent in the 'knowing' of the doctrine of the Trinity. The chapter concludes with an examination of event conceptuality. In the final chapter, I begin with an examination of the relation between the doctrine of the Trinity and concern for the Other and then take this into an analysis of the construction of Trinity–Church identity. This brings to a conclusion my concern to examine the possibility of the functionality of the doctrine of the Trinity in the present day.

Before commencing the first chapter, there are three matters I would like to explain. First, I have adopted the shorthand phrase 'Nicene orthodoxy'. This refers to the creedal statements of the Councils of Nicaea (325) and Constantinople (381/2) and to the interpretation of those statements by figures such as Athanasius, the Cappadocian Fathers and Augustine of Hippo. In using this phrase, my purpose is not to make any hegemonic claim but rather to suggest that the 'orthodoxy' that emerges from those councils and their interpreters is the product of a complex and sometimes tortuous process of reception and often highly nuanced reflection. Second, I have used numbers for dates without any use of the abbreviations of AD or CE. As both of these attributions have their problems, dates are stated on the basis that they are of the Christian era unless otherwise stated. Finally, I have frequently used the phrase 'God *in se*'. This is to avoid using a phrase such as 'in God himself' or 'in Godself'. '*In se*' in Latin can refer to him, her or it, so I have chosen this phraseology to avoid the constant repetition of a gender specific designation or 'Godself', which tends to veer away from a sense of the divine differentiation which after all is the focus of this book.

CHAPTER I

WHY 'THE TRINITY' AT ALL?

INTRODUCTION

Why does the Christian tradition include within it the doctrine of the Trinity? Indeed, some might say that the tradition is formed by the appeal to 'the Trinity'. Why 'Trinity'? And, if there is to be an understanding of diversity in the ultimate, why stop at three? or, why not two? The standard answer to these questions lies in an appeal to the Scriptures of the Christian tradition, in particular the New Testament. To a certain extent, such appeals also relate to the Hebrew Bible in so far as the New Testament itself depends upon the Scriptures of Judaism. Having said this, there will be those among biblical scholars who will challenge the very idea of reading the doctrine of the Trinity out of the New Testament; and, of course, there are those who simply reject the notion of a triune God altogether, and yet still see themselves as Christian theists. It is crucial, therefore, to understand that the 'standard answer' is itself a matter of hermeneutical tradition. In seeking to answer the question 'Why Trinity at all?', it is necessary to recognize that the doctrine of the Trinity is an 'ecclesiastical doctrine'; that is to say, it is the product of reflection on beliefs held by the believing community of Christians: the Church. The Church, the community of the faithful, is itself to be understood as a hermeneutical community. It has interpreted its own experience of encounter with that which it understands to be the divine mystery. It is from this encounter with mystery, as evidenced in the Scriptures, and as lived in contemporary experience, that the will to understand the Godhead as triune emerges. It is from this will to reflect upon and understand the encounter with the divine mystery that what is now received as the doctrine of the Trinity has been produced.[1] It is important to recognize that the doctrine is an ecclesiastical doctrine:

i.e., a belief system of the believing community. This enables the doctrine to be placed within a contemporary or 'postmodern' analytic of truth claims – what has been called the will to power or the will to knowledge or the will to truth.[2] The doctrine of the Trinity is, therefore, to be understood as the product of such 'will' and that this doctrine has been produced and handed on within the hermeneutical community of the Church. It needs also to be noted that at certain critical moments, the hermeneutical tradition has been shaped by particular forms of the will to power, not least the use of imperial or papal power, such as by Constantine who convened the Council of Nicaea (325) and Charlemagne who convened a council at Aachen (809), and the pope and emperors who convened the Council of Florence (1439). If it is accepted that 'truth' only emerges through the exercise of the will to power, then the formation of the Christian hermeneutical tradition in such a manner need not be a matter of concern. The question to be asked of the Councils is, Do the decisions that emerge from them remain faithful to the data of the Christian *kerygma* as witnessed in the Scriptures, particularly the New Testament? Athanasius, for one, was clear that what was perceived at the time as the 'novel orthodoxy' of Nicaea did reflect that to which he understood the Gospels to bear witness. In determining the appropriateness of the outcome of the councils, a dialectic is invoked between the will to power and truth, on the one hand, and the New Testament on the other, as a source of criteria for determining the truthfulness of the decisions elicited by the will to power.

In this chapter, I shall examine three areas which may be understood as primary sources for theological reflection on the human encounter with divine mystery. These three sources are crucial to the ongoing dialectical process of testing the reception of the conciliar decisions concerning the doctrine of the Trinity. Of the three sources, two are rooted in Scripture, mainly in the New Testament, and they are the 'Christ event' and the 'reception of the Holy Spirit'; and the third source focuses on the lived experience of the Christian community, in terms of worship and prayer: i.e., doxology.

THE PERSON OF CHRIST IN THE NEW TESTAMENT

In seeking to answer the question 'Why Trinity at all?', Christians have usually made appeal to the person of Jesus Christ as the cause for their understanding that there is differentiation in the divine being. Such an approach is already sophisticated and is working at a highly developed level. What does it mean to make such an appeal, and why should such an appeal continue? The answer lies not so much in the proclamation that 'Jesus is Lord' (Rom. 10.9 and 1 Cor. 12.3), which does not necessarily evoke a sense of differentiation; but rather in the claim that, 'in Christ God was reconciling the world to himself, not counting their trespasses against them, and entrusting the message of reconciliation to us' (2 Cor. 5.19, NRSV). It is on this basis that Harnack argues that, 'confession of Father, Son and Spirit is the unfolding of the belief that Jesus is the Christ'.[3] In other words, it has become generally accepted that the basis of the claims made in the Creed of Nicaea-Constantinople (381) are rooted in the New Testament.[4] What has also to be borne in mind is that this is a dialectical claim, made in relation to the interpretation of the experience of the Christian community, as well as its reading of the Scriptures.

The interpretation of the encounter with divine mystery as something that suggests or requires an understanding that the divine is differentiated may be traced to the Hebrew Scriptures, as well as to writings found in the Septuagint.[5] Scholars have argued that there are compelling reasons why both 'wisdom' and 'spirit' may be distinguished from 'God' in certain passages in these texts and that the appeal to the 'Word of the Lord' may also suggest some kind of differentiation. I do not want to suggest that such examples in any way lead necessarily to a Christian understanding of God as Trinity. They have, however, been interpreted as stages on a way towards such a development, with hindsight. The New Testament documents begin with a primary example of differentiation. This is the account of the baptism of Jesus, which is referred to in all four Gospels.[6]

Then Jesus came from Galilee to John at the Jordan, to be baptised by him. John would have prevented him, saying, 'I need to be baptised by you, and do you come to me?' But Jesus answered him, 'Let it be so now; for it is proper for us in this way to fulfil all righteousness'. Then he consented. And when Jesus had been baptised, just as he came up from the water, suddenly the heavens were opened to him and he saw the Spirit of God descending like a dove and alighting on him. And a voice from heaven said, 'This is my Son, the Beloved, with whom I am well pleased'.

Then Jesus was led up by the Spirit into the wilderness to be tempted by the devil. (Mt. 3.13–4.1, NRSV)

The descent of the Spirit and the designation of the 'Son' by the 'voice', inferring parental status to the voice, suggests a threefold differentiation, though not necessarily within the Godhead. The account of the Transfiguration provides a parallel narrative, but in this instance there is only twofold differentiation.[7] Another early example of differentiation, from a non-narrative context, is the concluding salutation from the second letter to Corinthians which provides a triadic formula at two levels: 'The grace (*charis*) of the Lord Jesus Christ, the love (*agape*) of God, and the communion (*koinonia*) of the Holy Spirit be with all of you' (2 Cor. 13.13, NRSV). The triads are: Jesus Christ, God and the Holy Spirit; and: grace (*charis*), love (*agape*) and communion (fellowship; *koinonia*). The triadic, horizontal juxtaposition of Christ, God and Spirit provides an intriguing imperative towards a threefold differentiated understanding of encounter with divine mystery. This demonstrates an implicit sophistication at work in the thought of the New Testament church, which may well be earlier in terms of being a written document than the Gospels themselves. The sense of differentiation is extended by the account of the coming of the Holy Spirit at Pentecost (Acts 2.1–13) and the passages concerning the Paraclete in the fourth Gospel.[8]

However, the testimony of the New Testament, and of the Gospels in particular, is capable of various and different, even opposing, interpretations. The Fourth Gospel, beginning with the 'Logos-Prologue', also contains passages that clearly suggest an inferior status of Jesus to the divine.[9] The classic subordinationist text in the Gospels is: 'You heard me say to you, "I am going away, and I am coming to you." If you loved me, you would rejoice that I am going to the Father, because the Father is greater than I' (Jn 14.28, NRSV).

There are other intriguing passages that suggest an otherness or transcendence about the figure of Jesus. John de Satgé draws attention to such passages, which suggest Jesus was feared, or held in awe.[10] There is a sense of a direct or physical otherness in the following passages, which leads to later reflection in terms of the ontological status, or difference to be attributed to Jesus: 'They were on the road, going up to Jerusalem, and Jesus was walking ahead of them; they were amazed, and those who followed were afraid. He took the twelve aside again and began to tell them what was to happen to him' (Mk 10.32, NRSV).

Then Jesus, knowing all that was to happen to him, came forward and asked them, 'For whom are you looking?' They answered, 'Jesus of Nazareth'. Jesus replied, 'I am he'. Judas, who betrayed him, was standing with them. When Jesus said to them, 'I am he', they stepped back and fell to the ground. Again he asked them, 'For whom are you looking?' And they said, 'Jesus of Nazareth'. Jesus answered, 'I told you that I am he'. (Jn 18.4–8, NRSV)

The interpretation of these passages is problematic, and I do not wish to suggest that they necessarily convey a 'high Christology'; these are further instances of the great diversity of expression of the person of Jesus within the New Testament account. Both these instances relate to broader understandings of Christ as an agent of divine salvation and of the coming of the end times (*ta eschata*). It is this role of Christ in terms of the bringing in of salvation that, in particular, leads to the sense of a differentiation: i.e., that Christ is not only an agent of divine salvation but also possibly a divine agent of that salvation. The redeeming work of Christ leads to reflection on his relationship to God (Father) and on the status of the Christ vis-à-vis the divine being.

The clearest examples of reflection on differentiation in the divine being in the New Testament relate to those passages expressing a 'higher' Christology, such as Paul's reflections on the Wisdom of God (e.g., 1 Cor. 1.17–31), and the Johannine prologue in which the divine Logos is understood to be pre-existent and the agent of creating the cosmos. In both instances, Word and Wisdom are used in order to stretch the received monotheism of Judaism towards an understanding of a differentiated Godhead. There are further examples in the letters, in which references to Christ in terms of equality with God and the fullness of deity are to be found (Phil. 2.6; Col. 2.9). These passages remain a long way from Nicene orthodoxy. Even this complex and sophisticated passage from Colossians (below), does not require a notion of pre-existence or divine equality to be understood; indeed, it seems to suggest a rather different status, possibly more akin to a notion that Jesus was adopted as God's Son:

He is the image of the invisible God, the firstborn of all creation; for in him all things in heaven and on earth were created, things visible and invisible, whether thrones or dominions or rulers or powers – all things have been created through him and for him. He himself is before all things, and in him all things hold together. He is the head of the body, the church; he is the beginning, the firstborn from the dead, so that he might come to have first place in everything. For in him all the fullness of God was pleased to dwell, and through him God was pleased to reconcile to himself all things, whether on earth or in heaven, by making peace through the blood of his cross. (Col. 1. 15–19, NRSV)

Reflection in the New Testament on the status of the Christ also includes references to being the beginning and the end: *arche* and *telos*, or Alpha and Omega (Rev. 22.13; Tit. 2.13). Perhaps most conclusively it is reflection on the change of the designation of 'God' to 'Father', which emerges from Jesus's 'Abba' experience of and address to God, which leads to the understanding that Jesus himself is in some way part of a differentiated Godhead. Jesus's address to God as 'Father' reaches its fullest expression in this Matthean passage (and its Lucan parallel): 'All things have been handed over to me by my Father; and no one knows the Son except the Father, and no one knows the Father except the Son and anyone to whom the Son chooses to reveal him' (Mt. 11.12, NRSV; see also Lk. 10.22).

The designation of God as 'Father' emerges from the existence and ministry of Jesus of Nazareth or reflection on that existence and ministry. But this designation remains some way from a later understanding of divine fatherhood as such. The testimony of the New Testament raises the question as to whether the Father–Son (Word) relationship belongs to the realm of the intra-divine being. In other words, do the Father and the Son mutually condition each other? Is there an eternal interdependence between them? Apart from the account of Christ's baptism and the triadic formula of 2 Cor. 13.13, the evidence examined so far only suggests a twofold or binitarian difference, a dialectic between God as father and Jesus as son. The New Testament also bears considerable testimony to a further third ingredient: the Holy Spirit.

THE HOLY SPIRIT IN THE NEW TESTAMENT

The New Testament witness refers not only to experience of the Christ event but also to the reception of the Holy Spirit. There is in the Christian *kerygma* the identification of both Christ and the Spirit with 'God'. As noted above, there are passages in the New Testament that clearly refer to a threefold designation of Father, Son and Spirit. It is possible that such designations may have been understood as transitional. God is now Father, then Son and, finally, Spirit.[11] The use of the words *theos* (God) and *kyrios* (Lord) in the New Testament may allow for the interpretation that these words have different referents, clearly offering the perception of a plurality in the divine being, a binitarianism. There are also occasions in the New Testament when reference is made not only to the Father and Jesus but when a distinction is also being drawn between Christ and the Holy Spirit, in the sense that the Spirit is not simply the Spirit of Christ himself. However, there are those who claim that the understanding of the Holy Spirit in the New Testament is rooted in the experience that the Holy Spirit and the Risen/Exalted Christ are the same.[12]

The interpretation of this relationship between Christ and the Spirit is central to whether later developments of a triadic understanding of the Godhead are rooted in the experience to which the New Testament bears witness or not. For if it could be demonstrated that in the experience of the Apostolic Age it was clear that the Spirit and the Exalted Christ were the same, suggesting only a binitarian understanding, that would create large-scale difficulties for those seeking to retain and justify later triadic formulation. In this regard, the account of the Baptism of Christ becomes a crucial reference point for later hermeneutical developments. In that the narrative distinguishes between Jesus, the Spirit and 'God' (Father/'parent' by implication), this suggests a threefold rather than twofold experience. There are other examples of ambiguity concerning the Spirit in the writings of both Paul and John. There are also texts that suggest that the Holy Spirit is the instrument of mediation in the relating of Father and risen/exalted Son. The narrative of Christ's baptism is an example of such mediating during the earthly ministry of Jesus. However, such references are mostly to be found in the post-Resurrection situation, in which the Holy Spirit may be designated as such, or as Spirit of God or Spirit of Christ, in which it is clear that the Spirit is an agent of Christ or sent by the Father.[13] The following passages from the Letter to the Romans would seem to demonstrate a threefoldness of Jesus Christ/God (Father)/Spirit:

> For God has done what the law, weakened by the flesh, could not do: by sending his own Son in the likeness of sinful flesh, and to deal with sin, he condemned sin in the flesh, so that the just requirement of the law might be fulfilled in us, who walk not according to the flesh but according to the Spirit. (Rom. 8.3–4, NRSV)

> For you did not receive a spirit of slavery to fall back into fear,
> but you have received a spirit of adoption. When we cry, '*Abba!*
> *Father!*' it is that very *Spirit* bearing witness with our spirit that we
> are children of God, and if children, then heirs, heirs of God and
> joint heirs with *Christ* – if, in fact, we suffer with him so that we
> may also be glorified with him. (Rom. 8.15–17, NRSV; italics
> mine)

The evidence of the New Testament witness concerning the relationship between God, Christ and Spirit can be interpreted in a variety
of ways, but for me it is clear that there are moments when an irreducible threefoldness is evident. Christ's own existence and ministry is
understood not only in relation to God (the Father) but also the
Spirit, e.g., Jesus's conception (Lk. 1.34–5); inauguration of ministry
(Lk. 3.21–2); and Christ's death understood as redemption (Heb.
9.14). That relationship is also understood to operate in a context
outside the 'historical' in a metaphysical realm, in which the Exalted
Christ and the Spirit have an existence which is construed on the
basis of sophisticated speculation. In the following text, the words
spoken by Christ suggest reflection upon the inner divine life: 'When
the Advocate comes, whom I will send to you from the Father, the
Spirit of truth who comes from the Father, he will testify on my
behalf' (Jn 15.26, NRSV).

The following text from the Letter to the Galatians might be interpreted in a similar fashion, though the conceptuality inherent in the
text refers more directly to experience in this world than to
elsewhere:

> But when the fullness of time had come, God sent his Son, born
> of a woman, born under the law, in order to redeem those who
> were under the law, so that we might receive adoption as children.
> And because you are children, God has sent the Spirit of his Son
> into our hearts, crying, 'Abba! Father!' So you are no longer a
> slave but a child, and if a child then also an heir, through God.
> (Gal. 4.4–7, NRSV)

These texts suggest to me that the understanding of an experience of
a threefoldness in the economy of salvation is an authentic interpretation of the Apostolic Age. While the formulations of later Trinitarian reflection leading to Nicene orthodoxy cannot simply be read out
of the New Testament, neither do they have to be read back into it.

The texts examined above clearly represent for me that later Trinitarian reflection is neither an aberration nor inauthentic. The development of Nicene orthodoxy, as Athanasius argues, is the securing of the Apostles' experience of Christ, to which the Gospels bear witness, rather than a radical misunderstanding.

THE CHRISTIAN LIFE

Worship

One of the contentions of those who perceive the doctrine of the Trinity as an irrelevance is that the doctrine does not relate to the 'ordinary' experience of Christians, that there is no Trinitarian experience to be had in living the Christian life. There is simply an experience of or encounter with the divine, which is undifferentiated. However, if the linguistic articulation of worship offered in churches is given even the most cursory examination, forms of expression that indicate differentiation will be found. Some churches will focus more clearly upon one of the persons of the Trinity: in a church with a charismatic or pentecostal tradition, there is likely to be a central focus on the Holy Spirit and the gifts or charismata of the Spirit. Such congregations are likely also to perceive the Church particularly in terms of the metaphor of a fellowship of the Holy Spirit. In other churches, there may be a clear focus on the person of Christ; evangelical traditions and sacramental traditions may have a strong devotion to Christ in the word and/or sacrament and may understand the Church in terms of the metaphor of the Body of Christ. While in other contexts there may be a focus on God as Father, perhaps having an emphasis on the transcendence of the divine and working with the metaphor of the People of God as a model for understanding the Church. Such pen sketches are inevitably caricatures, which barely stand up to scrutiny. They do illustrate that individual persons of the Trinity are addressed in worship, thus giving the lie to what, for me, is a mistaken view that there is no Trinitarian experience to be had either in the Christian life or in Christian worship. In most acts of worship, all three persons of the Trinity are likely to be invoked or addressed explicitly, and in many acts of worship, Trinitarian or triadic formulations will be used. Such phenomena do not necessarily guarantee any explicit Trinitarian understanding or devotion among members of a congregation, but such forms of address to God in worship are the stuff of which Trinitarian reflection can be made. More often than not, a Christian will have a sense of devotion to Christ or the Holy Spirit, which may be supplemented by a Trinitarian understanding of God and which may be reinforced by the liturgical practice of addressing most prayer to God the Father. There is, of course, an explicitly Trinitarian understanding of prayer, whether liturgical or personal: that prayer is offered to the Father, through the Son and in the power of the Holy Spirit, which relates to the passage in Rom. 8.15–17. Thus, in Christian worship and prayer, there are clear indications of a Trinitarian experience of the divine. The worshipper is invited to encounter Christ in word and sacrament and to be empowered with gifts of the Holy Spirit in living the Christian life of discipleship, with at least the implicit understanding that these experiences also relate to the Father. It is understood in the tradition that the Word and Spirit of God are agents of the divine creating, redeeming and recreating or transforming of the cosmos. In the past, when there were more widely accepted metaphysical understandings, the encounter with Word and Spirit in the creation as well as redemption might have been more widely appreciated and expected. The metaphysical understanding of the correlation of the Logos with the *logoi*, to be found in writers such as Origen, Gregory of Nyssa and Maximos the Confessor, was the basis for the expectation of encountering the divine three in the created order.[14] The understanding of the Spirit as the agent of Creation and the renewal of Creation was celebrated in the liturgical tradition and has experienced a revival in modern usage in relation to contemporary endeavours to relate the liturgy to ecological concerns.[15] However, generally speaking, in the present day, I suspect that if there is sense of God in creation, people are most likely to attribute this to the Father/Creator God. Such sentiments have been prevalent in Western culture from at least the time of the Enlightenment period in the thought of Deists and were reinforced in the Romantic movement by poets such as Wordsworth. In recent times, this has perhaps received a renewed impetus through the use of non-gendered language to refer to the three of the Godhead: e.g., Creator, Word, Spirit, in which the traditional understanding of the participation of all three persons in creating is obscured, by the first designation. I shall return to the critique of gendered Trinitarian language in Chapter 3.

The possibility of the experience of God as Trinity is then to be found in the Christian life and Christian worship. That experience is generally based upon the use of Trinitarian language, formulae and structures in worship. The Church community as a hermeneutical community inherits the tradition of Nicene orthodoxy that assumes and expects an encounter with the Holy Trinity in prayer and worship and life. This assumption has formed the basis of the ecumenical consensus, which is articulated in the constitution of the World Council of Churches that member churches should subscribe to a doctrine of the Trinity consonant with the Nicene–Constantinopolitan Creed. The inherited and lived tradition forms the Christian community in relation to 'Trinitarian expectations'. The sacramental traditions of the Church expressed in both Baptism and Eucharist set out these expectations most clearly.[16] Each Christian is admitted into membership of the Body of Christ, the Church, through use of the Trinitarian baptismal formula and the invocation of the Holy Spirit to fill each individual with equipping gifts in service of God's mission in the fellowship of the Church. In the Eucharist, the Church makes the memorial of Christ according to the injunction of the Institution Narrative and invokes the Spirit to equip those receiving the Body and Blood of Christ to be the Body of Christ in the world. Such understandings are, of course, highly developed and the product of long-standing tradition and reflection. Such 'Trinitarian expectations' as much assume a doctrine of the Trinity as explicate one. As Jean-Luc Marion has suggested, the narrative of the Emmaus story in the Gospel of Luke may be seen as a paradigm for the Church as a hermeneutical community,[17] a concept to which I shall return in Chapter 5. Marion makes the point that the hermeneutical tradition of the Church is based upon a sacramental encounter with Christ, which both informs and forms the Church as the Body of Christ, itself an incipient Trinitarian concept in the Pauline writings of the New Testament (1 Cor. 12; Eph. 4).

Reflection on worship as a source for theological understanding is an ongoing strand in Christian discourse across the centuries.[18] Such a doxological approach to reflection upon God as Trinity is to be found in many examples. One such instance is to be found in the writings of Basil of Caesarea. Basil reflected in particular on the use of Trinitarian formulae in Baptism and doxologies.

> For if our Lord, when enjoining the baptism of salvation, charged His disciples to baptise all nations in the name 'of the Father and of the Son and of the Holy Ghost' [Mt. 28.19] not disdaining fellowship with Him, and these men allege that we must not rank Him [the Spirit] with the Father and the Son, is it not clear that they openly withstand the commandment of God?[19]

Reflection upon the baptismal formula is also to be found in the writings of Gregory of Nyssa and Gregory Nazianzen. The Cappadocian Fathers understood that Christian discipleship did not simply consist in having the right understanding of God, it also meant worshipping God in the right way. (Orthodoxy means offering worship in the right manner.) In order to proclaim an authentic understanding of God as Trinity, the Cappadocians also taught that it was necessary for the Liturgy to be an authentic celebration of the Holy Trinity. As Pelikan argues, 'the doctrine of the Trinity, being a doctrine about why Father, Son, and Holy Spirit must (as the Nicene Creed required) "be worshipped and glorified together", was no exception to this rule.'[20] This was to be particularly evident in baptism:

> For the Cappadocians, baptism was in many ways the most cogent example of what Nazianzen called 'the spirit of speaking mysteries and dogmas' – which meant both mysteries and dogmas, and ultimately neither dogmas without mysteries nor mysteries without dogmas. This can, then, be taken as an enunciation of the principle, 'The rule of prayer determines the rule of faith' [lex orandi lex credendi].[21]

The Cappadocian Fathers found that the practice of baptism in particular provided the ground for reflection upon the equal status and deity of the Holy Spirit, because of the way in which the Spirit was understood in the doxological context of worship.

> For if He is not to be worshipped, how can He deify me by Baptism? But if He is to be worshipped, surely He is an Object of adoration, and if an Object of Adoration He must be God; the one is linked to the other, a truly golden and saving chain. And indeed from the Spirit comes our New Birth, and from the New Birth our new creation, and from the new creation our deeper knowledge of the dignity of Him from Whom it is derived.[22]

Who was the author of these words of thanksgiving at the lighting of the lamps, we are not able to say. The people, however, utter the ancient form, and no one has ever reckoned guilty of impiety those who say 'We praise Father, Son, and God's Holy Spirit'.[23]

The Cappadocian Fathers clearly understand that the reciprocity between worship and belief is inescapable for theological reflection and, in particular, Trinitarian theological reflection. This has left an ongoing mark on the tradition and its expression in the hermeneutics of the Christian community. This is reflected in such examples as the long-standing practice of invoking the Holy Spirit in a consecratory role in the Lord's Supper in the Reformed tradition, despite the overwhelming focus on the Word of God in that tradition.[24] Trinitarian hermeneutics are also to be seen at work in the widespread adoption of a Trinitarian structure to the Eucharistic Prayer, across many traditions as an outcome of the Liturgical Movement.[25] It is also important to recognize that within Christian experience there are strands of tradition which do not conform to this patterning, at least in a straightforward manner. So, I turn now to examine the understanding of those who suggest that the encounter with the divine is less easily differentiated, and how, if at all in their understanding, the differentiation which a doctrine of the Trinity requires is to be discerned and understood.

THE EXPERIENCE OF 'MYSTERY'

In the writings of those who reflect upon the Christian traditions of contemplative prayer and mystical experience, the doctrine of the Trinity does not always feature with a central role. Indeed, some commentators have suggested that the contemplatives and mystics place the doctrine of the Trinity at the margins of their writings. Their experiences of the divine often suggest that the Trinitarian experience and understanding of God is something to be left behind or is something that is constructed on top of a more primary and unitary encounter with the divine, or, indeed, that which is 'beyond the divine'. Michel Foucault has reflected that the experience of such 'mysticism' is a primary challenge to the status quo, particularly in the sphere of the political.[26] His reflections may also have a bearing on the power dynamics of the hermeneutical traditions of Trinitarian reflection. Mysticism provides access to experience which is not easily embraced or managed by the gatekeepers of the status quo but which challenges the assumptions of the received tradition and of those who defend it or benefit from it. I shall mention just two writers in this tradition, Pseudo-Dionysius (c.500) and Meister Eckhart (c.1260–1327). Dionysius 'the Areopagite', despite claiming to know characters from the New Testament, is usually not dated before the late fifth century. A philosopher as well as a theologian, Dionysius wrote works which have come to be accepted as classic examples of a mystical theology, which has its roots in both Platonism and Christianity. Central to his theological method is an understanding of contemplation (*theoria*), which is practised to attain to true knowledge. This has strong echoes of a Platonist understanding of knowledge. Dionysius clearly suggests that the Godhead, understood as triune, is something manifested in what the tradition understands to be the economy. The human capacity to know the inner reality of the divine is so limited that it is impossible to say what the being of God is:

> And the fact that the transcendent Godhead is one and triune must not be understood in any of our typical senses [. . .] no unity or trinity, no number or oneness, no fruitfulness, indeed, nothing that is or is known can proclaim that hidden-ness beyond every mind and reason of the transcendent Godhead which transcends every being [. . .] we cannot even call it by the name of goodness.[27]

This passage also demonstrates the radical apophaticism inherent in Dionysius' method. He is clear about the limits of human language and numeracy when it comes to expressing anything about the divine. This understanding is not new to Dionysius; it is clear that the Cappadocian Fathers also articulate such limitations to human expression.[28]

Eckhart has a parallel understanding of the revealed Trinity. The human mind might in some sense know and receive an understanding of the Holy Trinity in revelation, while the ultimate reality of the divine remains unknowable and hidden.[29] Eckhart uses a metaphor of divine 'boiling' or 'bubbling', *bullitio*, to explain the processions within the divine, which can be known in the creation and divine revelation, but he draws a distinction between the triune God and 'a distinctionless, nameless ground or Godhead that transcends this'.[30] Such understandings obviously pose significant challenges to the more typical approach and expectations of theologians who follow in the tradition of Nicene orthodoxy. The differences between the two Christian monks, Bede Griffiths and Abhishiktananda, who lived in India in the mid- to late twentieth century is illustrative of the tensions that emerge in the double appeal to contemplation and mystical experience, on the one hand, and the revealed God, understood as triune, on the other. Both men sought to engage with the Indian theological tradition of *advaita* (non-duality), which, in its radical form, is understood as a form of monism. While Abhishiktananda felt that his experience of contemplation took him towards the kinds of understanding seen in Dionysius and Eckhart, Bede Griffiths sought to retain an orthodox Christian understanding of God as triune.[31] In order to pursue the bearing of these tensions on Trinitarian theological reflection further, I will examine four writers from the twentieth century who also appeal to mystery.

The first writer, Rudolf Otto (1869–1937), had a profound influence upon theological discourse during the twentieth century, in particular in relation to his appeal to the 'numinous'. He invented this word and associates it with the Latin *numen*. Some commentators ascribe to it the meaning 'presence', while in classical Latin it might refer to a 'nod' and hence to a 'command', but also to a deity. In medieval Latin, it had the connotation of dominion or property. Otto makes considerable use of his new word to point to the human experience of the inexpressible and ineffable. The following is a significant description of numinous experience in Otto's writing:

> it grips or stirs the human mind [. . .] The feeling of it may at times come sweeping like a gentle tide, pervading the mind with a tranquil mood of deepest worship. It may pass over into a more set and lasting attitude of the soul, continuing, as it were, thrillingly vibrant and resonant, until at last it dies away and the soul resumes its 'profane,' non-religious mood of everyday experience. It may burst in sudden eruption up from the depths of the soul with spasms and convulsions, or lead to the strongest excitements, to intoxicated frenzy, to transport, and to ecstasy. It has its wild and demonic forms and can sink to an almost grisly horror and shuddering.[32]

Otto uses experience as the core of his understanding of mystery and the encounter with the ultimate or the divine. In so doing, he grants a fresh permission at the beginning of the twentieth century for theologians to be able to value mystical experience in theological reflection. Mystery, mystical experience and the appeal to the world of particulars are all enhanced in Otto's reclamation of the sense of that which is 'other' within the context of ordinary and everyday experience.

A second writer in this exploration of the appeal to mystery is Ian Ramsey (1915–72), who echoes Otto's understanding in his quotation from Joseph Conrad's description of a storm in *Typhoon* (1902). Ramsey goes on to reflect that

A gale – awesome indeed; and my claim is that in and around the gale occurred a cosmic disclosure; a situation which takes on depth, to disclose another dimension, a situation where I am confronted in principle with the whole universe, a situation where God reveals himself.[33]

Ramsey also suggests that prayer is a moment when such encounters or cosmic disclosures are to be experienced.[34] He broadens the appeal to mystical experience to include the more domestic activity of prayer, as well as the extraordinary moments of disclosure, such as a storm. Ramsey is also open to the understanding that Christian reflection may continue into a Trinitarian understanding of such disclosure.[35]

A third source of the appeal to ultimate or absolute mystery is to be found in the work of Karl Rahner (1904–84).[36] In *Foundations of Christian Faith*, he sets out his understanding of 'Man in the Presence of Absolute Mystery'.[37] Rahner sets out the basis of his understanding of epistemology in terms of the raw experience of mystery, which is accessible for all human beings. Clearly, the chapter title above does not include the word 'God', and in the chapter Rahner is focused on discourse concerning human being and human experience. It is also clear that the understanding of human being in the presence of absolute mystery raises the questions: What is absolute mystery? Why is it absolute?, and How it is present? So, although the word 'God' is absent from the title, the questions implicit in the word 'God' about the origin and destiny of life are clearly to be understood as questions which are being addressed in this discourse concerning the human experience of mystery. Rahner is seeking to understand whether human beings can know God. His answer lies in the suggestion that human beings encounter God in a transcendental experience of (God's) Holy Mystery. Whenever human beings experience their limits and imagine what lies beyond them, they begin to transcend those limits. In that experience, the mystery of human existence is to be discerned, the origin and destiny of which remain unclear. Rahner argues that to know 'mystery' is to know the source of transcendence. It is at this juncture that Rahner makes a crucial claim, particularly in relation to later Trinitarian reflection that this source of transcendence is not a blind and impersonal force. What is known is a personal God, and Rahner makes this claim in terms of analogy. God is not a person in the same sense that human beings are, but God is a person in the sense that God is not to be reduced to a 'thing'. Rahner proceeds to claim that God is the absolute ground of all things, 'absolute' because not reducible to anything else. Human beings relate to God as creatures to the source of their creation. Furthermore, human beings 'know' God by knowing themselves in relation to the mystery of being alive. This mystery is nothing other than that which gives human beings their place in time and invites them to fulfil the possibilities offered to them. Rahner thus argues that 'Holy Mystery' is present 'in' the world as its fundamental ground. It is 'holy' in that it enables a human being to become complete; i.e., it opens up the possibilities for human beings to be what they are meant in God's creating and redeeming purposes. Rahner allows that it may be possible to find God in historical religion and its holy places, people and things. He is clear that God is not confined to such phenomena. Rather, the phenomena of this world, including the holy symbols, sanctuaries and deeds of religion, mediate the presence of God and teach human beings how to discern it. Human beings can know God immediately as their transcendent ground. Rahner's appeal to Holy Mystery is something which he understands is available to and, indeed, part of every human life. In that he understands this in relation to an encounter with a personal God, this allows him by means of his axiom that the economic and the immanent trinities are the same (see below in Chapter 4), to claim that the encounter with Holy Mystery is encounter with the Holy Trinity.

The fourth writer in this exploration of 'mystery' is John Macquarrie (1919–2007) who argues along similar lines. He makes explicit appeal to Rudolf Otto's ideas:

> In what [Otto] calls 'creature-feeling' we can recognize [. . .] [a] mood of anxiety. This creature-feeling becomes awe in the presence of the holy. Otto's analysis is in terms of the *mysterium tremendum fascinans*, the mystery that is at once overwhelming and fascinating. The *mysterium* refers to the incomprehensible depth of the numinous presence, which does not fall under the ordinary categories of thought but is other than the familiar beings of the world. The *tremendum* stresses the otherness of holy being as over against the nullity of transience of our own limited being; it points to the transcendence of being. The *fascinans* points to what we have already called the 'grace' of being which has unveiled itself so that we understand that it gives itself to us, that it is the source of our being and strengthens our being with its presence.[38]

The encounter with mystery that these writers point to does not necessarily relate at all to the Trinitarian understanding of God of Nicene orthodoxy. Macquarrie's understanding of the gracious self-giving of the encountered mystery forms the basis for his later extrapolation from this place to a God who is triune. Macquarrie's description of mystery in terms of the phrase: 'it gives itself to us' has strong resonances with contemporary discourse on 'Gift' in the works of Derrida, Marion and Milbank.[39] This establishes an important connection between the appeal to mystery and recent attempts to reconfigure of the language of 'being'. I shall return to discuss the concept of gift in Chapters 3 and 5.

THREE SOURCES OF REFLECTION: A SUMMARY

In different ways, each of these writers suggests a return to the question with which I began: Why Trinity at all? In order to attempt an answer, it will be necessary to appeal not only to the primordial experience of mystery as variously understood but also to the scriptural witness and to the Nicene tradition. Reflection on scripture and tradition as well as on the primordial/everyday experience of mystery brings that experience of mystery into dialogue with its self-expression in the economy of salvation, in the Christ event and giving of the Spirit at Pentecost, as well as contemporary contexts of Christian worship and discipleship in which mystery may also be encountered. The remainder of this guide is, in a sense, an attempt to flesh out what that dialogue might look like. The self-expression of absolute mystery in the economy of salvation or revelation leads to reflection on the events of that revelation. Claude Welch has suggested that a recognition of the status of an event conceptuality is crucial in the task of constructing a doctrine of the Trinity.[40] In other words, the root of the doctrine of the Trinity is to be understood in relation to the activity of God in the Christ event and the event of Pentecost. Thus, God in Christ is both the agent and content of the event of revelation. Echoing the understandings of both Karl Barth and Ian Ramsey, revelation may be understood as a self-giving as well as a self-disclosure of God, of which the content is eternal.[41] This is also the understanding of Augustine. His reflection on the doctrine of the Trinity begins from the temporal sending of the Son and giving of the Spirit: understood as concrete historical events to which Scripture bears witness.[42] Later writers, such as Aquinas, received the tradition as a 'given' and accepted that the proposition that 'God is Father, Son and Spirit' is itself revealed. This meant that the concrete events of the missions of Son and Spirit in the cosmos are dealt with as the final stage of the construction of the doctrine of the Trinity in his work.[43] In this way, any appeal to event conceptuality is marginalized, particularly in the way in which the divine is understood as *actus purus*, i.e., a completed 'act' of absolute perfection beyond any contingent potentiality, which is implicit in the language of event. The rediscovery of the importance of the world of particulars and the economy of salvation and revelation during the course of the twentieth century leads back to the realization that it is necessary to begin with the concrete events, as well as with an event conceptuality. It is for this reason that I find Zizioulas's appeal to 'an event of communion' to be of such importance for reflection upon, and the construction of a doctrine of the Trinity.[44] There is, of course, a variety of ways in which event conceptuality may be received and interpreted. Ralph Del Colle has argued that either the event of revelation is of God *in se* or that Trinitarian language is simply the triadic representation of God in history according to the receptive capacity of the human subject and nothing more.[45] I find the tension in this claim to be misplaced. Surely the doctrine of the Trinity arises from human reflection upon the experience of encounter with mystery, the witness of the Scriptures to the events of revelation and the tradition of Nicene orthodoxy. There is no guarantee, beyond faith, that what is understood is of God *in se*. Rather, this emerges as axiomatic from the reflection. I shall return to look at this more fully in Chapter 4.

SUGGESTED READING

G. D. Fee, *God's Empowering Presence: The Holy Spirit in the Letters of Paul* (Peabody, Mass.: Hendrickson, 1994).
J. Hamilton, Jr., *God's Indwelling Presence: The Holy Spirit in the Old and New Testaments* (Nashville, Tenn.: Broadman & Holman, 2006).
U. Fleming (ed.), *Meister Eckhart: The Man from Whom God Hid Nothing* (Leominster: Gracewing, 1995).
K. Rahner, 'The Concept of Mystery in Catholic Theology', *Theological Investigations Vol. IV, More Recent Writings* (London: Darton, Longman and Todd, 1966), pp. 36–73.
P. L. Metzer (ed.), *Trinitarian Soundings in Systematic Theology* (London and New York: Continuum, 2005).

CHAPTER 2

MOMENTS OF INTERPRETATION

For a time during the last century, the question, 'Where to begin the construction of the doctrine of the Trinity?' could have been answered fairly straightforwardly in terms of two options: either from the unity of the Godhead or from the threefold diversity.[1] The options of the unitary or social models of Trinitarian doctrine still remain; the challenge to the appeal to social Trinitarianism, which I will trace below, means that the question of where to begin construction needs to be situated within the history of the hermeneutics of the doctrine of the Trinity. In this chapter, I will provide a sketch of four moments in that hermeneutical history. This will take the form of a reverse chronology or genealogy of these moments or vignettes. Of course, the moments themselves have long-standing prehistories, as well as long-term effects. It will be possible to research these moments more fully through the suggested reading. The four moments I will sketch are: (1) the de Régnon paradigm; (2) the problem with Socinus; (3) the Schism of 1054; and (4) Arius and Nicene orthodoxy. In my view, each of these 'moments' in the history of Trinitarian hermeneutics has led to a change not only in understanding but also in the 'direction' or 'shape' of Trinitarian theological reflection. Each of the three moments which are subsequent to the evolution and reception of Nicene orthodoxy, relate directly to that orthodoxy. This is a reminder that the doctrine of the Trinity is an ecclesial doctrine; it is an understanding, an interpretation of the Godhead that emerges from reflection upon Scripture, tradition and experience as received and lived in the context of the believing, worshipping Christian community of the Church. The reality of the fractured nature of the Church has meant that the reception of Nicene orthodoxy varies from church tradition to church tradition. Some churches understand themselves to be orthodox through the regular recitation of the Nicene Creed during worship, and others claim orthodoxy, without such liturgical or other regular recitation. Others still do not claim to stand in the tradition of Nicene orthodoxy and yet understand the Godhead to be differentiated, or simply claim to stand in the Christian tradition and do so as Unitarians. Against this background of diversity within the Christian tradition, broadly understood, the ecumenical movement of the twentieth century has endorsed the tradition of Nicene orthodoxy and made its acceptance as conditional for membership of its councils.[2]

The four moments in the history of Trinitarian hermeneutics testify to two ongoing realities. First, they testify to the reality that the reception of the decisions of Nicaea (325) and Constantinople (381), from which Nicene orthodoxy emerges is an ongoing process, which includes both reception and non-reception. As well as the ongoing need to reinterpret and receive the decisions of the councils, there remain those who are unconvinced either with the formulation of the doctrine in the councils or with the need to formulate at all. Second, they testify to the reality that the divergences of reception do not necessarily relate to doctrinal or hermeneutical issues per se. Often, these divergences relate to matters of church politics or to issues of church authority or, indeed, both together. The hermeneutics of the doctrine of the Trinity are manifestations of the will to power and the will to truth. How the doctrine of the Trinity is received, interpreted and understood is embedded in issues of authority and authorization and decision-making, and, thus, in the expression of power in the life of the Church. It is not my brief in this guide to explore these issues of authority and power per se; however, it is important to realize that the doctrine of the Trinity has been and continues to be shaped and constructed in relation to these issues. The four moments I will explore below clearly demonstrate this reality and offer some insight into the correlation of doctrinal formulation and the will to power.

THE DE RÉGNON PARADIGM

The key to understanding the doctrine of the Trinity was, for much of the twentieth century, stated in terms of asking a question about the place of commencing or constructing the doctrine. The choice offered was either to begin from the oneness of God or the threeness. This choice, it was argued, was part of the landscape of classical Trinitarian thought. The Eastern Fathers, writing in Greek, had, on the whole, begun with the three Persons in God, while the Western Fathers, writing in Latin, had begun with the divine unity. This choice was usually attributed to the 'Cappadocian Fathers' (Basil of Caesarea, Gregory of Nyssa and Gregory Nazianzen),[3] and Augustine of Hippo, who, it was argued, had 'begun' their reflections on the Christian tradition of the triune God from different, even opposite 'places'. Those places were deemed to be a social or communal starting place on the part of the Cappadocian Fathers, who were understood to root their reflections in the communal experience of worship. On the other hand, Augustine's starting place was deemed to be the experience of the individual, perhaps rooted in his own intense personal experiences, recorded in the *Confessions*; his approach was said to be psychological. This picture of the different starting places was perhaps always understood to be an oversimplification or caricature on the part of those who knew the patristic writings well. However, the caricature came to be accepted as a working paradigm among systematic theologians largely as a result of the interpretation of the work of the Jesuit author Théodore de Régnon,[4] by Eastern orthodox writers such as Vladimir Lossky.[5] Thus, the 'de Régnon paradigm' became the basis for the ascendancy of a so-called Eastern understanding of social Trinitarianism over against a perceived Western Trinitarianism, which was, in various aspects, deemed to be inadequate. In particular, it was argued that the focus on the unity of the Godhead had colluded with, or perhaps was responsible for, the development of individualism in the West. This polarization and valuation of East over and against West is now challenged by patristic and systematic theologians alike.[6] I will set out below the genealogy of these developments for the landscape of Trinitarian thought. Two concerns emerge for my own thinking about the Godhead as Trinity. What does the challenge to the de Régnon paradigm entail for social Trinitarianism? On what basis might a social understanding of the Trinity be upheld? And, second, what consequences are there for understandings of the Church, especially in relation to communion ecclesiology?

I begin with a genealogy of the appeal to social Trinitarianism. What this appeal means in detail undoubtedly varies among theologians. Those who sit within this framework appeal to relationality on the basis that there is some correlation between understandings of divine being, ecclesiality, human sociality and the relationship between God and creation. Leonardo Boff sets out a basis for this appeal in brief:

By the name God, Christian faith expresses the Father, the Son and the Holy Spirit in eternal correlation, interpenetration and love, to the extent that they form one God. Their unity signifies the communion of the divine Persons. There, in the beginning there is not solitude of One, but the communion of three divine Persons.[7]

Later in *Trinity and Society*, he suggests how the late-twentieth-century renewal in Trinitarian thought is empowered particularly by an appeal to context in a broad sense: to society, community and history, cosmic and human, as the starting point for reflection on the conceptuality of relationality.[8] 'So human society is a pointer on the road to the mystery of the Trinity, while the mystery of the Trinity, as we know it from revelation, is a pointer toward social life and its archetype'.[9] The methodological interplay between human experience and divine revelation is another feature of much of the theological reflection, which is manifested in a 'hermeneutic of relationality' and the appeal to social Trinitarianism.[10]

I shall not attempt to reconstruct a comprehensive genealogy of the appeal to social Trinitarianism in Christian thought, as that would be a task beyond the scope of this present work. What is attempted here is to identify some landmarks in the overall landscape of social Trinitarianism, which will include some allusion to the cross-disciplinary nature of the broader interest in and landscape of 'relation'/'relationality'. From some perspectives, at least, the appeal to relationality in terms of a social model of the Trinity has been seen as a 'stampede'.[11] Certainly, a focus upon *koinonia* and its attendant relational implications is to be found among theologians of widely different traditions and interests. In seeking to identify the major landmark publications in this 'turn to relationality',[12] there are those publications which have themselves sought to map this landscape; they include works edited by Christoph Schwöbel: *Persons, Divine and Human* and *Trinitarian Theology Today*, as well as his own more recent *Gott in Beziehung*.[13] Among this category of works, F. LeRon Shults describes a broader philosophical landscape in *Reforming Theological Anthropology: After the Philosophical Turn to Relationality*,[14] in which he traces the appeal to relationality from Aristotle to Kant, and from Hegel to Levinas. However, a comprehensive genealogy of the appeal to social Trinitarianism is a task still to be undertaken. The lack of a clear understanding of a theological or theological/philosophical genealogy of social Trinitarianism puts all discussion of this appeal to relationality and its attendant categories and implications at a disadvantage.

Second, there are those publications that clearly mark out the development of an appeal to a social Trinitarianism in Christian Trinitarian thinking in the second half of the twentieth century. On the whole, such monographs and collections of essays began to be published in the 1980s and 1990s. Jürgen Moltmann is a significant contributor in this field not only for *The Trinity and the Kingdom of God*,[15] but also for the influence he exercises on others such as Leonardo Boff in *Trinity and Society*.[16] Robert Jenson, in *The Triune Identity*,[17] traced the emergence of a theological relationality to the patristic era, in particular to Gregory of Nyssa, marking an ongoing appeal to the 'Cappadocian Fathers'. John Zizioulas contributed to the landscape in *Being as Communion*,[18] making an appeal to patristic (Cappadocian) sources as well as twentieth-century existentialist categories. The collection of essays *Trinity, Incarnation and Atonement*, edited by Ronald J. Feenstra and Cornelius Plantinga Jr.,[19] marks a stage in the dissemination and broader examination of the conceptualities inherent in the appeal to relationality. Catherine Mowry LaCugna, in *God for Us*,[20] rooted her exposition of relationality in the human reception of the divine self-communication. Colin E. Gunton contributed a number of works to the exploration and application of the appeal to relationality, but perhaps most clearly in *The One, the Three and the Many*,[21] set out his vision of the implications of the divine relationality. Evidently, there are other landmark works to which appeal could be made; what is offered here is by no means exhaustive. From the works selected, I want to explore further a possible (re)construction of a genealogy of the appeal of social Trinitarianism. The appearance of landmark works in the 1980s and 1990s is preceded by a period when the components of what may now be perceived as a turn to relationality were being crafted and assembled. One example of this is the development of the thought of John Zizioulas. His seminal article, 'Human Capacity and Human Incapacity: A Theological Exploration of Personhood',[22] published in 1975 and originally given as a paper in 1972 demonstrates the antecedents and components of Zizioulas's developed understanding. Zizioulas recognizes that his work stands in a continuity with such understandings of 'relationality' as those of Buber, Macmurray, Pannenberg and David Jenkins.[23] Zizioulas also appeals to the concept of *ek-stasis*, 'a movement towards communion',[24] which, he argues, is both a modern existentialist understanding (i.e., dependent upon Heidegger) as well as something he traces to the Greek Fathers such as Pseudo-Dionysius and Maximos the Confessor. In making this identification, he acknowledges the work of Christos Yannaras in bringing Heidegger's concepts into dialogue with Orthodox tradition.[25] In this brief exposition of the antecedents of Zizioulas's developed thought, a clear picture of the complexity of a genealogy of social Trinitarianism already emerges. It is also clear from such Orthodox writers as Nikos Nissiotis[26] that a focus on communion both ecclesial and divine was coming to be emphasized from the early 1960s. Writers such as LaCugna identify other earlier influences on the development of late-twentieth-century Trinitarian theology and explicitly appeals to the work of Théodore de Régnon.[27] Christoph Schwöbel points to the work of J. R. Illingworth[28] in the late nineteenth century as a point of departure for reflection, identifying a number of Anglican theologians who focused on the social model of the Trinity, exemplified in particular by L. S. Thornton.[29] Another stream of thought can be traced to the work of those in the *nouvelle théologie* of mid-twentieth-century Roman Catholicism, which emerges in the appeal to 'communion' in *Lumen gentium* of Vatican II.[30] This stream of thought may be identified in Louis Lochet's *Charité fraternelle et vie trinitaire*,[31] published in 1956; B. Fraigneau-Julien's *Réflexion sur la signification religieuse du mystère de la Sainte Trinité*, published in 1965;[32] and Klaus Hemmerle's *Thesen zu einer trinitarischen Ontologie*, first published in 1976.[33] Leonardo Boff acknowledges that not only Moltmann but also M. J. Scheeben[34] and Taymans d'Eypernon[35] explored the Trinity as 'supreme society' and as a model for human society. In these writings from the earlier twentieth century can be discerned a move, which fuels the shift to relationality in the fields of Trinitarian and ecclesiological exploration later in that century.[36] Focus on a relational conceptuality of the divine and ecclesial continued into the late 1990s and the new millennium and is witnessed in the writing of such as David Cunningham,[37] Paul Fiddes,[38] John Milbank and Catherine Pickstock,[39] Stanley Grenz[40] and the recent collection of essays *Trinitarian Soundings*.[41]

Developments in a broader philosophical context, which influence and undergird these developments in Christian theological thought, are again too complex to be dealt with in detail in this guide. The writings of Levinas are credited by some writers to be crucial for understanding the 'turn to relationality',[42] and in Levinas is to be found someone who clearly embraces the 'ethical relation to the other' as a central category. While not underestimating the contribution of Levinas to late-twentieth-century understandings, it is evident that philosophical discussion of 'relation' is by no means a recent development. Sara Grant argues that 'all men, have always argued about questions of relation'.[43] While not everyone would want to concur with these statements, they demonstrate that in constructing the genealogy of social Trinitarianism as it emerged in the latter part of the twentieth century, there are strands of thought which may be traced to early antiquity in both Europe and Asia. While the late-twentieth-century appeal to relationality may possibly be described as a 'stampede' in terms of its renewed application to Trinitarian thought and ecclesiology, this 'turn' should also be seen in terms of a much wider and longer genealogy. In the context of both shorter and longer views of this genealogy, it may be seen that both proponents of a social model of the Trinity and those who would offer a critique of this move would benefit from a clearer understanding of the long evolution behind late-twentieth-century conceptualities than is perhaps usually the case.

It should also be recognized that an element of this genealogy is also to be found within ecumenical conversation. I shall not attempt to provide a detailed analysis of the emergence of the use of *koinonia* (communion) in ecumenical dialogue; however, it is useful to indicate some features of that development and also where it is recorded. A possible starting place may be found in an encyclical of the Ecumenical Patriarch from 1920, in which appeal is made to the notion of 'fellowship' among the churches.[44] At the time of the founding of the World Council of Churches, the writings of Oliver Tomkins also bear testimony to growing understanding and articulation of the relationship between the Church as community and the life of the Trinity.[45] This conceptuality is given clear expression in the report *One Lord One Baptism* (chaired by Tomkins) in 1960.[46] After that time, the correlation of relationality ecclesial and divine becomes a strong theme in texts of the Faith and Order Commission and the World Council of Churches, which Mary Tanner traces in her address to the Faith and Order Conference in Santiago de Compostella in 1993.[47] In drawing this section to a close, I have sought in this genealogy to offer a guide to the appeal to relational and social understandings of the Godhead as they developed with particular reference to the emergence of the de Régnon paradigm, as initiated in the writing of Lossky and carried forward by Zizioulas.[48]

CRITIQUE OF RELATIONALITY

The resurgence of interest in the social model of the Trinity, together with an exploration of the consequences of the application of the category of *koinonia* to the Godhead and the Church, inevitably brought with it a counterpoise, a questioning of this resurgence and the potentially hegemonic use of relationality. A critique of the appeal to social Trinitarianism has been in evidence from at least the early 1990s. John Gresham, writing in 1993,[49] outlined four main perspectives from which critique of the social model of the Trinity could be offered; namely: terminological, monotheistic, Christological and feminist. These four perspectives highlight areas of concern that other writers have also identified. Another area posing a strong challenge to those who have sought to construct a doctrine of the Trinity in terms of the appeal to relationality is a question about the way in which patristic sources and terminology are interpreted, particularly in relation to the 'Cappadocian Fathers' and Augustine of Hippo.[50] Sarah Coakley argues that Gregory of Nyssa has been misread as an advocate of social Trinitarianism. She writes that Gregory does not begin to construct Trinitarian thought from threeness, as in the 'three men' analogy, but is 'more interested in underscoring the unity of the divine will in the Trinity.'[51] Coakley's assessment of Gregory of Nyssa is that he is better understood to stand in the tradition of so-called Western Trinitarianism, i.e., emphasizing the divine unity rather than so-called Eastern Trinitarianism, i.e., emphasizing the threeness.[52] The contemporary re-reading of Gregory of Nyssa and Augustine leaves the strong impression that Zizioulas has simply repeated the stock critique and rhetoric of Lossky,[53] which, in turn, rests upon the paradigm attributed to Théodore de Régnon,[54] concerning the models of the Trinity used in East and West. As noted already, de Régnon's paradigm and Lossky's argument have been challenged, and some response to this is required if the appeal to social Trinitarianism is to be sustained and developed.[55] Emerging from recent patristic scholarship, there is another layer of critique that also challenges the way patristic texts are used by systematic theologians. While Zizioulas may not necessarily see himself as a systematic theologian, the use to which he puts patristic material, I would suggest, falls into the category of material to which this critique refers. Scholars of patristic writers have gone so far as to challenge the notion of talking about 'patristic thought' or even 'Cappadocian thought'. Such revisionist or deconstructive tendencies raise many issues for the way in which historic sources are used in the writings of contemporary theologians. Furthermore, there is a question about the motivation for the resurgence of interest in relationality altogether. Concerns were raised by John Wilks in 1995,[56] especially in relation to Zizioulas's use of the Cappadocian Fathers. Fermer, writing in 1999,[57] reiterates these concerns, in particular focusing on the way in which Zizioulas extrapolates his conceptuality of the divine being as *koinonia* from the writings of the Cappadocian Fathers. Fermer argues that in the understanding of the Cappadocian Fathers the divine *ousia* was ineffable.[58] Anthony Meredith endorses this view.[59] This critique of the interpretation of patristic sources leads to a second challenge, which questions where the motivation for such interpretation is to be found. Writing in 1992, Nicholas Lash warns, 'Although the individualism which, in Western culture, infects our sense of what it is to be a human person is no help here, to exorcize [person] would not render the term more suitable for use in Trinitarian theology'.[60]

Implicit in Lash's argument is a critique of those who seek to reformulate a conceptuality of personhood in order to challenge the perceived effects of the Enlightenment on understandings of human personhood. Sarah Coakley reiterates this critique of the appeal to the doctrine of the Trinity as 'prototype of persons-in-relation' as made in particular by Zizioulas and Gunton in order to overcome Enlightenment 'individualism'.[61] James Mackey makes a similar point but argues more explicitly that in the social modelling of the Trinity is to be found a projection of current ideas of human relationships into the immanent Trinity,[62] resulting in what he deems to be too much certainty about the inner life of God.[63] Indeed, he suggests, there are 'crypto-ideologies that must always lurk in those social Trinities which have not quite abjured all knowledge of the inner being of God'.[64] Agreeing with Mackey, Fermer reinforces the attack, arguing that the relational interpretation of the divine and ecclesial to be found in the work of Zizioulas and Gunton suggests the collapse of the distinction between God and the world.[65] Metzler argues that a possible solution to the recognition that relational understandings of the divine and ecclesial are based upon contemporary understandings of persons and relationships, rather than patristic understandings, is to accept that the divine is relational in the economy but not in the inner life of the divine.[66] In this solution, he rejects the axiomatic concept that the economic and immanent

Trinities are identical, which underpins so much of the social modelling of the divine and ecclesial.[67] Furthermore, Krempel argues that relation, 'has in modern times replaced "substance" or "the absolute" as the ultimate category of reality'.[68] David Cunningham raises parallel concerns, questioning whether the appeal to social Trinitarianism leads to an authentic expression of Christian monotheism: 'contemporary Trinitarian theology has simply presented a "kinder gentler" substantialist metaphysics. The fault lies in the assumption that the doctrine of the Trinity necessarily implies an ontology of any kind – which, in my view, it does not'.[69]

In response to this challenge, Cunningham recommends an appeal to 'participation' rather than 'relationality', for he argues that participation (*perichoresis*) achieves what relationality sets out to do but without the pitfalls. His concern to overcome ontology, which finds support in the work of Milbank and Marion,[70] is, it seems to me, a proper concern; whether that concern finds a solution in making a distinction between relationality and *perichoresis* is another matter, particularly when so many proponents of social Trinitarianism set so much store by *perichoresis*.[71] Jens Zimmermann also reiterates this strand of critique but also offers a means of rehabilitating a 'hermeneutic of relationality':[72]

> Clearly, the Trinitarian conception of the human subject is important for the recovery of theological hermeneutics. There is, however, one significant problem: most presentations of the communal model of subjectivity are not very hermeneutical. They begin in the speculative realm with the doctrine of the Trinity rather than with God's self-revelation in history. Instead of beginning in time and history, speculation begins in the eternal. The danger is that metaphysics begins to shape theology. While much of the Greek Orthodox speculation on the Trinity and personhood is attractive, its tendency to determine human subjectivity primarily through the Trinity rather than through God's self-expression in Christ is in danger of shaping God himself in our own image . . .[73]

Zimmermann's solution is to appeal to Bonhoeffer's conceptuality of personhood,[74] as understood in relation to the Incarnation and the Cross. Earlier, Jean Galot made similar suggestions, rooting his appeal to relationality in the 'Relational Being of Christ',[75] while also anchoring his argument in the doctrine of the Trinity. This appeal to the self-expression of the divine in Christ is echoed in the typology of Trinitarian thought set out by Sarah Coakley, in particular in relation to 'the Trinity construed from reflection on the death of Christ', as well as in her appeal to 'religious experience'.[76] In using Coakley's typology to analyse and interpret the critique of the social modelling of the divine and ecclesial, two alternative approaches to 'relationality' emerge. On the one hand, it would be possible to be satisfied simply with a 'hermeneutic of relationality', while, on the other hand, it would be possible to argue that the hermeneutic leads to an ontology of relationality.

In pursuit of this question concerning relationality, Rowan Williams's essay on 'Trinity and Ontology' is instructive. In his appropriation of Donald MacKinnon's appeal to the tragic in the life of Christ, Rowan Williams points to the need to begin reflection on relationality from the 'world of particulars', rather than from an *a priori* understanding of the Godhead: 'what we first know is the reality we subsequently come to know as derivative, transposed from what is prior'.[77] Sustaining this position is evidently problematic, for as both Williams and Coakley point out, despite the appeal to the 'particularity' of the Cross, in the Trinitarian thought of Moltmann, the interpretation of the world of particulars is construed against a background of 'more than a whiff of Hegelian dialectics';[78] i.e., that the concrete particular is set aside by the overall metaphysical context of the argument. A parallel critique might be offered of others who defend the appeal to social Trinitarianism, such as Zizioulas. In seeking to clarify how the category of *koinonia* might be used, the question must be posed as to whether a relational understanding of the divine and ecclesial communion is to be construed upon *a priori* understandings, be they scriptural, patristic or contemporary; or upon 'the world of particulars' as evidenced in the Scriptural witness and experienced in the lived tradition of praxis and worship. Some would argue that the latter is preferable, being less open to charges of importing extraneous ideologies.

Alan J. Torrance suggests a possible way forward in terms of understanding the connections to be made between the interpretation of the world of particulars and the interpretation of the God who reveals himself. He argues that, 'Theologically interpreted, communication presupposes the category of communion, and not the other way round'.[79] That leaves him open to the charge of appealing to *a priori* understandings rather than a direct appeal to the revelation in the Christ event. Nonetheless, his appeal to the use of *mirifica communicatio* (miraculous communication) as an interpretative tool in relation to the *mirifica communio* (miraculous communion) mediated through what he understands as the *mirifica commutatio* (miraculous exchange) may still hold useful possibilities. The main issue in asking the question regarding metaphysics is the way in which the role of the mediating *mirifica commutatio* is construed. Does the encounter with the Christ event in the 'world of particulars' take us by means of the *mirifica commutatio* to the *mirifica communio?* Or is there an *a priori* understanding of 'communion'?

Christoph Schwöbel also points to the dissatisfaction with non-Trinitarian thought, which gives no proper account of the person and work of Christ as well as 'disappointment with the inability of many versions of Christian theism, conceived in terms of a metaphysics of substance or a philosophy of subjectivity, to do justice to the relational "logic" of such central Christian statements as "God is Love" '.[80] Against this critique of 'a metaphysics of substance', a hermeneutical rather than ontological account of relationality may be more pertinent in seeking to give an account of the category of *koinonia*.

In conclusion, I would suggest that the sustained critique of the appeal to social Trinitarianism can be answered through an appeal to the 'world of particulars'. Such an appeal would focus on Christology, as rooted in an understanding of the concrete events of revelation in the economy. There need be no rush to formulate ontological claims. Nonetheless, the conceptuality of relationality rooted in an appeal to *koinonia* can still be endorsed. This relates to claims for the relevance of the doctrine of the Trinity. As I shall outline below, Pecknold has argued that Augustine understood the doctrine in functional terms. If such an understanding can be defended as authentic, then what is to prevent putting the doctrine of the Trinity to a non-ideological functional use in addressing concerns about the impact of individualism in contemporary Western society?

THE PROBLEM OF SOCINUS

A second major feature in the history of Trinitarian hermeneutics is the dispute surrounding Socinus and Socinianism. In particular, the identification of Socinian thought with Arianism led in the era following the early years of the Reformation to a major bifurcation in the interpretation of the development of ideas in the pre-Nicene Church. On the one hand, there were those who held that the emergence of Nicene orthodoxy was a natural development from the pre-Nicene traditions evident in the Early Church fathers, while, on the other, it was perceived that the understandings of Arius and Arianism were those which were predominant in the period before Nicaea. While such divergence could make a considerable difference to the ways in which the Nicene Creed and tradition were received, authors on either side of the bifurcation often drew unexpected conclusions from their interpretations, which I will explore briefly below.

As part of the left-wing Reformation, Socinianism emerges as a direct assault on orthodox teaching concerning the Godhead as triune and takes its name from Laelius Socinus (d. 1562 in Zurich) and his nephew Faustus Socinus (d. 1604 in Poland). The Socinian sect they formed began as a secret society to evade the concerns of the ruling authorities of the state and the mainstream churches. In 1574, the sect proclaimed itself as Unitarian, publishing a *Catechism of the Unitarians*, which set out their views on the singularity and undifferentiated nature of the Godhead. It was not long before those whose theological interests lay in the area of the history of Trinitarian doctrine perceived a parallel between the teachings of Socinianism and Arianism. This identification can be seen in scholars on both sides of the Reformation divide. It became a matter of division between Catholic and Protestant, once the Jesuit scholar Dionysius Petavius (Denis Petau) (d. 1652) had also made this identification. In his *Theologicorum dogmatum* (Paris, 1644), he was perhaps one of the first of his generation to offer the interpretation that the pre-Nicene writings were more often in sympathy with an Arian understanding than with the Nicene orthodoxy defended by Athanasius. Unlike the Socinians, Petavius reached different conclusions, offering a clear defence of Nicene orthodoxy. Furthermore, Petavius offered a critique in particular of the Socinian writer Johannes Crellius and identified Socinian ideas with the radical views of Erasmus.[81] From these interpretations, Petavius drew the conclusion that the Church is always in need of a strong central authority and clear-sighted leadership; in other words, his interpretations of the pre-Nicene Church and of sixteenth- and seventeenth-century heterodoxy led him to a strong affirmation of papal authority. This sets the specifically Trinitarian doctrinal controversy in the domain of inter-church politics and questions of church authority and governance. In terms of the wider controversy concerning post-Reformation heterodoxy, it meant that not only those who explicitly denied the three-foldness of the Godhead but also others, such as Melanchthon, who were sceptical about so-called speculative doctrines such as the Trinity or, indeed, the two natures of Christ,[82] were drawn into this fierce debate.

P. Louis Maimbourg, also a Jesuit, in his *History of Arianism* (1673) clearly identifies the Socinians of his day with Arius and Arianism, arguing that a recognition of Nicene orthodoxy should have been sufficient to persuade Socinus that his view were erroneous. This understanding is challenged by Pierre Bayle in his *Philosophical Commentary* (1686–7).[83] Bayle, a Huguenot, wrote in response to the Revocation of the Edict of Nantes, a defence of free conscience for pagans, Muslims, Jews, atheists, Catholics, Protestants, Anabaptists and Socinians. He argued for a doctrine of 'errant conscience', in which 'error disguised as truth must be allowed all the privileges of truth, i.e., must be permitted to be believed by those convinced they had found truth.'[84] While Bayle himself clearly disputed Socinian understandings of God, his doctrine of toleration clearly perturbed those of a more traditional or orthodox point of view and only served to intensify disputes between defenders of Trinitarian orthodoxy and those who espoused Unitarianism of one sort or another. Such radical appeals for the toleration of heterodoxy are part of the context in which the defenders of orthodoxy sought to interpret not only those of a different perspective of their own time but also of the past and, in particular, of the pre-Nicene church and, of course, the person of Arius. For example, Christopher Sand, a Socinian, argues in his *Nucleus historiae ecclesiastic* (1668) that the writings of the pre-Nicene Fathers were often more in line with Arius than with Athanasius. This echoes the conclusions which Petavius had reached, though each reaches radically different conclusions. The Anglican Bishop, George Bull, writing in *Defensio fidei Nicaean* (1685) interpreted the pre-Nicene fathers very differently from both Sand and Petavius, arguing that they stood in line with the Nicene orthodoxy of Athanasius. Daniel Waterland (d. 1730) is another Anglican defender of Nicene orthodoxy. In his work *Vindication of Christ's Divinity* (1719)[85] he offers insightful and learned essays and sermons in defence of the orthodox doctrine of the Trinity against those who had espoused a fashionable Arianism or Socinianism during the late seventeenth century.

Controversy concerning the interpretation of the pre-Nicene fathers was not only a matter for the interpreters of the history of Trinitarian doctrine in the seventeenth and eighteenth centuries. John Henry Newman and other nineteenth-century writers also engaged in fierce disputes concerning Trinitarian hermeneutics. In 1833, the same year as Keble's *Assize Sermon*, John Henry Newman published a controversial work, *The Arians of the Fourth Century*.[86] Newman revised this work several times and was clearly unhappy with it in his post-conversion life. Rowan Williams, in his *Introduction* to the work from 2001, argues that Newman interprets the pre-Nicene church in relation to his own current concerns about the Church of England. Nonetheless, Newman's work illustrates the core issues surrounding nineteenth-century concerns over the continuing influence of Socinianism as well as the interpretation of the Church Fathers prior to the Council of Nicaea. In what is a highly perceptive essay, Newman sets out the ambiguity of the language and formulations used to speak of the Godhead before the fourth century. While some of the conclusions that Newman draws from his study may now be seen as no longer tenable, his work allows the reader to value the processes of the development of doctrine. Newman's understanding that Nicene orthodoxy emerged as much from a rejection of an abundance of metaphors and a widespread understanding of the Godhead akin to that of Arius meant that a decision needed to be made in terms of the hermeneutics of that development towards orthodoxy. On the one hand, those of the High Church Party in the Church of England feared that Newman's views might evoke sympathy for Unitarianism or Deism, while, on the other hand, his views could have played into the hands of Dionysius Petavius, who was still at that time considered a leading Roman Catholic writer and who had argued that the chaotic situation before Nicaea suggested the necessity for a firm central authority: i.e., the Papacy.

What becomes clear from this brief overview of the disputes around Socinianism is that, first of all, these disputes shaped not only the interpretation of the contemporary discourse of the sixteenth to nineteenth centuries but also the interpretation of the Early Church. Second, it becomes evident that Petavius occupied a central place in this discourse, both in terms of his scholarship and also as a symbol of the disagreement between Catholics and Protestants concerning religious toleration, questions of authority and, above all, the Papacy. Petavius was often quoted either as an adversary or as an ally in contemporary discourse concerning Arius or Socinus. He was appealed to by some Anglican authors and is cited by writers as disparate as Isaac Newton, in his work *On Arius and Athanasius*,[87] and Gibbon in *The History of the Decline and Fall of the Roman*

Empire[88] as an authority on the interpretation of the doctrine of the Trinity. In the period before de Régnon and the promotion of the 'de Régnon paradigm', Dionyius Petavius may be seen to be just as influential in shaping Trinitarian hermeneutics. What is perhaps surprising is the relative neglect of Petavius in the writings of those who chronicle the development of the doctrine of the Trinity during the twentieth century. Not surprisingly, Rahner, himself a Jesuit, does make a brief mention of him; but writers such as Karl Barth, Wolfhart Panneberg, Robert Jenson and David Brown do not refer to this period.[89] Indeed, they appear to avoid tackling the influence of Socinianism on the interpretation of the doctrine of the Trinity, perhaps assuming that the reassertion of Nicene orthodoxy is all that is necessary. An example of an exception to this is to be found in the *Christian Dogmatics*, edited by Carl E. Braaten and Robert W. Jenson, in which Braaten himself clearly recognizes that Socinianism influences the development of doctrine in general.[90] But he does not explore this specifically in relation to the doctrine of the Trinity. I believe that this avoidance of the history of Trinitarian hermeneutics can no longer be sustained. A recognition of the various features of the developments in this history is crucial if the (non-)reception of the tradition is to be understood in a holistic way. The disputes concerning Socinianism or parallel manifestations have influenced the ways in which Nicene orthodoxy is perceived and received. To the extent that the perceived irrelevance of the doctrine of the Trinity can be traced to these controversies, at least in part, in the sense that the doctrine is seen as part of an Establishment Christianity over against a more Free Church understanding, with all the implicit ramifications of hegemonic claims and counterclaims and appeals to freedom and toleration, it is possible to see the out-workings of a combination of the views of Socinus and Melanchthon in the views of the Deists and in the writings of Schleiermacher, Ritschl and Harnack[91] and, more recently, in a work such as *The Myth of God Incarnate*.[92]

THE SCHISM OF 1054

The third major feature of the history of Trinitarian hermeneutics is centred upon the dispute concerning the addition to the Creed of the Council of Constantinople 381, of the words 'and the Son' (in Latin *filioque*) by churches in the West. Such an addition to the text of an Ecumenical Council had been strictly forbidden. A disagreement between the Latin and Greek churches emerged, at first in relation to questions of authority and only subsequently in terms of doctrine. But a sense of difference in doctrine and practice was established both officially and, one might say, 'psychologically' too. The conceptuality of there being a difference between East and West as expressed in the 'de Régnon paradigm' is deeply embedded in the psyche of the Christian tradition(s), even if the de Régnon paradigm itself is a misconstrual of that divergence. The addition to the Creed evoked indignation on the part of the authorities in the East and, to some extent, incomprehension in the West. Nonetheless, the disputed addition has created two competing interpretations in terms of the explication of the understanding of the relationship of the Holy Spirit to Father and Son: the East claimed that the Father alone is the origin of the Spirit, while the West claimed that both Father and Son could be understood to be the origins of the Spirit. Evidently, both positions rest upon highly abstract and speculative understandings of the inner life of the Godhead. I shall return to examine something of these doctrines in Chapter 3. I would suggest that the arguments are to be understood at least in their origins as responses to misunderstanding and that the attempts at reconciliation and mutual understandings during the Middle Ages demonstrate that this was recognized, at least to some extent. It may be the case that the *filioque* dispute has become more clearly understood and perhaps more entrenched as a result of ecumenical dialogue during the twentieth century.

There is some evidence that a phrase akin to the *filioque* was introduced by a council into the Creed in Persia in 410, which stated that the Spirit proceeds from the Father 'and from the Son'. Thus, the issue is not simply a matter of conflict between the Latin West and Greek East. A theology of *filioque* is often attributed to Augustine of Hippo; however, this is anachronistic, and, while his writing may be read in support of the development, it is doubtful that his theology would inevitably lead to such a development. The first evidence for the use of the *filioque* in the West is in Toledo in Visigothic Spain in 587, without any consultation or agreement. It has been suggested that it was added to counter a local heresy. The history of the spread and use of the phrase is mixed. For instance, at a council held at Aix-la-Chapelle in 809, called by the Emperor Charlemagne, Pope Leo III forbade the use of the *filioque* clause and had the original version of the Nicene–Constantinopolitan Creed engraved on silver tablets to be displayed in St Peter's in Rome. Later in the ninth century, the Pope was asked to adjudicate in a dispute over the succession of the Patriarch of Constantinople. This concerned the appointment of the Patriarch Photius and led to what has been called the 'Photian Schism'. The addition of the *filioque* to the Creed became an issue in the dispute, which Photius claimed was a sign that the Pope had exceeded his authority. The issues of papal aggrandisement and the *filioque* became intertwined, foreshadowing the issues of the schism of 1054. In 879–80, at the Fourth Council of Constantinople, *filioque* was effectively condemned, and, although this Council was accepted by the contemporary pope, Photius had initiated an Eastern understanding that Rome had fallen into heresy.

During the first millennium, no creed was used in the Papal Eucharistic Liturgy. It was as a result of journeying to Rome for his coronation that the Emperor Henry II, in 1014, discovered that the Creed was not used during the Mass. He requested that the Nicene Creed be added in the version which included the *filioque*, after the Gospel. Thus, the Papacy became committed to the inclusion of the *filioque* almost by accident. The arguments between East and West came to a head in 1054 and resulted in schism. Various moves towards reconciliation between East and West were attempted during the Middle Ages. One such attempt was made in 1274, at the Second Council of Lyons. Thomas Aquinas, and others, were commissioned to write doctrinal treatises in search of clarity and possible reconciliation. Accordingly, Aquinas produced his version of *Contra erroes Graecorum* (*Against the errors of the Greeks*), which included his explication of the *filioque*. Such progress as was achieved by the Council did not last. Another attempt was made in 1439 at the Council of Florence, when the Byzantine Emperor John VIII Palaeologus, Patriarch Joseph of Constantinople and other bishops from the East travelled to northern Italy in hope of reconciliation with the West, probably with the intention of seeking political and military help against the Ottoman Turks. Doctrinal accord was reached on the basis of accepting that there was divergence between the Latin and Greek Fathers of the Early Church, which justified ongoing differences of expression, in what was understood to be a common faith. A decree of union between East and West, *Laetentur Coeli*, was issued in 1439. However, many in the Orthodox community refused to accept the reunion, and, after the fall of Constantinople in 1453, there was effectively a situation of both separation and schism.

Despite the focus on the *filioque*, it has been argued that there are other more fundamental differences to be negotiated between East and West. As I have argued above, this is not to be seen in terms of the caricature of the Latins' appeal to *unitas in trinitate* and the Greeks' to *trinitas in unitate*. While there is some truth in the distinction to be drawn between a unitary modelling (the unity in distinction of persons) and a social modelling (the distinction of persons in the unity) in the construction of Trinitarian doctrine, such a distinction does not necessarily describe the differences between East and West. Indeed, such a distinction may be found in writers from both traditions. It is important to remember that both West and East agree that the Godhead is to be understood in the classic terminology of *mia ousia, treis hypostaseis* (one substance, three hypostases) or *tres personae, una substantia* (three persons, one substance), to which I will return in Chapter 3. Rather, it can be argued that the main differences between East and West concern their epistemological approaches and ontological affirmations about the being and nature of God. These were articulated by the leading theologians of the High Middle Ages, Gregory Palamas and Thomas Aquinas.

Gregory Palamas, the Orthodox theologian, builds on the traditions of the East and draws a clear distinction between the essence and energies of the Godhead. In his understanding, the essence of God is utterly inaccessible and unknowable for human beings. Thomas Aquinas, in the West, argued that the divine essence might be known through the *habitus* (habit or state) of created grace, enabling the human mind to perceive divine truth. The separation of East and West as a result of the 1054 Schism in a sense accentuates this difference in epistemological approach. However, even in this area of dispute, there are common strands to be discerned. Both Palamas and Aquinas were clear that even a redeemed human being does not actually know or participate in the very being of God. The ultimate mystery of the Godhead does not become comprehended or accessible through God's revelation in the economy of salvation. That being the case, what is accessible to human knowing in revelation? Palamas replied that the uncreated energies are to be understood as divine, in that they are known in the three hypostases of God's revelation. Aquinas replied that as a consequence of the *habitus* of created grace there could be a real human knowing of God in the beatific vision. God's supernatural assistance enabled the human mind to see God, and of this there is a foretaste 'now' through the reception of sanctifying grace. Despite the differences concerning epistemology, writers from East and West in the Middle

Ages understood that a graced knowledge of God was available to human beings, which was God's threefold personal identity.

Despite the high profile of the schism and its effects on the communion between the churches of the East and West, the issues are in many ways more about perceived than material doctrinal differences and more about issues of jurisdiction and authority than issues of doctrinal hermeneutics. The longer-term effect has been to ingrain the tradition with the perception that there are deep-seated doctrinal differences to be negotiated and overcome. I would suggest that these surface in the so-called 'de Régnon paradigm', and continue to shape Trinitarian doctrinal discourse to the present day. The serious misunderstandings concerning the construction of the doctrine of the Trinity between East and West are matters both for ecumenical dialogue as well as academic discourse. In both cases, the will to power needs to recognized and taken into account in the process of each side seeking to (re)understand the other's hermeneutical stance.

ARIUS AND NICENE ORTHODOXY

The fourth feature of the history of Trinitarian hermeneutics to be discussed concerns the possibilities for the interpretation of the effects of Arius and Arianism, and the reception of the Councils of Nicaea (325) and Constantinople (381). The association of Arianism with Socinianism in the minds of the seventeenth-century scholars, as noted already, led to an ongoing debate concerning the interpretation of the understanding of Godhead in the pre-Nicene Church. It is the question of the interpretation of the pre-Nicene Church, as well as the reception of the response to Arius and Arianism in the Councils of Nicaea and Constantinople, that I shall now examine.

A pre-Nicene ecology of language

Patristic scholars are generally agreed in the present time that even when writers such as Irenaeus and Tertullian were seeking to respond to what they understood as heretical views, they did so in ways that were open and exploratory in terms of the language and formulations that they used. It is usual to assume that the writings of the early patristic period are characterized by a fluidity of language and expression and employed an imaginative and multiple use of metaphor to describe the 'persons' of the Godhead. It would be a mistake to look for and find any kind of systematic conceptuality of the 'Trinity' in the first three centuries. Rather, forms of expression emerge from the culture of the times. Some scholars have interpreted these phenomena in terms of inculturation. If it is inculturation, then I would suggest that it is unintentional; that is to say, the writers borrowed the terminology that they employed from the thought world which they inhabited. Indeed, could they have done anything else? It is clear from the evidence of Philo of Alexandria that Jewish as well as later Christian writers reached for terminology and conceptualities that were to hand, that probably were as much their own as anyone else's. The use of *logos* by the author of the fourth Gospel and later writers demonstrates a connection to both Stoic and Platonist conceptualities, as well as a connection to the tradition of the Hebrew Bible and the understanding to be found in its writings of 'the Word of the Lord'. Early patristic writers were often creative and imaginative in the way they used and stretched metaphors, such as sunlight, fire, heat and so forth. As far as the understanding of 'divine generation' is concerned, a plethora of metaphors were used, often by the same writer: for example, well, spring and stream. Rowan Williams argues that the profusion suggests that none of them was supposed to be taken literally or in isolation.[93] An 'ecology' of doctrinal language emerged within the attempt made by Christians to give an account of the God whom they understood they had encountered in Christ: 'Within the whole system of Christian speech, words receive their proper sense, balanced by others, qualified and nuanced by their neighbours.'[94] Equally, the conceptualities, which in the final outcome came to be deemed erroneous, had been used initially to express key understandings of the Godhead. Monarchianism can be said to have been used to safeguard the unity of God. Dynamic or adoptionist Monarchianism, attributed to Paul of Samosata, understood that the power (*dynamis*) of God had descended on Jesus, inspired him and given him divine honour. Some would argue that such an understanding can be read out of the Apostles' Creed. There were other forms of Monarchianism: such as modalism, patripassianism and Sabellianism,[95] in which the three names used in relation to the Godhead: Father, Son and Spirit represented one *hypostasis* or *persona*, which was manifest in a succession of modes. There was no understanding of any real distinction within the divine being. These understandings of the divine led to the asking of crucial questions about how God *in se* was related to the revelation and redemption given. It is out of these concerns and the perceived threats of misunderstanding or heresy that the imperatives towards definition emerge.

The reception of Nicene orthodoxy

The perceived threat of Arius and Arianism led to a process of clarification, which, in some senses, can be seen as bringing about an impoverishment of language and formulations. The clarification or definitions are of course stated in the Creeds of 325 and 381. The discourse and disputes which occurred between the Councils demonstrates that decisions have always to be received and lived with. In this section, I want to examine something of the effects of defining and also of the receiving of that defining. John Henry Newman wrote in his essay on doctrinal development that, 'no doctrine is defined till it is violated'.[96] In the fourth century, the emergence and development of orthodoxy was clearly a dialectical process: 'The dialectic moves towards "definition" which is regulative in character as it makes rules to protect previously "undifferentiated" beliefs'.[97] Bernard Lonergan argues that such a process was probably inevitable, but, in agreement with Petavius, he argues that what emerged was essentially a novel understanding of the divine being, which is both speculative and ontological in character.[98] Furthermore, Lonergan argues that the Creeds of the fourth century and the disputes that gave rise to the imperatives for them

> mark a transition (as the gospels themselves do) from the particular to the universal, and from 'a whole range of problems to a basic solution to those problems.' The entire process is seen as a movement 'from naive realism, beyond Platonism, to dogmatic realism and in the direction of critical realism.'[99]

In the pre-Nicene period, there are two main developments in the Church's understanding: (1) a development towards understandings of the triune Godhead and of the Person of Christ; and (2) the development of the very notion of dogma.[100] As Pecknold recognizes, 'It is important to notice that all of these developments occurred in response to regulative needs. That is to say, Trinitarian doctrine was moving towards formalization because it quite simply needed rules'.[101] However, with Augustine of Hippo, it has been argued that a different kind of development or reception began to take place.[102] Following on from the Council of Constantinople, Augustine receives and uses the doctrine as set out in the Creed and other documentation of the Council. Pecknold argues that Augustine did not receive the tradition passively but actively studied the evolution of the newly found orthodoxy of Nicaea and Constantinople. The first eight books of *De trinitate* (written between 399 and 416) demonstrate that Augustine engaged critically with the tradition.

Most interesting is the way in which Augustine sees the tension between the early economic theologians (*De trinitate*, I–IV) and the so-called 'metaphysical' ones of the fourth-century controversies over Arianism and Nicaea (*De trinitate*, V–VII). It may be overstating it to find Augustine's genius primarily in his brilliant synthesis of the economic and metaphysical Trinitarians, as this synthesis was also a concern of most pro- and neo-Nicene theologians.[103]

Augustine assimilates much from the teaching of the Cappadocian Fathers, for instance, Gregory of Nazianzen's understanding that, 'The name Father is not one of substance (*ousia*) or activity (*energia*), but relationship (*schesis*)' (Orationes 29, XVI). Augustine continues to reflect upon and develop the Cappadocians' concern for the relations in the unity of God. Evidently, Augustine modified the Greek terminology of the Cappadocians for the Latin context in which he lived and worked but preserved their basic insights. Pecknold argues that Augustine was the first theologian to use the doctrine of the Trinity to perform functions in theology other than regulative ones. Augustine marks a post-formal shift to the 'functionalization' of doctrine.[104] This did not entail a reformulation of the doctrine but its reception in ways which were novel and creative. Augustine draws a distinction between the terms *frui* (enjoyment) and *uti* (use). *Frui* is 'the attitude we entertain towards things we value for themselves'. *Uti* is 'the attitude we entertain towards things we value for the sake of something else'.[105] Pecknold argues that the *De trinitate* is shaped to reflect the way Augustine viewed history. The first half clearly deals with *frui* in relation to the Trinity, and the second half seeks to understand the Trinity in terms of *uti*. Indeed, the 'inter-relation between *frui* and *uti* in Augustine should also suggest something of the way in which the immanent and the economic are interrelated in his thought'.[106] Augustine's treatment of the doctrine of the Trinity, moving to a 'functionalization', allows doctrine to become redemptive as well as regulative. Thus, doctrine can operate on a number of different levels such as hermeneutic, systematic and salvific. By appealing to the salvific, Augustine is able to remove the doctrine of the Trinity from merely being a rule by which to judge statements and turn it into something which has a functionality which is both existential and redemptive.

> Augustine uses the Trinity in the analogies to draw the reader through a process of spiritual conversion in which the journey inward may invite the journey upward. [. . .] The conversion itself is the point, so that the believer may be drawn out of himself and into a relationship of remembering God, understanding God, and loving God.[107]

The shift to a functionality of doctrine, which Augustine achieved in his understanding of the Trinity, is something that continues to set a challenge down to the present time. Does theological discourse encourage and enable first-order reflection on God? Much recent Trinitarian theology has understood the doctrine to have a clear functionality in the present-day context. Indeed, I noted above that this has often been the cause of sharp criticism. But perhaps it is time to take stock and ask if this newly discovered relevance is not an echo of the achievement of Augustine? I would suggest that Augustine's appeal to function can be used in support of the contemporary appeal to relationality, including Zizioulas's own construction and use of the doctrine of the Trinity. An implication of Augustine's use of the doctrine of the Trinity might entail an issue of divergence or separation from the Eastern apophatic approach. This is something which would need to be explored with theologians from the Eastern tradition.

In taking stock of these four moments in the history of Trinitarian hermeneutics, it becomes clear that the development of doctrine is never simply a matter of 'pure' theological reflection. Reflection always takes place in a context, and part of that context may include other disputes, questions of authority and certainly some form of the manifestation of the will to power. This is clearly the case in the way in which the Councils of Nicaea and Constantinople respond to the perceived threat of Arius and Arianism. This is reiterated in the post-Reformation period in terms of the fear of Socinianism, though this is inscribed on the tradition in a different way: in this instance the hermeneutics of the fourth century become part of the will to power concerning the Papacy. This is also the case in terms of the dispute concerning the *filioque* in the Schism of 1054. The appeal to de Régnon made by Lossky in a sense reinscribes each of these disputes in terms of the desire to cultivate the perception that there are profound differences between East and West. Arius, the Schism, Socinus and de Régnon have each made profound marks upon hermeneutical history and produced markers in the ongoing reception of Trinitarian hermeneutics to the present day.

SUGGESTED READING

F. LeRon Shults, *Reforming Theological Anthropology: After the Philosophical Turn to Relationality* (Cambridge and Grand Rapids, Mich.: William B. Eerdmans, 2003).

K. Ware, 'Byzantium: The Great Schism', in *The Orthodox Church* (Harmondsworth: Penguin, 1983), pp. 51–81.

M. Wiles, *Archetypal Heresy: Arianism through the Centuries* (Oxford: Clarendon Press, 1996).

J. H. Newman, *The Arians of the Fourth Century* (1833; Leominster and Notre Dame, Ind.: Gracewing and University of Notre Dame Press, 2001).

L. Ayres, *Nicaea and its Legacy: An Approach to Fourth Century Trinitarian Thought* (Oxford: Oxford University Press, 2004).

S. Coakley (ed.), 'The God of Nicaea: Disputed Questions in Patristic Trinitarianism', Special Issue, *Harvard Theological Review* 100, 2 (April) (2007).

CHAPTER 3

EXPRESSING THE INEXPRESSIBLE?

INTRODUCTION

The words, formulas and concepts used to express the understanding that God is three yet one are always going to be used in an attempt to bring to expression something which is not only a logical impossibility but also a mystery beyond the competency of human language. The Council of Constantinople in 382 declared that the Godhead should be understood in the following terms: one substance, three 'persons': *mia ousia, tres hypostaseis*. This is the technical language of Nicene orthodoxy, which has been received and sometimes restated over the past sixteen centuries. This chapter will examine the complex landscape of the attempts to express the inexpressible. Sometimes the focus will be on single words and, at other times, on complex frameworks involving the (re)statement of terminology and concepts. There are two sections to the chapter. The first traces the development of the doctrine of the Trinity up to and including the construction of Nicene orthodoxy. The second examines the reception and refinement of that orthodoxy. In the first part, I will discuss the pre-Nicene ecology of terms and formulations, the decision at Nicaea to use the *homoousion*, the expression of the Divine Three following on from Nicaea and the emergence of the discourse concerning 'relations of origin'. In the second part, I will examine the problematic of personhood in modernity, focusing in particular on the formulations of Karl Rahner, Karl Barth and John Zizioulas. Arising from the discussion of personhood, I will discuss the appeal to communion (*koinonia*) and the conceptuality of indwelling (*perichoresis*). In conclusion, I will discuss the use of gendered language in the doctrine of the Trinity, examining the feminist critique of such language, the notion of 'sophiology' and the conceptuality of 'iconic language'. In parallel with this analytical examination of terminology, the reader should also continue to bear in mind that the use of these terms is only an attempt to express what is ultimately inexpressible: the being of God. Questions of the relation of language and terminology to the nature of God *in se* need also to be asked. In what sense can the language of finite human beings reflect the infinite and eternal being of God? The use of language may be deemed analogical or metaphorical. The question remains to what extent does the language used refer to the being of God? I shall return to examine some aspects of this problem in the following chapter. For the time being, it is important to hold on to the vision that God is and remains 'mystery'.

PRE-NICENE ECOLOGY

In this first section, I consider the periods before the Council of Nicaea and between Nicaea and Constantinople and ask how does the conceptuality emerge that God is both one and three: one *ousia* and three *hypostases*? As I noted in the previous chapter, there was considerable fluidity in the use of language during the first three centuries. The forms of expression and formulation used draw upon a multiplicity of metaphors in an attempt to understand the threefold revelation of God, witnessed in the Scriptures and encountered in worship. One of the major features in the theological landscape of the early Church was the appeal to *logos* (word or reason). Used already by Philo of Alexandria (c.20 BC–c.50 AD)[1] and in the Fourth Gospel with reference to the divine being, the appeal to *logos* demonstrates that theological reflection in the Judaeo-Christian tradition was being done within the cultural and philosophical mind-set of the Hellenistic world. Such usage may be understood as a kind of inculturation. Philo and the author of the Fourth Gospel used *logos* as a means of communicating with adherents of their traditions, as well as with those outside those traditions, what they understood about the divine and also the relationship of the divine to the created cosmos. The practice of using the language and terminology of the contemporary cultural milieu in theological reflection was, on the one hand, a tactical ploy of apologetics, but, on the other hand, that very usage itself formed the identity and self-understanding of those traditions, and their theological conceptualities. The Johannine statement that the Word (*logos*) was made flesh, which undoubtedly connected with the conceptual understandings of both Stoic and

Platonist traditions, in the long term committed the Christian tradition to an understanding of the person of Jesus Christ and of the relationship of the divine to the cosmos in terms of the conceptuality of 'incarnation'. The controversies within the Christian tradition that led to the calling of the ecumenical councils in an attempt to solve them, arise from legitimate questions concerning that interface between the Christian *kerygma* and the expression of that *kerygma* in Hellenistic language and terminology, as the Johannine appeal to *logos* demonstrates. Of course, the notion that these can be separated is itself a vexed question, since the *kerygma* is already expressed in such terms in the New Testament. The crisis which emerges around the figure of Arius and, later, the semi-Arians, is a crisis with its roots in Scripture. If the writers of New Testament literature were content to 'borrow' from the thought-worlds of the surrounding cultures and philosophies, how is one to determine where Gospel ends and philosophical traditions begin? Arius' claims that the *logos* was inferior to and different from the Godhead are mainstream understandings of the relation of the divine to the cosmos in the context of later Platonist philosophizing. At one level, the main issue which the councils of Nicaea and Constantinople faced is the question of the extent to which, when borrowing terms from culture and philosophy, one was also bound by the preconceptions attached to those terms.

The beginnings of post-Apostolic reflection on the threefoldness of the revelation of God in the economy are witnessed in the attempt made by Theophilus of Antioch (d. c.185) to speak of the *logos* in terms of the *logos* in relation to God *in se: endiathetos* and put forth: *prophorikos*, in relation to the world (economy).[2] This attempt raises the question of how the use of terminology relates to God *in se*. Theological reflection is already engaging with the need to ask whether divine revelation is something which is only within the world and external to God, which would sit more easily with standard philosophical assumptions; or did revelation relate to the (inner) divine being? Irenaeus of Lyons (c.130–c.200) continues in the tradition of making an explicit appeal to the threefoldness of divine revelation. He uses the metaphor of God having two hands: the Word and the Spirit in the economy.[3] Most scholars would agree that this does not amount to an exploration of intra-divine reality, but he does have an understanding of 'Son-ship' as being eternal. Irenaeus' idea of the two hands of God, in turn, raises a question concerning the unity of divine action in creating and redeeming the cosmos: does God have one or three wills; one or three activities, so to speak?

And are the two hands subordinate to 'God'? Tertullian (c.160–235) takes Trinitarian theological reflection to another stage of development, arguing that God is to be understood as three persons (*personae*) and one substance (*unius substantiae*).[4] This raises the broader questions: what is a *persona*, and what does Tertullian's use of the terms *trinitas* and *trias* in relation to God infer? What is tri-unity? Tertullian's use of *persona* is drawn from the law courts and stage; 'person' refers to a participant in a dispute or a role in a drama. It is likely that Tertullian understood the *tres personae* as three roles in the divine economy: Father, Son, Spirit, with the main stress on the unity of God. Such an interpretation of Tertullian's views resonates with the then prevalent views of modalism and Sabellianism, in which the one divine being is understood to have three names. Welch argues that Tertullian understands that, 'God is three not in condition (*statu*) but in degree, not in substance but in form, not in power but in aspect (*specie*); yet of one substance and of one condition, inasmuch as he is one God, from whom these degrees and form and aspects are reckoned'.[5] If Welch's interpretation is correct, there is already a highly nuanced understanding of the relation between the one and the three in Tertullian's work. In the writings of Origen (c.185–c.254) are to be found the beginnings of the 'relations of origin'. Origen understands that God (the Father) is without origin,[6] while the Son is generate, through an eternal begetting. The divine being is conceived as a 'community' of three by Origen, but this is a descending hierarchical threefoldness,[7] which the Cappadocian Fathers would develop and transform into an egalitarian and co-eternal co-equal threefoldness. This would become the stuff of Nicene orthodoxy.

NICAEA AND THE *HOMOOUSION*

The decision of the bishops at the Council of Nicaea (325) to include the non-Scriptural and non-traditional term *homoousios* (of the same substance)[8] to express both differentiation and unity between Father and Son was not received without controversy. That the term was not in Scripture and not part of the core tradition meant that many had reservations about its use, if not its inferred meaning. In addition, there were many who also struggled with this newly inferred meaning. It was generally understood among the early fathers that *ousia* was too materialistic a term to be applied directly to the Godhead. Eusebius and Origen[9] are typical of those who accepted the philosophical convention that God is 'beyond substance'. Tertullian had been content to apply *substantia* to the Godhead,[10] which he understood as a distinguishing property, i.e., eternity.[11] Origen was content to speak of the Son as 'substance of substances and Idea of Ideas',[12] while the Father is 'beyond all these', and the Spirit was understood as an 'active substance, not an activity'.[13] The reluctance to use *ousia* in relation to the Godhead in Trinitarian theological reflection was only gradually overcome because its materialistic overtones remained. Furthermore, since the *homoousion* introduced at Nicaea was novel and controversial, it came to be received and interpreted in a variety of ways.

During the reception of the conciliar creed of Nicaea in the period between 325 and 381, among the responses there were those who took a 'semi-Arian' approach, and there were also the spirit-fighters or 'Pneumatomachians'. The semi-Arians sought to promote the term *homoiousios*, implying that Father and Son were different, different in *ousia*, and, by implication they were not equally divine. The spirit fighters denied the divinity of the Holy Spirit and sought to exclude the Holy Spirit from the *homoousion* Godhead. It is in response to the semi-Arians and the spirit fighters that much of the remarkable theological work of the Cappadocian Fathers was written. The Cappadocians themselves inhabited the world of semi-Arianism and were, at heart, conservative in their approach. But, on the whole, history has seen the Cappadocians as contributing creatively and innovatively to the tradition in the period of the reception of Nicaea and in the conciliar decisions of Constantinople in 381 and 382. Not only the promulgation of the Creed of 381, but also the agreement of qualifying terms and concepts, is influenced, to a considerable extent, by the work of the Cappadocians Fathers. This forms the basis of what has come to be perceived as Nicene orthodoxy: i.e., that the Godhead is one substance and three persons, and that Father, Son and Holy Spirit are *homoousion*. In this latter claim, what had previously been understood about the Godhead in terms of a descending hierarchy was transformed into an understanding of the Godhead as an horizontal egalitarian communion of three. For some, all this can seem a long way from that to which the New Testament bears witness and removed from Christian experience of the activity of God in the economy of salvation. However, Athanasius (c.293–373) would champion the view that the decision to use the *homoousion* at Nicaea made explicit the claims for the divinity of Christ, which are to be discerned in the New Testament.

This became and remains the commitment of the mainstream churches: that the decisions made at Nicaea and Constantinople do not create a new orthodoxy but, rather, clarify three centuries of theological reflection in its dialectic with Hellenistic thought and proclaim afresh the heart of the Christian Gospel, that 'God was in Christ reconciling the world to himself'.

THE DIVINE THREE

While in the Latin West there was general agreement that the three-foldness encountered in the economy of salvation was to be designated by the word *persona*, there was more variety of use in Greek. That being said, the word *proposon* is clearly an equivalent of *persona*. Both words refer to drama; the Greek word *prosopon* was used to refer to an actor's mask. Indeed, *prosopon* remains the word most commonly used in Greek to this day to refer to the individual human being. Perhaps because of its dramatic reference, and, therefore, the possibility of a connotation resembling, or colluding with modalism, the word 'hypostasis' came to be used in 382 to state the threefold in God. This was not without controversy on a number of levels, not least because there had been a widespread and uncontroversial use of *mia hypostasis* among theologians to refer to the single divine reality or being. Alongside this usage, the Cappadocian Fathers also used the term *tropos hyparxeos* (mode of existence), although infrequently. This latter use was picked up by Karl Barth, as he struggled to deploy the term 'Person' in relation to the divine being. I shall return to this below. Apart from *prosopon*, the other terms, *hypostasis, tropos hyparxeos* along with *ousia/homoousion* each in different ways express something about existence or being (substance or essence). What is communicated in the phrase: one substance, three persons, in English is very different from what is implied in the Greek: *mia ousia, tres hypostaseis*. It is perhaps best to be clear from the outset that the Greek is not addressing what is implied in a modern Western sense of 'person', nor in an ancient understanding of *persona/prosopon*. The Greek terms suggest a play on the conceptuality of being and existence. God is a being, one being, who is also three beings; or God is a single substance, which is expressed in or exists in the form of three substances or subsistences. The nuances of the Greek are very difficult to render in English: there are no direct (modern) equivalents. Nonetheless, the terminology of the Council of Constantinople has been received and understood (in English) in terms of one substance and three persons – i.e., the divine being – because the experience of and witness to the threeness revealed in the economy of salvation is understood to be both one and three. In other words, the threefoldness experienced is a threefoldness which refers not to an enacted drama and the changing of masks by one actor but to three 'existents', in a differentiated but nonetheless single Godhead.

The differentiation of the Godhead came to be expressed in the conceptuality of relation (*schesis*) in terms of the origins of the Divine Three. The relations of origin will be discussed below. For now, it is important to recognize that the appeal to relation produces reflection on the three in relation to each other and in relation to the divine being *in se*. In the later part of the twentieth century, such reflection was the origin of a large-scale rediscovery of relationality and personhood, which has had a profound effect on Trinitarian theological endeavour. This is to be seen among those who commend this endeavour as well as among those who have come to offer a critique of the 'shift to relationality'. In the West, writers such as Augustine, Boethius (480–c.525) and Richard of St Victor (d. 1173) are often cited as the main sources for a classical Western understanding of the person, whether human or divine. Boethius produced an understanding of Person, which became perhaps more influential than it might otherwise have done, in that Aquinas takes the definition as a given: 'a person is an individual substance of a rational nature' (*rationalis naturae individua substantia*).[14] Richard of St Victor, on the other hand, argues that a person (in the Godhead) is the 'incommunicable existence of the divine nature' (*divinae naturae incommunicabilis existentia*).[15] Augustine reflects on persons in terms of the faculties of memory, intellect and will and has typically been categorized as producing a psychological understanding of both personhood and the Godhead. There is now an extensive revision of this interpretation of Augustinian teaching. Rowan Williams has argued that Augustine has been read through the perspective of Descartes in order to produce such an understanding.[16] The interpretation that Augustine's understanding of the Divine Three leads him to a non-communal conception of God's being is difficult to sustain when he writes of the Spirit as the *communia* of the Father and the Son.[17] Rather than a conceptuality that focuses the unity of the Godhead exclusively on the monarchy of the Father, Augustine understands the divine unity in terms of the communion of the Father and the Son. Rather than neglecting the Spirit, of which Augustine is sometimes accused, it seems that he is better understood as placing a unifying emphasis on the Spirit. Some recent commentators have argued that John Zizioulas's title *Being as Communion* could as easily be applied to Augustine's understanding of the Trinity as it was to the Cappadocians' understanding, for it is clear in *De trinitate* that Augustine had learned, from the Cappadocians especially, the importance of the real relations of the three.[18] Thus, for Augustine, the Divine Three are 'subsisting relations'.

The issue of whether the differentiation of the Divine Three is to be found only in the economy or also refers to the divine being *in se* remains an ongoing question. Underneath that question is another: Does the divine being in its mystery 'guarantee' divine self-communication in the economy? Athanasius and the Cappadocians argue that what is experienced in and borne witness to in the saving economy does point to the reality of intra-divine relations. Not everyone accepts this conceptuality. I shall return to this issue in the following chapter with a discussion of the relationship between the immanent and economic in conceptualizing the Trinity in contemporary discourse.

RELATIONS OF ORIGIN

Despite the Church having established an orthodox understanding of the oneness and threeness of the divine being, those engaged in theological reflection have continued to ask what the threefoldness is. Gregory Nazianzen uses the term *schesis* (relation) to evoke a sense of the mutual relations between the three, an understanding that influenced both Greek and Latin thinking. The problem of conceptualizing what each of the three might be and how each relates to the others is highlighted by Augustine, who claimed that *persona* was an 'obscure' word to use and did not necessarily add any further clarification. He wrote that the word was used, 'because we wish some one word to serve for that meaning whereby the Trinity is understood, that we might not be altogether silent, when asked what three, while we confessed that they are three'.[19] There is a further question underlying the designation of the 'three' and 'one': What sort of unity and what sort of distinction are to be understood in the Godhead? One way in which to answer this is to understand that the Divine Three are to be distinguished on the basis of one principle and two criteria. The principle of identity and non-identity is to be found in Gregory Nazianzen and Athanasius: there is an identity of the three with the divine nature; while there is a non-identity of the three with each other. The two criteria are that the distinguishing characteristics of the three are relation and relationality. The first, relationality, consists in paternity, sonship and sanctity and is founded upon the experience of and witness in the economy. This is important for a renewed understanding in the present day of an appeal to the world of particulars. The second criterion, also in the economy, is the revelation of the origins of the relations of each to the others. Gregory Nazianzen appeals to the mutual relations between the three in order to distinguish each of the three hypostases. He does this by building on Gregory of Nyssa's teaching that the three are related by their relations of origin: i.e., the Father unbegotten (*agennetos*), the Son begotten (*gennetos*) and the Spirit breathed forth (*ekporeusis*)[20] and the Son and Spirit each having their origin from the Father.

The understanding that the Father is the unbegotten, the Son the begotten and the Holy Spirit the breathed is something held in common by both East and West. However, there are differences between the Latins and the Greeks concerning these relations of origin. A major area of dispute, acknowledged already in Chapter 2, concerns the origin or procession of the Holy Spirit and the addition in the West to the text of the Creed of 'and the Son' (*filioque*). This, in turn, relates to whether one understands the role of the Father as the principle or origin (one might almost say 'beginning') of the Godhead or whether one understands that the Godhead is 'the Trinity'. Some scholars have argued that the main difference between East and West on the issue of the relations of origin is not so much the *filioque* as the monarchy of the Father.[21] In the West, the relationships of the Spirit and Son to Father are understood in a different way from that of the East. The *homoousion* guarantees the equality of the Divine Three, while the principle of non-identity distinguishes them. Athanasius was clear that one entity could not be *homoousion* with itself. In a sense, the *homoousion* implies both difference and relation, while, at the same time, guaranteeing equality. The development of the conceptuality of relation consolidates this understanding, as is witnessed in the writings of Augustine. The writers of the West could agree that the Father is the 'principle' (*arche*) by which the Son is generated and the Spirit breathed forth, but for the Latin writers, relation is qualified more by opposition than origin. In this understanding, the *filioque* is required (and is not just an ad-hoc addition) to maintain the distinctions of the Godhead: i.e., the Spirit is distinct from the Father and the Son, because 'it' is from the Father and the Son.

In the later Western Trinitarian reflection of Thomas Aquinas, there emerges what has been called 'a virtual Trinitarian metaphysics'.[22] Aquinas develops a highly sophisticated understanding of the relations. Del Colle argues that in Aquinas, 'The relation of the other (*ad alium*) for example, the Father actively generates the Son, and the Son is passively generated by the Father, is coincident with subsistence in oneself (*in se*)'.[23] In contrast, in the East, a much clearer conceptuality of the Divine Three as 'persons in communion' was sustained. The Father is understood to be the principle (*arche*), source (*pege*) and cause (*aitia*) of the Godhead and of the Divine Three. The Father communicates his being to Son and Spirit, preserving the personal distinctiveness of the three. From this perspective, the argument for the *filioque* is seen to destroy this asymmetrical vision of the Godhead by a construction that allows Father and Son conjointly to be the principle of divine unity. In an article from 2004, Pecknold has argued that there are problems in the speculative conceptualities of East and West but that both traditions were much nearer to each other than is often assumed:

> I will not comment on either monopatrism or *filioque*, except to say that I think both present problems are inadequate to express the radical co-inherence of the Three in the One and also to say that I think both Augustine and the Cappadocians were seeking to express this very same co-inherent unity. In any case, the charge that Augustine finds a prior essence in God is a profound misunderstanding. Mary Clark writes, 'There is no evidence in *De Trinitate* that Augustine asserted divine unity to be prior to the Trinity, nor Trinity to unity.'[24]

These disputes concerning the theological construction of the inner divine life are rooted in complex and highly speculative conceptualities. Reflections on the Divine Three and their relations of origin tended to become more and more removed from the experience of the divine in the economy of salvation. This, in turn, led to feelings that the doctrine of the Trinity was irrelevant, which is witnessed not only in the Enlightenment but also by some theologians in the Reformation period. However, it is quite clear that Zizioulas's whole theological edifice of relationality is built upon an appeal to a specific understanding of the paternal *arche*, which I will examine below.

In this instance, Zizioulas's construction is not only speculative but also directly applied to the needs of Church and human society at the present time, which echoes Pecknold's understanding of the potential functionality of Trinitarian reflection. In going on to look at modern understandings of personhood, among other understandings, I shall examine the idea of self-donation as a designation of personhood, which also seems to echo the concept of the paternal *arche*.

PERSONHOOD IN MODERNITY

The exploration of social Trinitarianism and the appeal to relationality during the course of the twentieth century has been accompanied by a renewed discourse on person/personhood. This discourse was manifest in two different streams, one in which the 'turn to person/personhood' is understood in relational terms and another in which person/personhood is seen in individualistic terms. The appeal to a social or relational understanding of the human person is often grounded in a dialogical and dialectical understanding of the person rooted in the ancient understanding that the human person is *zōon logon echōn* (living being having the word). In the modern context, McFadyen expounds the view that the human person is formed in dialogue, which entails being in dialectic relations with other persons,[25] and Macmurray argues that the basic condition of community is communication, placing his relational understanding on a dialogical footing.[26] This dialogical and dialectical understanding of human personhood has been understood analogically to refer to the divine personhood. Kasper argues that

> the divine persons are [. . .] infinitely more dialogical than human persons are. The Father is a pure self-enunciation and address to the Son as his Word; the Son is a pure hearing and heeding of the Father and therefore pure fulfilment of his mission; the Holy Spirit is pure reception, pure gift. These personal relations are reciprocal but they are not interchangeable.[27]

Joseph Ratzinger (now Pope Benedict XVI) also understands that such a dialogical conceptuality of the divine personhood has fundamental implications for the understanding of the relationality of the Godhead.[28]

The exploration of a relational understanding of person/personhood in the 1970s may be found not only in the work of Zizioulas but also in the work of Johann Auer[29] who raises the question of personhood in relation to the 'person' of Jesus Christ and the Trinity and, by extension, to the Church. The work of Karol Wojtyla (later Pope John Paul II) also contributes to the richness of the discourse concerning a relational understanding of the human subject. Alfred Wilder,[30] reflecting on the work of Karol Wojtyla, situates his work in the post-Enlightenment context in relation to understandings of person found in Feuerbach, Marcel and Buber, over against the exposition of the Absolute Ego found in Fichte, Schelling and Hegel. Lawerence B. Porter,[31] writing in 1980, focuses his attention in particular on the divine 'persons', arguing that the attempt to avoid the language of 'person' in Trinitarian doctrine made by both Barth and Rahner does not take into account patristic innovation, found particularly in the work of Tertullian. He argues that the self-relatedness of the Godhead requires the ongoing and unresolved tension, which the language of person/personhood brings to the doctrine of the Trinity.[32] The mid-1980s saw a number of publications outlining the emergence of and need for a relational understanding of person/ personhood, of which Zizioulas's *Being as Communion* is a prime example.[33] In 1986, Hans Urs von Balthasar[34] wrote on the concept of person, setting out something of a genealogy of the term itself as well as of those who have defended a relational understanding of it. In counterpoint to this development among theologians, an alternative discourse is manifest in other disciplines, especially among philosophers, who have argued either that the self or the person is a construct or have continued to defend the Enlightenment individualist understanding of person/personhood.[35] Over against this tendency in philosophy an appeal to relationality has been made by theologians.

Emerging from the discourse on the relationality of personhood, two themes may be discerned: first, an understanding of person in terms of act, and, second, that 'act' is to be understood in terms of (self-)donation. An underlying strand to these themes may be traced to the influence of Husserl.[36] The human person is to be understood as living subject; thus, human subjectivity is defined in terms of consciousness, self-knowledge and self-possession, which are to be recognized in human freedom.[37] Another influence is traced to Whitehead, mediated in the Christian reception of his thought by Hartshorne and Cobb.[38] In this conceptuality, 'God is not to be understood as a unique non-temporal actual entity but rather as a personally ordered society of actual occasions'.[39] The divine act of being is understood as an activity rather than as a state; and that activity is understood as the 'interrelating' of the divine 'persons'. Bracken argues that, 'this activity of interrelating is never exactly the same in two successive moments. The three divine persons, in other words, experience change in their ongoing relationality to one another.'[40]

Such an understanding of person/personhood and relationality has particular resonances with the discourse on *différance* and repetition to which I will return in Chapter 4.

Writing on the understanding of person/personhood to be found in the work of Karol Wojtyla, Robert A. Connor argues that the philosophical/theological tradition has failed to provide 'a satisfactory ontological model to explain the ever-emerging awareness of person as an intrinsically relational being'.[41] He suggests that in the thought of Karol Wojtyla, such a model may be emerging, through his use of a phenomenology of the acting subject, which Connor interprets as 'a model for growth by relating'.[42] Here the suggestion that the person is 'ever-emerging'[43] resonates with the conceptuality of difference and repetition. An interesting extension of this understanding of person/personhood in terms of act is to be found in the writing of Joseph Ratzinger. Writing in relation to the doctrine of the Trinity, he discusses the personhood of the Father: 'the first person does not generate in the sense that to the complete person the act of generating a son is added, but the person *is* the act of generating, of offering oneself and flowing out [. . .] the pure actuality.'[44] He reiterates this understanding in a later work arguing that, 'The person is identical with this act of self-donation'.[45] The richness of discourse on person/personhood adds further to the sense of the complexity of the appeal to relationality. The appeal to 'act conceptualities' may assist in seeking to address the question of an ontological expression of relationality.

The effects on understandings of person and personhood which arise from 'the shift to the subject' attributed to Kant, and to be seen in the epistemology of Descartes, combined with a modern psychological focus on the individual, have given rise to a general notion that a person is perhaps above all a centre of consciousness. To the understanding of self-consciousness there has also been added the modern notion, perhaps obsession with 'personality'. When such a set of pre-understandings meet with the statement that the divine being is one substance and three persons, there are inevitably questions to be asked and complications to be unravelled. In short, is it possible to conceive of a single being which is three persons: i.e., three centres of consciousness or three personalities? This conundrum has been the focus of a considerable amount of theological reflection during the twentieth century. Add to this the arguments of those who doubt that there is any such entity as person or personhood and the picture becomes even more complex and a resolution even more doubtful.[46]

During the nineteenth century, some theologians appealed to the social analogy of the Trinity as a means by which to challenge the view of certain idealists that 'the Absolute' was not a person. Idealists objected to the attribution of personhood to the Absolute because they understood that 'personality' was implicitly a relational term and therefore a relative condition. Those who appealed to the social analogy did so on the understanding that personality could be understood as *permeable*, rather than relative. In the twentieth century, Moltmann advocated a social or communitarian analogy for the Trinity in order to seek to overcome the Absolute Subject of Hegelian idealism.[47] Joseph Bracken, a Roman Catholic theologian, also argued for a social analogy for the Trinitarian Godhead, as a challenge to the idealist concept of a single divine subject, and replaces it with three divine subjects that share a single consciousness.[48] Lionel Spencer Thornton[49] argued for a similar understanding of the Godhead. He also appealed to the social analogy, constructing his concept of the Trinity upon an understanding of divine fellowship. However, he rejects the notion that the three persons are 'Three Centres of One Consciousness'. Thornton argues that solutions such as William Temple's phrase, 'Three Centres of One Consciousness', belie the reality of the human lack of knowledge and understanding either of consciousness or of the divine persons. Rather, he suggests that the persons are 'Three Centres of One Activity', 'The three centres of relationship are here comprehended within the unity of One Absolute Activity'.[50] Thornton's argument holds together divine agency and consciousness so that in his view there is only 'one mental life' in the Godhead. He also bases his construction on the understanding that the primary encounter with the threeness of God arises from the experience of revelation, so that in his view the social analogy provides the basis to adapt the idealists' understanding of the Absolute.[51]

PERSONHOOD IN THE THOUGHT OF KARL RAHNER

The understanding of person and personhood in the writings of Karl Rahner presents an intriguing example of a modern response to the questions surrounding the expression of the Divine Three. Paradoxically, Rahner's construction of the doctrine of the Trinity is clearly dependent upon the concept of the Absolute Subject of Hegelian idealism, and yet Rahner sets himself the task of offering a decisive critique of the psychological or unitary model of the Trinity. In Rahner's understanding, what is encountered in the divine self-revelation is the threefoldness rather than the oneness.[52] Thus, he argues that the threefoldness of the Godhead is something which is known in faith through the divine self-utterance. This leaves Rahner with a problem concerning the designation of that threefoldness encountered in the economy. He too finds the use of the word 'person' to be impossible in his own context. Emerging from his axiom that the economic and immanent are to be identified in the understanding of God as Trinity, he suggests that, 'The one self-communication of the one God occurs in three different manners of givenness, in which the one God is given concretely for us in himself, and not vicariously by other realities'.[53] He goes on to argue that each of the three should be designated as a 'distinct manner of subsisting'. This designation

> would then be the explanatory concept, not for person, which refers to that which subsists as distinct, but the 'personality' which makes God's concrete reality, as it meet us in different ways, into precisely this one who meet us *thus*. This meeting-us-thus must always be conceived as belonging to God in and for himself. The single 'person' in God would then be: God as existing and meeting us in this determined distinct manner of subsisting.[54]

Whether Rahner has solved a problem or made it worse, I leave to the reader to decide.

The question of self-consciousness in relation to any model of the Trinity remains an ongoing issue and may never be finally resolved. If personhood and personality are understood in terms of a modern understanding of consciousness, then there has to be some recognition that there is a problem to be addressed if this is applied to the Godhead. In the social model, there is a tendency to ascribe self-consciousness to each of the Divine Three. While in the unitary model, if the deity is Mind, then that single mind will be conscious of itself. Some writers who have sought to work with both models have sought to relate consciousness to the threeness and the oneness of the Godhead, with such concepts as intersubjectivity, interpersonality and shared consciousness.[55] For example, Bourassa argues for an understanding of divine self-conscious which mediates between the two models of the Godhead by attributing consciousness to each person and to the three persons in common:

> Consciousness in God is both an *essential* act of knowledge and love common to the three persons, and *personal* consciousness, exercised by each person, as consciousness of self, according to the personal action of each which is infinitely conscious and free, as pure and spontaneous love, in the most perfect reciprocity.[56]

PERSONHOOD IN THE THOUGHT OF KARL BARTH

In the work of Karl Barth, another instance of the difficulty over person and personhood emerges in relation to the Godhead as expressed in the formula of the Council of Constantinople. While Barth sought to be faithful to the orthodoxy of the early councils and Creeds, his pre-understandings of 'person' led him to the view that God is one person, in terms of consciousness and 'personality'. This leaves him, as it does Rahner, with the question of the designation of the Divine Three, if he is to attempt to be faithful to Nicene orthodoxy. Barth decided upon the term *Seinsweise* (mode of being), the English in particular immediately raising fears of 'modalism'. Barth is sensitive to this charge and is at pains to argue that this is not his intention, that he is motivated only by a concern to express the formula *mia ousia, tres hypostaseis* in a modern idiom. His concern also demonstrates an awareness that the *hypostasis* in the ancient world did not carry the connotations that 'person' carries in the West in the modern period. Barth's preference for *Seinsweise* in expressing the divine threefoldness emerges from his view that 'person' or *hypostasis* had always been opaque throughout the history of reflection on the doctrine of the Trinity. Indeed, he rejects any idea that it is part of the theologian's task to understand what the 'persons' of the Trinity are.[57] Furthermore, Barth argues that the problems with the ancient terminology are complicated by the modern understandings of personality and consciousness.[58] Barth seeks to clarify his position when he argues that

The truly material determinations of the principle of threeness in the unity of God were derived neither by Augustine, Thomas nor our Protestant Fathers from an analysis of the concept of person, but from a very different source in the course of their much too laborious analyses of this concept. We prefer to let this other source rank as the primary one even externally, and therefore by preference we do not use the term 'person' but rather 'mode (or way) of being', our intention being to express by this term, not absolutely, but relatively better and more simply and clearly the same thing as is meant by 'person.'[59]

Barth argues that *Seinsweise* is to be understood as the equivalent of the patristic usage, *tropos hyparxeos*, which is to be found, albeit infrequently, in the writings of the Cappadocian Fathers.[60] This choice relates to the Reformed as well as the Cappadocian tradition.[61] However, the way in which the term *tropos hyparxeos* was understood in the patristic period is another matter. It has been argued that the way the term was used by the Cappadocian Fathers had connotations of origin and derivation. Prestige argues that *tropos hyparxeos* should be understood to mean 'mode of existence', which carries an implicit understanding of the beginning of what is denoted.[62] 'When the phrase "mode of hyparxis" is applied to the divine Persons, it may, at least in the case of the second and third Persons, originally have contained a covert reference not merely to their existence, but to the derivation of their existence from the paternal arche'.[63] *Tropos hyparxeos* might equally be translated 'mode of existence' or 'mode of obtaining existence'. Once it is understood that the persons of the Godhead are co-eternal and co-equal, these two meanings effectively become the same:

The term mode of hyparxis was applied, from the end of the fourth century, to the particularities that distinguish the divine Persons, in order to express the belief that in those Persons or hypostaseis one and the same divine being is presented in distinct objective and permanent expressions, though with no variation in divine content.[64]

In *Church Dogmatics*, Barth uses *tropos hyparxeos* to denote the differentiation of the Godhead which is known in the divine event of self-revelation,[65] and understood in terms of the divine self-repetition or reiteration.[66] In so far as the modes of being are to be understood in terms of the divine *self*-repetition, they may be understood in terms of the different ways in which each of the modes possesses the divine being or essence.[67] An implication of this understanding would be that the divine essence is something which is prior to the threefoldness. While Barth is quite clear that there is no fourth hidden *thing* behind the three,[68] he does use the phrase 'the one undifferentiated divine essence'.[69] There is also imprecision in way in which Barth uses *tropos hyparxeos*. The term may allow the identification of personality and self-consciousness with the one divine Person, but it raises problems surrounding the relation of the threefoldness to the divine *ousia*. Barth argues that, 'God is manifest and is God in the very mode or way that He is in those relations to Himself'.[70] While Barth may argue that the modes of being are permanent expressions of the God who acts, identical with the divine event-essence, the term *tropos hyparxeos* does not convey with clarity what the threefoldness of the Godhead is, and Barth himself readily admits this.[71]

Barth's usage of the term *Seinsweise* (*tropos hyparxeos*) has consistently been the subject of adverse criticism. Moltmann perceives the use of the term 'mode of being' to describe the threefold repetition of the one divine Lord as confirmation of his view that Barth remains firmly rooted in the idealist tradition of the single self-conscious divine subject.[72] Kasper argues that Barth's uncritical acceptance of the modern understanding of the person which led him to the terminology of mode of being inevitably means that the three 'persons' of the Godhead are given a treatment which is more negative than it is positive.[73] Gunton also argues that Barth's usage of *tropos hyparxeos* meant that he remained within the 'Western tradition' of the Trinity and of personhood, rather than setting him in the Cappadocian tradition.[74] Although there may have been a degree of correspondence between the terms *tropos hyparxeos* and *hypostasis* in patristic usage, the distinction between the context in which Barth uses the term 'mode of being' and that in which the Cappadocian Fathers employed *tropos hyparxeos*, makes any comparison problematic.

PERSONHOOD IN THE THOUGHT OF JOHN ZIZIOULAS

It is John Zizioulas's great achievement that he has been able to bring Byzantine Orthodox tradition concerning persons and personhood into contemporary theological discourse and ecumenical dialogue.

What is especially striking about Zizioulas's treatment of the Orthodox tradition is his ability to relate it to the concerns of the modern
West. It is Zizioulas's pre-understanding that person and personhood are not qualities which are added to human beings: human
beings do not have personhood, rather they *are* persons. 'Personhood,
in other words, has the claim of absolute being, that is, a metaphysical claim, built into it.'[75] Nonetheless, Zizioulas recognizes that
the content and description of personhood have legitimately been
explicated in the modern terms of consciousness and dialogue.[76] His
understanding of the ontology of personhood also takes into
account the philosophical concept of 'being there' (*Dasein*).[77] He
brings to the interpretation of *Dasein* the centrality of the Liturgy in
the Orthodox tradition when he argues that, 'To assert "being there,"
is to assert that you are overcoming not being there. It is a trium-
phalistic cry, or if you wish a doxological/eucharistic one, in the
deepest sense of acknowledging being as a sort of victory over non-
being'.[78] This assertion of being by the person implies the recognition of a *beyond* and therefore is to be understood as a movement of
transcendence. Zizioulas also appeals to a philosophical (perhaps
existentialist) and theological understanding of freedom. In particular, he explicates the claim of the Orthodox tradition that the
unoriginate status of the Father is true freedom. The being and
communion of the Trinity are constituted in the radical freedom of
the person of the Father: 'True being comes only from the free person, from the person who loves freely – that is, who freely affirms his
being, his identity, by means of an event of communion with other
persons.'[79]

Embedded in this ontological understanding of the person,
according to Zizioulas's construction, are the existentialist categories
of *Dasein* and freedom, which are to be received within a philo-
sophical/theological framework of a classical metaphysics and a conceptuality of transcendence. This leads to an understanding of the
person (*hypostasis*) as an ontological rather than a functional entity.[80]

(a) The person is no longer an adjunct to a being, a category
which we *add* to a concrete entity once we have verified its ontological hypostasis. *It is itself the hypostasis of the being.* (b)
Entities no longer trace their being to being itself – that is, being is
not an absolute category in itself – but to the person, to precisely
that which *constitutes* being, that is, enables entities to be entities.
In other words from an adjunct to a being (a kind of mask) the

person becomes the being itself and is simultaneously – a most significant point – *the constitutive element* (the 'principle' or 'cause') of beings.[81]

Zizioulas extends this understanding of hypostasis by applying it directly to the Godhead. Thus, he claims, that the substance never exists in a 'naked' state, that is, without hypostasis, without 'a mode of existence.'[82]

And the one divine substance is, consequently, the being of God only because it has these three modes of existence, which it owes not to the substance but to one person, the Father. Outside the Trinity there is no God, that is no divine substance, because the ontological 'principle' of God is the Father. The personal existence of God (the Father) constitutes His substance, makes it hypostases. The being of God is identified with the person.[83]

His concept of being is inseparable from his concept of the person, and out of this understanding of ontology and relationality emerges Zizioulas's notion of an 'event of communion'. The permanent and unbreakable status of the relationships between Father, Son and Holy Spirit means that the particular beings of each are never isolated individuals. There is 'a reality of communion in which each particular is affirmed as *unique* and irreplaceable by the others'.[84] Zizioulas combines the outcome of Nicene orthodoxy achieved in the terminology of Constantinople and the theological reflection of the Cappadocian Fathers, with a modern understanding of consciousness, *Dasein* and freedom. In so doing, he creates the possibility of retaining the classical terminology of *hypostasis* and the monarchy of the Father within contemporary theological discourse.

This achievement is not without its critics, who have offered insightful and challenging critiques of Zizioulas's construction of personhood. The questioning of the conceptuality of personhood and the interpretation of patristic usage of terms among those who appealed to a relational understanding of the divine, was signalled by André de Halleux in the mid-1980s. De Halleux rejects as simplistic the division of Trinitarian conceptualities between a social Eastern model and a psychological Western model, traced to de Régnon. He argues that in the understanding of Basil of Caesarea there was perhaps never a real distinction between *hypostasis* and *ousia*.[85] From this critique, Halleux suggests that Zizioulas's interpretation of the Cappadocian Fathers' understanding of *koinonia* as dialogical is a misunderstanding.[86] He concludes that the personalism of the Cappadocians does not have to be opposed to the language of 'essence' (*ousia*).[87] Norman Metzler[88] argues that despite the values in the social modelling of the Trinity, nonetheless the use to which the term *persona* is put in these relational understandings cannot bear the weight being put upon it.[89] The most developed critique in this area is offered by Lucian Turcescu,[90] who argues that the conceptuality of personhood for which Zizioulas argues is not to be found in the writing of the Cappadocian Fathers but is rather a 'newly minted concept of person (which) rests on an understanding of the Christian Trinity mainly as prototype of persons-in-relation'.[91] The questions and challenges which these critics of relationality pose are not to be set aside. They have to be faced and a considered response offered. It is beyond the scope of this guide to make such a detailed response. However, I would suggest that while the specific critiques are sustained, they do not necessarily curtail the theological project of Zizioulas and of those others who have sought to develop a contemporary understanding of *koinonia*, personhood and relationality. The question of how to transpose *hypostasis* into modern usage remains an ongoing conundrum which may never be answered. The theological project to understand the divine in terms of communion and relationality is surely one worth defending and extending; and I have suggested that one way in which to do to this might be through an appeal to a 'hermeneutic of relationality'.

COMMUNION AND THE DIVINE

The appeal to communion (*koinonia*) has become axiomatic for those seeking to expound a relational understanding of personhood, whether human or divine. This raises several questions including the conceptualization of the divine substance or being 'as communion'. Most attempts to construct a social Trinitarian understanding of the divine in recent times have appealed to the category of communion or community as a necessary counterpart to the stress placed on the Divine Three. An exposition of Zizioulas's understanding of the divine communion will provide a useful example of contemporary discourse.

It is Zizioulas's understanding that the use of communion as a theological category was introduced into theological reflection in the writings of the bishops of the early church, such as Ignatius of

Antioch, Irenaeus and Athanasius. Zizioulas suggests that this was so because they 'approached the being of God through the experience of the ecclesial community, of *ecclesial being*. This experience revealed something very important: the being of God could be known only through personal relationships and personal love. Being means life, and life means *communion*'.[92]

Theological reflection on the being of God in the context of the ecclesial community was developed especially in the writings of Athanasius and the Cappadocian Fathers. From their reflection on the eucharistic experience of the Church, Zizioulas argues that they developed an ontological understanding of communion. Athanasius and the Cappadocian Fathers formulated a concept of the being of God as a relational being, expressed in their use of the terminology of communion. In using this terminology, the Cappadocian Fathers sought to express what they perceived was evident in the economy and in the Scriptures that the Godhead was both simplicity and multiplicity, both a unity and a communion. The God who is encountered in the revelation in Jesus Christ is to be understood as interrelated being, sharing in a common essence. Basil in Letter 38 expounds his understanding of this conceptuality of being.[93] He writes that the Father, Son and Holy Spirit are a fellowship: 'but in them is seen a certain communion (*koinonia*) indissoluble and continuous'.[94] Later in the same letter, he explains what this communion means in relation to belief in a single God and also in terms of the inner divine life. The Godhead is to be understood 'as being both conjoined and parted, and thinking as it were darkly in a riddle, of a certain new and strange conjoined separation and separated conjunction'.[95] This conceptuality of the inner divine life was not to be understood as the result of fanciful speculation but, rather, as the explication of the encounter between God and humanity in the revelation in Jesus Christ. This concept of God's inner life is understood to be related directly to the divine activity in the economy. Out of this understanding, Zizioulas goes on to reflect that 'The substance of God, "God," has no ontological content, no true being, apart from communion'.[96] He expounds his understanding of communion as an ontological category further when he writes

Nothing in existence is conceivable in itself, as an individual, such as the τόδε τί of Aristotle, since even God exists thanks to an event of communion. In this manner the ancient world heard for the first time that it is communion which makes beings 'be': nothing exists without it, not even God.[97]

This is a crucial passage that expresses Zizioulas's understanding of communion very clearly and, furthermore, is an instance of where he makes appeal to the concept of *an event of communion*. This appeal to event conceptuality is an important feature of Zizioulas's theological project, and it is also critical for the reception of his construction of relationality in the contemporary context. I shall examine event conceptuality in Chapter 5.

Another crucial feature of Zizioulas's construction of relationality is his understanding that only a person, the person of God the Father, is the cause of communion and ultimate relationality:

> this communion is not a relationship understood for its own sake, an existential structure which supplants 'nature' or 'substance' in its primordial ontological role – something reminiscent of the structure of existence met in the thought of Martin Buber. Just like 'substance,' 'communion' does not exist by itself: it is the *Father* who is the 'cause' of it.[98]

All existence is not only relational (of communion: *koinonia*) but also personal (of the person: *hypostasis*). Zizioulas seeks to structure the ontological category of communion as it emerges from Athanasius and the Cappadocians in relation to a number of controlling factors and concepts. The ontological status of the concept of communion has emerged in relation to an understanding of the Godhead as a threefold communion, i.e., the Holy Trinity; a communion which is a communion of three *hypostases*; a communion of three *hypostases* whose relations are understood in terms of a mutually constituting relationality; but nonetheless a communion which does not supplant the notion of substance (or being); and, finally, a communion whose mutuality is not a prior thing brought to bear on the persons from outside, but whose mutuality is rooted in the personhood of the Father. In other words, the subtlety of the Cappadocian understanding removes communion and relationality from the danger of becoming an absolute category in itself which would be prior to and therefore condition the being of God. Indeed, Zizioulas is at pains to avoid anything which might be understood to condition the Godhead, and this is particularly evident in his discussion of the divine freedom. He argues that the Father as a free person brings the divine communion and substance into being, *freely*. Neither communion nor substance are pre-existing categories which are imposed upon the deity by some external necessity. Both are freely chosen by the Father. This means that 'not only communion but also *freedom*, the free person, constitutes true being. True being comes only from the free person, from the person who loves freely – that is, who freely affirms his being, his identity, by means of an event of communion with other persons.'[99]

It is evident that Zizioulas does not understand the Godhead in terms of the self-realization of a single subject. For, even though the Father is conceived of as the logical cause of the Trinity, the understanding that all three persons are both co-equal and co-eternal means that *being as communion* is also eternal. The Father's freedom is untrammelled by any 'necessity'.[100] Zizioulas goes on to argue that the freedom of God is not to be understood in terms of the uncreated divine nature or substance. Indeed, such a concept would leave humanity without any hope of attaining to true personhood. Rather, he argues that

the ground of God's ontological freedom lies not in His nature but in His personal existence, that is, in the 'mode of existence' by which he subsists as divine nature. And it is precisely this that gives man, in spite of his different nature, his hope of becoming an authentic person.[101]

The divine freedom is, therefore, to be understood as the freedom of Father who chooses in love to live as Trinity. This may be seen as an event of self-realization and affirmation, but it is not the realization of a single absolute subject, nor of the individual seeking to assert freedom against the necessity of finite existence.

In the discussion of the category of communion and of the concept of freedom, I have already noted that Zizioulas employs the phrase 'an event of communion' to denote the dynamic quality of the communion and freedom of the Godhead, which he understands, finds expression in a mutually constituted communion of the Divine Three. Zizioulas is careful to guard against substituting *being* with the concept of event. Rather, event is used to explicate the dynamic quality of the relational ontology of *koinonia*. The Godhead is not understood either in terms of an event which has no ontological reference, or in terms of a static classical monism. Zizioulas seeks to draw together the multi-level understanding of being which is to be found in the Cappadocian Fathers by his use of the phrase 'an event of communion' and in so doing adds a further level to the traditional view by this appeal to the concept of event. This brings the Cappadocian tradition into dialogue with a modern understanding of the dynamic process of existence and life. The Cappadocian Fathers' understanding of the *ousia* of the Godhead as *koinonia* is to be understood also in terms of a concept of event. In other words, the *koinonia* of the Godhead is both *energeia* (energy, work or action) and *dynamis* (power, ability or potential), which resonates with the triadic language of Maximos the Confessor. The being of the Godhead as communion is something which happens. It happens because the person of the Father freely loves and chooses that the Divine Being should be a dynamic relationality, a communion of three persons. The communal or relational being of the triune God is understood to be an event of life and love, *an event of communion*. I shall return to explore this appeal to event further in Chapters 4 and 5. As I have noted already, there are those for whom this construction of divine communion is unacceptable. Some argue that the patristic evidence does not support Zizioulas's claims, while others see in this the projection of a particular ecclesiological or sociological agenda. The reader will need to weigh the arguments in order to determine whether this construct of communion continues to be persuasive.

INDWELLING/PERICHORESIS

Another component in the construction of social Trinitarianism and a relational understanding of the Godhead is the appeal to the concept of 'mutual indwelling' or 'interpenetration', in Greek: *perichoresis*. The extent of this appeal in recent times has been remarkable. For example, it has been used by Moltmann, Boff, Fiddes, Cunningham and LaCugna[102] to suggest the applicability of the doctrine of the Trinity both to the Church and to the wider human community, as a model and inspiration for human coexistence. The *perichoresis* of the Divine Three has been held up to be emulated in some sense by human beings in the sociality and reciprocity of persons in communion or fellowship with God and each other. The Trinity becomes the archetype of the human community, which is explicated in terms of interdependence, equality and mutual accountability, hospitality and inclusion. As I have made clear already, this endeavour has evoked a strong critique of such applica-

tion. On the other hand, Pecknold points to Augustine's development of the functionality of the doctrine,[103] which suggests that the
attempt to construct the doctrine of the Trinity in terms of relationality and *perichoresis*, in order to promote and celebrate its relevance
in the present day, may not be improper.

It is often argued that the use of the term *perichoresis* is an extension of the Nicene orthodoxy of 'one substance, three persons'.
Current evidence suggests that it was used explicitly in relation to the
doctrine of the Trinity only from the seventh or eighth century. But
many scholars have argued that the conceptuality of 'mutual indwelling' or 'interpenetration' in terms of the Divine Three is implicit in
the thinking of both the Cappadocian Fathers and Augustine. *Perichoresis* has been articulated to reinforce the unity of God while also
claiming the radical differentiation of the three. In particular, it has
been applied to the question of the centre of consciousness in the
Godhead. The concept has been used both in the East and West but
probably with different emphases. The Greek term *perichoresis* has
two equivalents in Latin, *circumcessio* and *circumincessio*. Some have
argued the former *circumcessio* has more of the dynamic connotations of the Greek term, while the latter *circumincessio* has more the
sense of a static repose. An evaluation of these distinctions would
require careful reading and interpretation of the writings of Thomas
Aquinas.[104]

Most scholars would agree that the term *perichoresis* was first used
in Christian theology in reflection on the two natures or *prosopa* in
the person of Christ.[105] It was employed later to designate the mutual
indwelling of the Divine Three in the work of John of Damascus.[106]
The conceptuality underlying the term may be traced back in the
writings of the Fathers to Athenagoras,[107] and is related to the passage below from the Fourth Gospel: 'The words that I say to you I do
not speak on my own authority; but the Father who dwells in me
does his works. Believe me that I am in the Father and the Father in
me' (Jn 14. 10–11).[108]

The doctrine of the mutual indwelling (*perichoresis*) of the Divine
Three in one another represents a further stage of theological reflection on the problem of conceptualizing the unity of the divine will
and the divine substance, in relation to the understanding that the
Godhead is both one and three.[109] The development of such a terminology happened slowly. Basil, in a typically conservative stance,
argues that the persons are to be understood as 'being with', rather
than 'being in' one another.[110] Hilary develops an understanding that

the persons contain one another,[111] and Gregory of Nyssa begins to find a form of expression from an established philosophical term, *chorein* (to hold or contain)[112] to designate the relationships of the persons. The developed use of the *perichoresis* in John of Damascus' *De fide orthodoxa*[113] rests upon the Johannine passage cited above. The Divine Three are understood to indwell and interpenetrate one another in such a way as to be able to say that there is one divine *ouisa*, and that the Holy Trinity is truly one God,[114] and the divine *hypostases*, while indwelling one another, do not coalesce. The endeavour to seek a relational ontology of the particular is developed in this expression of mutual indwelling (*perichoresis*) of the Divine Three. 'Each one of the persons contains the unity by this relation to the others no less than by this relation to Himself.'[115] John of Damascus' exposition of the perichorectic relations of the persons with one another has been interpreted as a further expression or extension of the conceptuality of the divine being as communion, while the Latin usage of the *circumincessio* of the Divine Three has tended to be interpreted as an expression of the relations subsisting in the single divine essence.[116]

The reception of the concept of the *perichoresis* in modern times has been mixed. Some dismiss it as a complete departure from what may be understood to be the Gospel,[117] while others accept the underlying concept but seek to provide a modern interpretation of it.[118] In the early twentieth century, the main reason for an appeal to a concept of *perichoresis* was in relation to the question of the location of the consciousness of God. Thornton argues that the divine personality and, therefore, the divine self-consciousness are shared among the three persons, and the unity of the divine personality and consciousness is to be understood in terms of the 'complete mutual indwelling and interpenetration of the Three Persons in the Godhead'.[119] This kind of understanding has been a recurring theme in contemporary theological reflection.[120] McFadyen has developed an understanding of *perichoresis* with particular reference to the question of the subjectivity of each of the persons. He writes that:

[t]he triune life is marked by the most profound interpenetration. Yet it is precisely in this interpenetration that the Persons have their distinct being, and it is only through their unique individual identities that this interpenetration is possible. The unique subjectivities of each Person are formed through the unique form of intersubjectivity which pertains to them. Like all living things

they are neither fully open nor fully closed systems. It is their radical openness to and for one another (in which Personal closure still retains a place) which constitutes their existence in this unique community [. . .][121]

McFadyen's restatement of the doctrine of *perichoresis* allows the question of the divine subjectivity and self-consciousness to be addressed in the contemporary context. It also permits a clear commitment to the endeavour to construct an understanding of relationality as found in the writings of Zizioulas, Jenson and Gunton. In such a restatement, the particular is safeguarded as an ontological category, and the being of God is understood as communion.

Alongside his appeal to the terminology of *Seinsweise*, Barth also makes an unequivocal appeal to the doctrine of *perichoresis*. His purpose in using the concept is a defence of the unity of the Godhead. He argues that the difference, which the relations of origin of three modes of being produce, is the ground for the divine fellowship, for the relations of origin imply 'a definite participation of each mode of being in the other modes of being, and indeed, since the modes of being are in fact identical with the relations of origin, a complete participation of each mode of being in the other modes of being'.[122]

Barth recognizes that this understanding is rooted in Scripture and makes particular reference to the Johannine passages. He also acknowledges the statement of the doctrine in *De fide orthodoxa* and interprets what is to be found there, in the following comment:

the divine modes of being mutually condition and permeate one another so completely that one is always in the other two and the two in the one. Sometimes this has been grounded more in the unity of the divine essence and sometimes more in the relations of origin as such. Both approaches are right and both are ultimately saying the same thing.[123]

This shows that Barth appreciates that the doctrine of *perichoresis* may be understood in different ways and makes it plain that he is not claiming any particular interpretation for himself. This may relate to Barth's discussion of the relations of origin of the three on a number of occasions;[124] in none of these does he discuss their 'relations of communion'.[125] Alan Torrance argues that the 'relations of origin' point to the ways in which the Divine Three relate to each other, while, by the phrase 'relations of communion', he draws out Zizioulas's concept of their grounding or ordering, that is their *taxis*.[126] Alan Torrance argues that 'the irreducible mutuality of relations of communion [is] essential to the three in their incommunicable distinctness [. . .] as they constitute the communion which is ontologically intrinsic to God'.[127]

This is an asymmetrical conceptuality of the Godhead in which the three are expressed in an ordered distinctness properly understood as a horizontal rather than a vertical ordering. This ordered communion of the Divine Three requires a highly developed understanding of the construction of the divine *koinonia* and of the concept of *perichoresis*, which is to be found much more clearly in the writings of Zizioulas than of Barth.

This divergence of understanding typified in the works of Barth and Zizioulas over the conceptualization of the Divine Three in terms of the divine communion and their mutual indwelling raises crucial issues from understanding the divine being in terms of relationality. This is demonstrated in Barth's further use of the concept of *perichoresis* in his discussion of the origin of the Holy Spirit. He argues that

> the one Godness of the Father and the Son is, or the Father and the Son in their one Godness are, the origin of the Spirit. What is between them, what unites them, is, then, no mere relation. It is not exhausted in the truth of their being alongside and with one another. As an independent divine mode of being over against them, it is the active mutual orientation and interpenetration of love, because these two, the Father and the Son, are of one essence, and indeed of divine essence, because God's fatherhood and sonship as such must be related to one another in this active mutual orientation and interpenetration. That the Father and the Son are the one God is the reason why they are not just united but are united in the Spirit in love.[128]

Serious reservations have been expressed about such a use of the concept of *perichoresis*. Moltmann makes the following critique of the attempt:

> to constitute the Spirit as We-Person from the I of the Father and the Thou of the Son, [which] seems like a personalistic postulate, as long as the counterpart for that 'We' cannot be named in inner-

Trinitarian terms; for the first person plural, like the first person singular, is related to a counterpart, to the 'you.' If the Spirit forms the 'We' of the Trinity, then he himself is the perichoresis. The Tri-unity is then only a duality: I + Thou = We.[129]

The resolution of the question of whether Barth has made the Spirit the 'We-Person', and also 'the *perichoresis*' of the Trinity, may be focused on his statement that the Spirit is 'an independent divine mode of being over against them' (Father and Son).[130] Is this a convincing statement of a third mode of being in the Godhead?[131] There is an element of ambiguity in Barth's formulation of the doctrines of the Spirit and of *perichoresis*, at least where these two doctrines overlap. Nonetheless, I would strongly suggest that the Spirit is a distinct mode of being and not the We-Person of Father and Son, nor simply the *perichoresis* of the two of them.[132] As well as this highly technical usage of the notion of *perichoresis*, there have been those who have 'used' the concept in ways that are highly imaginative and evocative. It is important to note this usage as well as the more analytical and technical. In the examples below, there are instances in which *perichoresis* is used in effect to clinch the argument that the doctrine of the Trinity is relevant and useful and, indeed, the explanation of the reality of the cosmos.

The retrieval of and revival of interest in the doctrine of *perichoresis* in the latter part of the twentieth century is marked in particular by those whose interests lie in liberation: liberation from domination of one kind or another, be it patriarchy, wealth or oppression, so that, despite the highly speculative nature of the concept of *perichoresis*, it has consistently been 'used' to stress the relevance of the doctrine of the Trinity, often on the basis of highly imaginative constructions of the concept or of its outcomes. Indeed, the language used often borders on the poetic.

Moltmann interprets the conceptuality of indwelling and interpenetration in terms of 'the circulatory character of the eternal divine life' and uses this understanding to reinforce his construction of the intra-divine life as an egalitarian community of love.[133] Moltmann also speaks of the perichoretic 'circulation' as a means whereby the divine glory is shared and 'manifest'. He speaks of the divine *perichoresis* as the means whereby the divine beauty and 'the sacred feast of the Trinity' are realized. However, he does not leave this construction in the realm of speculation. He argues that 'it is only this doctrine (*perichoresis*) that corresponds doxologically to "the glorification of the Spirit" in the experience of salvation'.[134] In other words, he sees this crowning concept in the construction of the doctrine of the Trinity at least as an echo of soteriological concerns: in this, he stands in parallel with Pecknold's appeal to functionality and to the interpretation of Augustine's own 'use' of the doctrine.

From the outset of *Holy Trinity: Perfect Community*, Leonardo Boff is clear that *perichoresis* is useful because it makes the doctrine of the Trinity useful. For Boff, the Holy Trinity is his 'Liberation Program'. He argues that *perichoresis* 'opens up for us a fruitful understanding of the Blessed Trinity'.[135] The conceptuality of inter-penetration expresses the life and love that is the divine *ousia*. 'Thus, the divine Three from all eternity find themselves in an infinite explosion of love and life from one to the other'.[136] From this basis, Boff contrues the being of the triune Godhead as 'a mystery of inclusion',[137] creating the possibility of employing the concept in the service of his liberationist agenda for the reformation of human society. He concludes the section dealing with *perichoresis* with a quotation from *Tao of Physics* by Fritjof Capra.

> In the new world-view, the universe is seen as a dynamic web of interrelated events. [. . .] All natural phenomena are ultimately interconnected, and in order to explain any one of them we need to understand all the others. [. . .] In that sense, one might say that every part 'contains' all the others, and indeed, a vision of mutual embodiment seems to be characteristic of the mystical experience of nature.[138]

In this, Boff highlights an element in the retrieval of *perichoresis*, which is the potential for connecting the inner life of God with the reality of the cosmos. Such a connection might be conceived in terms of a pantheistic or panentheistic understanding, or possibly on the basis of 'process thought'. Such conceptualities have been seen as problematic in terms of the potential for or perhaps inevitable conditioning of the divine by the created order. Those who have appealed to *perichoresis* in this way do so knowing that they are deliberately pushing at the boundaries of speculative Trinitarian reflection. A more sustained critique is offered by those who question whether much of this construction is projecting onto God the aims and purposes which the writers have already embraced, rather than allowing Scripture and tradition to inform the construction of the doctrine of the Trinity.

Catherine Mowry LaCugna also makes appeal to the term *peri-choresis*. She examines some of the different analogies and metaphors used historically to explain the concept, such as a light in one house illuminating another, or of perfume sprayed into the air permeating the local environment. She argues that the main weakness with such pictures is that they remain impersonal and fail to convey the dynamic and creative energy implicit in the eternal movement of *perichoresis*. So, she suggests that the idea of *perichoresis* as a 'divine dance' emerged in order to convey the personal and dynamic dimensions of the concept and, indeed, of the Godhead. 'Choreography suggests the partnership of movement [. . .] In interaction and intercourse, the dancers (and the observers) experience one fluid motion of encircling, encompassing, permeating, enveloping, outstretching.'[139] Again, for LaCugna, the concept is useful in that it builds up the potential relevance of the doctrine of the Trinity. She sees the perichoretic divine dance as an instance of a model of an egalitarian human community, freed of hierarchical oppression. She reflects further that the usefulness of *perichoresis* would be greatly enhanced if it were rooted more clearly in the economy than in the inner divine life.

'The divine dance' is indeed an apt image of persons in communion: not for an intradivine communion but for divine life as all creatures partake and literally exist in it. [. . .] Everything comes from God, and everything returns to God, through Christ in the Spirit. This *exitus* and *reditus* is the choreography of the divine dance which takes place from all eternity and is manifest at every moment in creation. There are not two sets of communion – one among the divine persons, the other among human persons, with the latter supposed to replicate the former. The one perichoresis, the one mystery of communion includes God and humanity as beloved partners in the dance.[140]

LaCugna expressed the mystery of the Godhead in terms of the relationship between God and the created cosmos in terms of the metaphor of a dance: a perichoretic dance. This has all the problems of necessity inherent in it, which she recognizes and attempts to guard against. The language she uses is evocative and 'poetic' in the ways in which it pushes against the limits of human concepts to express a vision of the relationship of the divine and the cosmos, a vision which has profound resonances both within and beyond the

Christian tradition. The understanding of God as 'lord of the dance' is a vision shared by Christianity, evoked for example in Sydney Carter's hymn and by Hinduism, manifest in the dancing Shiva, the Lord Nataraja, whose cosmic dance sustains the universe in being.[141] LaCugna has employed *perichoresis* in her construction of the doctrine of the Trinity, in order to create a relevant and functional doctrine which addresses the needs she has diagnosed as a feminist theologian.

David Cunningham also writes of the concept of *perichoresis* in terms of a dance. He is less enthusiastic about this picture as, for him, it overemphasizes the three involved in the dance and promotes too strong a sense of relationality between three 'individuals'. Cunningham recognizes the riches of the term *perichoresis* but laments the need to use it, in the sense that he perceives that its use was coined in order to prevent a sense of tritheism.[142] This reflects his overall agenda to offer a critique of the appeal to relationality in the latter part of the twentieth century.

In concluding this section, I want to draw attention to Paul Fiddes, who makes some particularly pertinent reflections on the concept of *perichoresis* regarding its usefulness in constructing a doctrine of the Trinity that is 'relevant'. Like LaCugna, he recognizes and celebrates the metaphor of a dance in construing the notion of *perichoresis*. He also recognizes that dance was 'a widespread image for the participation of all created beings in God',[143] which was used by philosophers such as Plato and Plotinus to suggest how created intelligence was held in harmony with the single divine mind. Fiddes is able to endorse the use to which *perichoresis* has been put by liberation theologians concerned with inequality, discrimination and oppression.[144] Fiddes' most important contribution to the structuring of *perichoresis* is in relation to suffering and death, both the suffering and death of Christ and of humanity. The divine perichoretic dance has most often been understood in terms of love and joy. He argues that suffering and death need also to be part of the dance.

> The negative movement of perishing is, accordingly, a separation entering into the heart of God's relationships. The dance of perichoresis can be disturbed; [. . .] a gap can open up between the movements of the dance. [. . .] if the dance is to absorb this interruption, to weave this very brokenness into the dance and make death serve it, transforming the movement to nothingness into a movement of possibility, we have to think carefully about the

nature of the breach. [. . .] if the dance of perichoresis already has this gulf at its heart, we can begin to understand how God in extravagant love allows death itself to enter that space.[145]

Fiddes draws upon the work of Moltmann and von Balthasar in drawing out these reflections on *perichoresis*.[146] In making these connections, Fiddes has structured the concept of *perichoresis* in such a way as to be able to include within it the core elements of the economy of salvation and has established in a creative and innovative way the soteriological functionality of the concept and of the doctrine of the Trinity. In this achievement, he has retrieved a core element of the tradition from irrelevance, without surrendering to the force of the critique of projection. The cumulative effect of these several reflections on the concept of *perichoresis* from the latter part of the twentieth century demonstrates that the creativity of those who espouse the appeal to relationality has the potential to achieve a functional doctrine of the Trinity which, on its own terms, is relevant to the concerns of the contemporary context and faithful to Scripture and tradition.

This concludes the identification of core concepts in the terrain of Trinitarian language. The exploration of mutual indwelling, communion and personhood used in the endeavour to express the riddle of the divine threefoldness and divine oneness, and in relation to Nicene orthodoxy and the reception of that orthodoxy down to the present time, has demonstrated that bringing the encounter with God in the economy of salvation to articulation is an ongoing task, in the stretching of language by metaphor and analogy to present the ultimately inexpressible in each new generation. Before moving to the next chapter, I will discuss two further examples of the articulation or symbolization of the Divine Three.

GENDERED LANGUAGE

I began this chapter by suggesting that alongside the examination of terminology the reader should also bear in mind that the use of the terms is always an attempt to express what is ultimately inexpressible: the being of God. So, in concluding the chapter, I will examine in particular the use of gender-specific language and ask how such use relates to the nature of God *in se*. For some, clearly the use of language is analogical or metaphorical. But others hold that the language used refers directly to the being of God. The expression of a Christian understanding of the being of the triune God in terms of male language in the formulas of worship and doctrine will be addressed in relation to these two different approaches: the feminist critique of such language and its defence in relation to 'iconic language'. The expression of the divine in male-gendered language has been recognized as problematic in theological reflection for many centuries, not in the terms of modern-day feminist critique but in recognition that all language falls short of describing the divine and that the divine being is not gendered in the sense that human beings are gendered. There is a historic and ongoing recognition within the Christian tradition that all language about God is analogical, including the designations 'Father' and 'Son'. Gender is not to be attributed to God in any literal sense. It is evident in the Scriptural witness that both male and female analogies have been used and offer profound disclosures of God and God's relationship to human beings. It is important to remember that St Paul refers to Christ as the wisdom (*sophia*) of God.[147] *Sophia* is a feminine noun in Greek and provides a gendered diversity in terms of the person of Christ. It is something which on the whole is lost, along with the *logos* designation of the second person of the Trinity. To this day, there remains a survival of the *sophia* designation in the name of what was once the greatest church building in Christendom: the Church of Hagia Sophia (Holy Wisdom) in Constantinople.

FEMINIST CRITIQUE OF GENDERED LANGUAGE

The feminist critique of the doctrine of the Trinity is at once part of a wholesale reassessment of the Christian theological tradition and so is concerned with more than the question of gendered language. Underlying the feminist critique of the doctrine of the Trinity is a prior question of how the system(s) of thought emerged that led to the construction of the classical doctrine. The result of asking such questions has brought about a feminist reinterpretation of Western monotheistic traditions. The basis of this reinterpretation or reconstruction has been the introduction of non- or multi-gendered language for God. It is a fundamental preconception of feminist critique that language is a powerful medium that not only permeates belief about the essence and character of God but that also profoundly influences human behaviour and social interaction. One strand of the feminist critique asserts that any notion that God has a male gender is to be rejected, and male pronouns are not to be used when referring to God. Anything which might suggest that the divine being is authoritarian or disciplinarian is to be avoided. As an alternative, some feminist writers have tended to emphasize 'maternal' attributes such as nurturing and acceptance in relation to the divine. A core understanding of the critique is that not only is the male gendered language of the classic doctrine of the Trinity a reflection of a patriarchal context but that it has also sustained and empowered patriarchal relationships between men and women. In other words, the Father–Son relationship that implies a form of subordinationism in the Trinity has provided an ideological warrant for the subordination of the female to the male. The doctrine of the Trinity has been seen by some feminists as a framework for working out theological perspectives on gender and difference. Not all theologians accept these premises and question whether a relatively obscure doctrine such as the doctrine of the Trinity could in reality be seen to authorize a general understanding of gender relations. Others have asked whether there is something like maleness and femaleness in God that provides a reference point for the human understanding of gender.

Catherine Mowry LaCugna has argued that the traditional doctrine of the Trinity has been damaging as a model for earthly relationships among human persons.[148] She perceives that men have modelled social hierarchy, including their domination over women, on the basis of understanding the triune God as an archetype for human interactions, legitimating oppression and domination. LaCugna's understanding is rooted in her interpretation of the Cappadocian tradition of a hierarchical relationship among the three members of the trinity, i.e., a powerful Father-Godhead figure and subordinate Christ and Holy Spirit figures, which has led to hierarchical domination of certain persons, namely men over women. Mary Daly echoes these concerns:

The Judaic-Christian tradition has served to legitimate sexually imbalanced patriarchal society. For example, the image of the Father God, in the human imagination and sustained as plausible by patriarchy, has in turn rendered service to this type of society by making its mechanisms for the oppression of women appear right and fitting. If God in 'his' heaven is a father ruling 'his' people. then it is in the 'nature' of things and according to divine plan and the order of the universe that society be male-dominated.[149]

In the present social and political context, where equality and inclusivity have come to be valued over hierarchy, the feminist diagnosis of the problems inherent in the classic doctrine of the Trinity clearly need to be addressed. LaCugna suggests that a reunderstanding of the Trinity can be achieved through a thoroughly relational and reciprocal understanding of the relationships among the Divine Three, which can provide a more acceptable model for human relationships. LaCugna also argues that an understanding of the equal love and freedom that exists in the relatedness of the members of the Trinity can also be a model for earthly communities of inclusivity. The use of non-gendered God language such as 'Creator, Redeemer, Sustainer' can assist the community of faith to respond to God's relationality, but she is not in favour of replacing the traditional language of 'Father, Son and Holy Spirit'. The loss of the personal aspect of the Divine Three would be detrimental to the understanding of God as a personal saviour, friend and comforter. Other writers have suggested that the worship of the male god (father) should be replaced with that of the goddess (mother). However, this suggestion is not part of the agenda of most Christian feminist theologians. On the whole, their concern has been to reaffirm the generally accepted theological understanding that all language about God is analogical and that God is beyond gender. From a more radical perspective, Mary Daly argues that the power of language is not to be underestimated:

> Sophisticated thinkers, of course, have never intellectually identified God with an elderly parent in heaven. Nevertheless it is important to recognize that even when very abstract conceptualizations of God are formulated in the mind, images have a way of surviving in the imagination in such a way that a person can function on two different and even apparently contradictory levels at the same time. One can speak of God as spirit and at the same time imagine 'him' as belonging to the male sex.[150]

Two further aspects of the classical formulations of the doctrine of the Trinity have caught the attention of feminist theologians. Among some feminist theologians there is a growing perception that the shift in the medieval West, usually attributed to Thomas Aquinas,[151] from the doctrine of the Trinity as the foundation of Christian theological reflection to the focus on God as a unitary supreme being who is only subsequently understood to have Trinitarian aspects, is a highly problematic turn for theology. This turn is interpreted as having empowered 'a hierarchal monistic understanding of reality-monarchism, and a correlated individualistic and elitist view of human social structures'.[152] Alternatively, Christian feminist theologians have been arguing that a Trinitarian understanding of God based upon a relational reading of Nicene orthodoxy leads to much healthier understanding of social structures and human interaction.[153]

The second aspect of Trinitarian thought concerns the person of the Holy Spirit who has often been thought of as female, either analogically or indeed literally. Feminist theologians on the whole have not sought any literal identification of the Spirit as female, because of an analogical understanding of God-talk, though some writers have promoted the notion of a female model of God as Spirit. There are major concerns over the attempt to 'feminize' the Holy Spirit, for it is argued that the Spirit has too often 'been construed through a patriarchally distorted image of the feminine as being quiet, recessive and dependent'.[154] This does not sit well with the evidence of the Scriptural witness, particularly of Pentecost, where the Holy Spirit was portrayed in terms of the power of God: the tongues of flame and the 'rushing mighty wind'. However, it is possible, on the basis of the Pentecost story, to construct an understanding of the Spirit's work was inclusive; that is to say, that the Spirit gives gifts equally to both women and men. In this case, feminist theologians might welcome a feminine understanding of the Spirit, as a reversal of the power structures inherent in a traditionally patriarchal reading of the doctrine of the Trinity.

There has also been constructive feminist critique of the doctrine of the Trinity. For example, Diana Neal has proposed a feminist reading of the relationality of father and son,[155] building on Moltmann's reference to the Council of Toledo in 675. 'It must be held that the Son was created, neither out of nothingness, nor yet out of any substance, but that he was begotten or born out of the Father's womb (*de utero Patris*), that is, out of his very essence.'[156] It is the view of Neal and Moltmann that only through a Trinitarian understanding of the divine is it possible to go beyond a patriarchal understanding of God and construction of society, despite the male-gendered language of the traditional doctrine of the Trinity. Neal refers, in particular, to the crucifixion of Christ as the reinterpretative lens through which to re-read the tradition: 'the trinitarian event of the cross presents Christians with a symbolic framework which, far from being necessarily patriarchal in nature, subverts patriarchal relations of power between fathers and sons, This, in turn, would lead to a deconstruction of the binary definition of maleness with divinity and femaleness with materiality'.[157]

Neal goes on to argue that there can be a new symbolization of God, through a re-reading of the doctrine of the Trinity. She suggests that Luce Irigaray is correct to argue that symbolic changes follow on from psychological changes. The change from passivity to agency that women have begun to experience is reflected in this re-reading, bringing with it a symbolic diversity. 'A plurality of symbols of the divine will provide us with a more modest, but inevitably truer experience of God. These symbols will find their sources in the rich fullness of human ways of being.'[158] In a sense, this is a further example of a functional reception and use of the doctrine of the Trinity. A constructive re-reading on a much broader scale is to be found in Gavin D'Costa's *Sexing the Trinity*.[159] He also appeals to the work of writers such as Lacan and Luce Irigaray. D'Costa uses the possibilities raised through their works to explore the symbolization of Christ in terms of the phallic and vaginal in order to transcend stereotypical understandings of gender and the idea that the doctrine of the Trinity necessarily has to be understood in patriarchal terms. In particular, he explores the notion of the non-phallic in relation to the feminine and argues that idea of the 'Phallic Mother' pushes back the boundaries of symbolization for the divine. The understanding that phallic symbolization is by no means exclusively male is a welcome addition to the conceptualization of the doctrine of *perichoresis* with its imagery of interpenetration.

SOPHIOLOGY

By way of a codicil to the feminist critique of the doctrine of the Trinity, I would like to mention briefly the notion of 'sophiology', which is associated in particular with the work of Sergei Bulgakov.[160] Bulgakov was influenced in this regard by Vladimir Soloviev,[161] and, at least to some extent, finds an echo in contemporary feminism. Sophiology, coming from the Greek *sophia*, is a concept rooted in the traditional understandings of theology concerned with the Wisdom of God. Sophiology involves speculative reflection on the relationship between the visible and invisible worlds, the role of nature, as well as teleology, and has its roots in wisdom theology and in Russian theology of the nineteenth century. The Russian Orthodox theologians Georges Florovsky and Vladimir Lossky have vehemently opposed this appeal to *sophia*. Vladimir Lossky has argued that sophiology is a mistaken concept in which the Holy Spirit and the Virgin Mary are united as a single deity or *hypostasis* of God.[162] Bulgakov himself describes the wisdom of God as the 'interior organic unity' of the divine ideas.[163] He associates wisdom with love in terms of the substance of the Trinity.

> Belonging, giving, yielding: these are terms of love. And more especially, these words suggest that the Wisdom of God may be best spoken of by feminine metaphors, since in the deepest and most abiding love we know, the married love of human beings, they are words that suggest the attitude of the bride more than the bridegroom.[164]

This is perhaps an appeal to an unreconstructed stereotyping of gendered relations. But of its day, it was an attempt to associate the feminine with the heart of the doctrine of the Trinity. Bulgakov also understands that there is a role for the Divine Wisdom in the creating of the cosmos. The creation 'is, or was meant to be, a *sophianic* creation, a creation filled with the wisdom of God'.[165] It is beyond the scope of this guide to examine this concept in detail. Bulgakov's appeal to a *sophianic* creation suggests that his outlook on the created order is panentheistic. His work has received renewed interest in recent times and demonstrates that Trinitarian theological reflection, even within an appeal to Nicene orthodoxy, can be highly imaginative and creative in seeking further symbolization of the divine.

ICONIC LANGUAGE

In distinction from the understanding that God-talk in general, and specifically in relation to the doctrine of the Trinity, is to be understood as contingent, constructed out of Christian theological reflection, in faithful dialogue with the witness of Scripture, tradition and the experience of the economy, there is another view that God-talk about the Trinity is to be understood as 'iconic language'. Such 'iconic language'

> is given by revelation and based on the fact that theology is not based on the distinction between subject and object, like analogies and metaphors, but on the unique character of the ecclesial *koinonia*. In this context the use of metaphor poses difficulties,

given that it is grounded exclusively in human experience. We cannot separate iconic language from the fact of revelation, expressed in Holy Scripture and ecclesial tradition. Unlike symbolic language, iconic language is not rooted in human experience.[166]

An implication of this understanding is that the expression of the Godhead as Father, Son and Holy Spirit is held to be non-negotiable. This concept of 'iconic language' represents a very different understanding of the workings of language from that which is usually understood both in terms of everyday conversation and of theological reflection. The concept is often associated with Eastern Orthodox writers, but there are parallels to be found in writers from various other traditions. For example, Robert Jenson has argued that the Church's 'primary Trinitarian talk' are 'dense signs', that is, sacramental gifts that enable participation in the heavenly liturgy:

> It is throughout eternity that we will be initiated into the pattern of the life among the divine Three; if we are now able to shape our liturgy by the 'begetting' and 'sending' constitutive of that life, it can only be that we are permitted to trace a life not yet of this world.[167]

And T. F. Torrance argues that knowledge of God is only possible by 'sharing in some way in the knowledge which God has of himself'.[168] The human knowledge of God does not emerge from a centre in the human being but from a centre in God, not on any human ground of being, but on the ground of God's being. The human ability to know God does not arise from some innate human capacity but from divine activity in which God allows himself to be known through his Word. In the historical particularity of Jesus of Nazareth this becomes an actuality:

> In Jesus we encounter the very EGO EIMI [I AM] of God, so that in him we are summoned to know God in accordance with the way in which he has actually objectified himself in our human existence and communicated himself within the structure and modes of our human knowing and speaking.[169]

DiNoia also argues that the specific Trinitarian language is part and parcel of the gift of the triune God's very self, 'the incorporation of created persons into personal communion with the uncreated Trinity'.[170] He argues that only God himself is able to supply language appropriate to the divine mystery.

> 'When we cry "Abba! Father!"' it is that very Spirit himself bearing witness with our spirit that we are children of God' [Rom. 8.15–16, (NRSV)] [. . .] The speakability of the otherwise unspeakable mystery of the triune God presupposes the gift of God's very self and depends on resources that come with that gift.[171]

The construction of an understanding of 'iconic language' means that the designation of the Divine Three as Father, Son and Holy Spirit is non-negotiable. Does such an understanding stand up to scrutiny in terms of the human experience and perception of the workings of language? It is beyond the scope of this guide to offer a detailed analysis of different understandings of human language in theology and philosophy. Broadly speaking, the approaches in the feminist critique of the gendered language of the Divine Three and in the defence of iconic language set out the polarities for understanding the workings of human language in doctrinal constructions. There is a detailed and nuanced analysis of the relationship of human language to divine self-expression in Barth's work, *The Word of God and the Word of Man*.[172] This work sits at one end of the polarity. Janet Martin Soskice's work, *Metaphor and Religious Language*, which also represents a nuanced analysis sits at the other end.[173] Once again, I leave this matter to the reader to resolve.

In this chapter, I have sought to identify the core words and concepts in the complex landscape of Trinitarian technical language. The emergence of Nicene orthodoxy and its reception and re-reception down the centuries is a story of human endeavour in the pursuit of giving an account of the faith of the tradition. The quest to articulate and interpret the human encounter with the divine in human language has been pursued, often against a background of misunderstanding, controversy or conflict. Out of these conflictual occasions, the Church was 'forced' to set out particular signposts, in the decisions, formulations and creeds of the councils. In more recent times, the resolution of the impact of modernity and postmodernity has on the whole rested in the hands of individual theologians. In this case the signposts have tended to be more disputed and provisional. This is particularly the case over the expression of personhood. The appeal made to relationality during the course of the twentieth century has itself now been challenged and questioned. The landscape of Trinitarian language remains as complex and intriguing as ever. It is a reminder of the need to receive the tradition anew in each generation and bring it to expression in language forms of the day, just as those who appealed to *logos* did in the first centuries. Similarly, it is necessary to re-receive and re-understand revelation in each new generation, and it is to this that I shall turn in the next chapter.

SUGGESTED READING

M. Wiles, *The Making of Christian Doctrine: A Study in the Principles of Early Doctrinal Development* (Cambridge: Cambridge University Press, 1967).

F. M. Young, *From Nicaea to Chalcedon: A Guide to the Literature and Its Background* (Philadelphia, Pa.: Fortress Press, 1983).

M. Carrithers, S. Collins and S. Lukes (eds), *The Category of the Person: Anthropology, Philosophy, History* (Cambridge: Cambridge University Press, 1985).

C. Taylor, *Sources of the Self: The Making of Modern Identity* (Cambridge, Mass.: Harvard University Press, 1989).

A. I. McFadyen, *The Call to Personhood: A Christian Theory of the Individual in Social Relationships* (Cambridge: Cambridge University Press, 1990).

J. D. Zizioulas, 'On Being a Person: Towards an Ontology of Personhood', in C. Schwöbel and C. E. Gunton (eds), *Persons, Human and Divine* (Edinburgh: T. & T. Clark, 1991), pp. 33–46.

C. M. LaCugna, *God for Us: The Trinity and the Christian Life* (New York: HarperCollins, 1991).

G. D'Costa, *Sexing the Trinity: Gender, Culture and the Divine* (London: SCM Press, 2000).

CHAPTER 4

THE RECEPTION OF REVELATION

INTRODUCTION

The question at the heart of this chapter relates not only to how the doctrine of the Trinity is supported evidentially, i.e., what data is there to support a doctrine of the Trinity, but also how is the doctrine to be received by the individual and the Christian community of the Church? These questions echo the divergence over language, which I discussed in the previous chapter. Is language a set of human phenomena that are culturally and historically conditioned, so that the designation of the divine as Father, Son and Holy Spirit is contingent and replaceable? Or is the human language capability part of God's gift-giving in the creating and redeeming of the cosmos, thus justifying the claims made for 'iconic language'? In a sense, this tension is another presentation of the polarity I have already noted between the claim that divine revelation is either of God *in se*, or Trinitarian language is the triadic representation of God in history according to the receptive capacity of the human subject and nothing more.[1] It may be possible to find a middle way, a *via media* between these two poles, that recognizes claims to insight and truth in each stance while also moderating the tendency towards absolutist claims in each polarity. This resonates with the possibility expounded by Lindbeck that the understanding of doctrine can be held in a synthesis of cognitive and experiential-expressive perspectives, as perhaps Rahner and Lonergan may be said to do.[2]

In this chapter, I will examine how the reality, which the doctrine of the Trinity is understood to symbolize, is known and received in the context of the believing ecclesial community. I shall attempt to do this through the analysis of four different but overlapping conceptual frameworks: the first analysis will be of the epistemological constructions of divine (self-)revelation. The second will examine the epistemological implications of the classical construct of divine activity: 'the external works of the Trinity are undivided' (in Latin, *opera ad extra trinitatis indivisa sunt*). The third analysis will examine the implications of the axiomatic claim articulated by Rahner that, 'The "economic" Trinity is the "immanent" Trinity and the "immanent" Trinity is the "economic" Trinity'.[3] The final analysis will focus on the noetic and ontic implications of event conceptuality.

EPISTEMOLOGY AND REVELATION

Doctrines of revelation emerge from reflection on the experience of the divine in the world as it is understood to be received and lived by the Church. Epistemological constructions of divine (self-)revelation, are made to provide a conceptual framework for the experience of 'knowing' that to which the doctrine of the Trinity refers or symbolizes. An example of the question of how God is known, in particular how God is known as Trinity, is to be seen in the divergence of understanding between Thomas Aquinas and Gregory Palamas, based upon the Orthodox understanding of the distinction to be drawn concerning the divine essence and energies, which I discussed in Chapter 2. I shall reiterate that discussion briefly: one way of looking at the different perspectives of the churches of East and West is to claim that the divergence is not so much that the Latin church understands the doctrine of the Trinity as a claim of *unitas in trinitate* while the Greek church understands *trinitas in unitate*, as that there is divergence between them concerning the epistemological approach and ontological affirmations which can be made about the being and nature of God. The Palamite tradition of the East perceives that the essence of God is inaccessible to creaturely knowledge, and God is known by human beings only by means of the divine energies, while the Thomist tradition of the West suggests that the divine essence is knowable through created grace, allowing the human mind to be enabled to grasp divine truth. The ongoing schism between East and West reinforced this sense of divergence and difference. As suggested already, and as is often the case, if these arguments are examined carefully in terms of the goal to which doctrinal constructs point, there is ground for arguing that the two traditions have more in common than was perceived in the past. Both traditions seek the goal of a limited human knowledge of the divine, and of the divine as Trinity; there is a sense of caution and reserve in each exposition in recognition of the inadequacy of human language and conceptuality and in the face of ultimate divine mystery. Both traditions demonstrate a realization that especially in the case of the doctrine of the Trinity, the task and process of theological reflection is one of contemplation rather than of precise definition. The consequences of the Enlightenment challenge to epistemological certainty meant that it became necessary once more to ask the question, 'Is it possible to know God and in particular to know God as Trinity?' Theologians had to ask themselves whether it was possible or preferable to 'begin' with God or with the works of God in creating and redeeming or the knowing of the human subject. One manifestation of anxiety about the consequences of the Enlightenment is to be seen in the debates concerning Socinianism and Deism in the seventeenth and eighteenth centuries, which I discussed in Chapter 2. Another response to the Enlightenment challenge or perceived threat to traditional ways of constructing epistemology, and particularly the knowledge of God, was the effective marginalization of reflection upon Trinitarian theology. It has often been argued that this arises out of a combination of Enlightenment philosophy with the soteriological emphasis of mainstream Protestant thought. Melanchthon had argued that 'to know Christ is to know his benefits', and that there was no need for speculation about the nature or natures of Christ.[4] Immanuel Kant argued that there are clear limits to (human) knowledge: things are not known in themselves, but only as they appear to the knowing subject.[5] The acceptance of Kant's diagnosis of human knowing among some theologians leads to the marginalization of Trinitarian understandings of the Godhead among liberal Protestants. A good example of this development is to be found in the work of Adolf Harnack.[6] The one obvious exception to this trend is found in the work of the philosopher Hegel. In his *Phenomenology of Geist*, he constructs a metaphysics on a Trinitarian basis.[7] Hegel expounds the view that the Absolute Spirit is revealed in history in a dialectic of thesis, antithesis and synthesis, which mirrors the Christian understanding of God as Trinity. Hegel's construction has undoubtedly influenced many Christian theologians, particularly those who stand in the German idealist tradition.[8]

It was in response to this diagnosis and proscription of human knowledge, made by Kant, that Karl Barth and Friedrich Schleiermacher constructed their very different theological frameworks.[9] Both theologians reflect on the doctrine of the Trinity, and their treatment of the Trinity clearly demonstrates how they are responding to the Kantian proscription of knowledge. Schleiermacher treats the doctrine of the Trinity only at the end of *The Christian Faith* almost as an afterthought,[10] whereas Barth begins the *Church Dogmatics* with an exposition of divine revelation in terms of the triune God.[11] An interpretation of these responses would be to suggest that Barth and Schleiermacher typify Lindbeck's designations of creed and doctrine in terms of 'cognitive' and 'experiential-expressive'. This may be an oversimplification, but Schleiermacher is certainly to be credited as the originator in modern times of an understanding of theological reflection in aesthetical terms.

For Schleiermacher, 'doctrine' emerges from a critical examination of human religious affections. Schleiermacher constructs his doctrine of the Trinitarian being of God on the basis of being able to contrast the hidden and revealed God.[12] The hidden God remains unknown to human beings. There is, however, divine revelation. This is construed in relation, first, to a Christological confession and, second, to the divine indwelling in the community of faith. On the basis of these two experiences, Schleiermacher allows that a Trinitarian understanding emerges. In each instance, the Christological and the ecclesial, he understands that there is a union of divine essence with human nature. Such a perception does not necessarily entail a doctrine of the Trinity or a threefold understanding of the divine. However, the divine is experienced and received by human beings through Christ and the Spirit. Trinitarian reflection and doctrinal exposition are contingent upon receiving the experience of the divine in the context of Christian religious consciousness or tradition. Some commentators have argued that Schleiermacher is best understood as standing in line with Sabellius. In other words, the divine being 'happens' in the economy of revelation without necessarily referring to inner divine reality. There can be no certainty about who God is *in se*; however, it is possible that God 'is' threefold in the economy. Maybe Schleiermacher's construction of the doctrine of the Trinity is to be understood as an off-shoot of the Socinian branch of Protestantism. In relation to Claude Welch's categorization of three levels of Trinitarian reflection: (1) economic (2) essential (3) immanent; where (1) relates to an understanding of the revelation of God through Christ and the Spirit in the history of salvation (economic); (2) accepts the doctrines of the *homoousion*, and the co-eternity and co-equality of the three hypostases (essential); and (3) accepts the account of the divine internal relations of the filial generation and Spirit's procession, and the *perichoresis* of the three (immanent), Schleiermacher's understanding of the Trinity may be interpreted in terms of (1) and perhaps to some extent of (2), but certainly not (3). Indeed, Schleiermacher warns against such speculation.[13] Karl Barth's approach to the question of the knowledge of God is also grounded in a response to Kant. Barth begins from the understanding that human beings cannot know God, as Kant indicates, which leads to his vehement rejection of 'natural theology'.[14] He declares that only God can make God known. This making known is what has happened in Christ and comes to articulation in the Church doctrine of the Trinity. Barth's reconstruction of a theological epistemology in response to Kant's diagnosis is largely responsible for the twentieth-century revival of interest in and appeal to the classic doctrine(s) of the Trinity. Barth constructs his epistemological framework on the doctrine of the Word of God and the Trinity, in which he appeals to a divine threefoldness designated by the terms: 'Revealer, Revelation, Revealedness'.[15] This is the polar opposite of Schleiermacher's response to the same epistemic problematic. There is a caution in Barth's exposition in that he clearly recognizes that revelation is mediated. God reveals himself; that is to say, this relates to God *in se*, the immanent Trinity, in order that revelation is really the revealing of God; i.e., that it is divine self-revelation. For Barth, there is clearly no hidden God: a *deus absconditus*, who lies behind the God known in revelation. This claim in part relates to a divergence in Protestantism. Luther does make reference to the idea that there is a sense in which God ultimately remains a mystery,[16] or in part remains hidden from human knowledge and enquiry. In Barth's affirmation that there is no hidden God, nothing of the divine that is ultimately unknown, he is reiterating a Reformed stance over against a Lutheran perspective. A further example of this divergence may be seen in Paul Tillich's work: writing from a Lutheran perspective, he expounded an understanding of the God beyond God.[17] It is evident from this brief analysis of various sources and traditions that there is no consensus in the Christian tradition concerning the construction of a theological epistemology, no consensus about the role of experience and the economy in the creation of an epistemological framework. This lack of consensus impacts particularly upon the construal of the doctrine of the Trinity. Barth made the Trinity an instrument of epistemology, with the work of the Holy Spirit as the subjective element of revelation within the knowing human subject, as the personal stage of the reception of the revelation of the Word encountered in its witnesses Scripture and Church proclamation.[18] This instrumental construction of the doctrine of the Trinity is another example of a functional take on Trinitarian reflection. This construction might be understood to be excessively and mistakenly instrumental, if it were to be seen as strictly 'cognitive', perhaps as a mechanical transaction between the human and divine. Indeed, there are many questions to be raised about the apparent subjugation of a primary doctrine such as that of the Trinity to a secondary doctrine such as revelation or epistemology. However, it may be that Barth's construal of the doctrine of the Trinity is a proper recognition of the centrality of epistemic problems in the post-Enlightenment context, which remain in the postmodern context. Furthermore, his construction of the doctrines of Trinity and revelation in terms of the objectivity and subjectivity of Word and Spirit in relation to the knowing human subject may demonstrate an 'experiential-expressive' understanding of doctrine. For myself, it is a false juxtaposition to suggest either that revelation is the revelation of God *in se* or that Trinitarian language is the triadic representation of God in history according to the receptive capability of the human subject and nothing else. Attempts to set these two sides of Trinitarian reflection against one another suggest a false dichotomy between the divine and the human, which, as Kathryn Tanner has argued, is long overdue recognition and can be overcome through a reading of Chalcedon that does not polarize divine over against human.[19] This reflects Barth's later understanding of the relation of the divine and human in Christ.[20] I would suggest that this move towards a synthesis of the different approaches to epistemology in Trinitarian reflection is not about finding more certainty and clarity. Rather, it suggests that in the divine approach to the human and in the human attempts to express the encounter with the threefoldness of the divine, a certain epistemic and linguistic reticence or apophaticism is part of responsible Christian theological reflection: one might almost call it a kind of agnosticism or 'unknowing'.

DIVINE ACTION AND REVELATION

This second analysis will examine the epistemological implications of the classical construction of divine activity *ad extra* as undivided for the knowing and receiving of divine (self-)revelation by the believing ecclesial community. In the patristic period, one of the overriding concerns among those who sought to promote or defend the idea of a differentiated Godhead was with the expression of divine unity, alongside diversity. There may have been a radical shift in the conceptualization of monotheism early in Christian tradition, in the perceived encounter with the divine three; nonetheless, there was no serious attempt to suggest there was more than one ultimate being. Modern suggestions that there might be three gods were more or less unthinkable for the Christian in the context of Hellenistic Platonism.[21] The conundrum for those engaged in Trinitarian theological reflection was how to suggest both unity and diversity in the Godhead. One means of ensuring the unity of divine being was to appeal to an understanding that in the Godhead there was only one will, and in relation to the world only one 'centre of activity'. It is perhaps no coincidence that John of Damascus expounds the notion of *perichoresis* in the Islamic context in which he finds himself, as means of securing the expression of a differentiated monotheism, in order to counter Islamic propaganda that Christians worshipped three gods. Despite the very notion of 'Trinity' arising from what is perceived as a threefold encounter in the economy of salvation and in the experience of worship, divine action in the world, the action of creating, redeeming and revealing comes to be understood as 'undivided'. This is expressed in the doctrinal formula: *the external works of the Trinity are undivided* (*opera ad extra trinitatis indivisa sunt*). Many commentators have understood this to be the working assumption of Augustine,[22] although Stephen T. Davis is clear that the phrase itself is not found in Augustine's works.[23] Examples of similar understandings can be found in Gregory of Nyssa's *Ad Abablium*, and the phrase itself comes to be used in some of the later councils, such as the councils held at Toledo in 638, 672–6, 693 and the Council of Venice in 796/7.[24]

The understanding of the unity or indivisibility of divine activity *ad extra* was probably first expounded by Athanasius in opposition to those who denied the deity of the Holy Spirit. His construction of the doctrine of unified divine activity in the world rests on a set of philosophical presuppositions inherent in contemporary Platonism. The main thrust of this understanding is that energy or works or actions (*energeia* in Greek) (*opera* in the Latin phraseology of the doctrinal statement) is revelatory of *ousia* or essence. This philosophical understanding arose from the concept of *energeia* in the thought of Aristotle but had been developed in the writings of Platonists such as Philo, Porphery, Galen and Iamblichus.[25] Athanasius argues that the witness in Scripture is to God's acts in the world, which are always being accomplished by all three persons of the Trinity at the same time. On the basis of the understanding that an undivided 'external act' (*energeia*) reveals an 'inner' essence (*ousia*) then God who is Trinity is one in his very (inner) essence. The purpose of Athanasius' argument achieves its goal: the Holy Spirit is to be understood as being divine. The notion of the indivisibility of divine action in the world also relates to the development of the Eastern conceptuality of essence and energies. A particular consequence of the teaching that God's works *ad extra* are undivided is that only one kind of distinction can be attributed to the Godhead and that is the internal relations of origin. This outcome is somewhat ameliorated in the light of the doctrine of *perichoresis* as formulated in the works of John of Damascus but what may be said of this, is also highly speculative. Expounding the notion of the perichoretic action of the divine three acting together, Davis writes that, 'the persons are fully open to each other, their actions *ad extra* are in common, they "see with each other's eyes," the boundaries between them are transparent to each other, and each ontologically embraces the others.'[26] This is a highly evocative picture, but it is important to receive it as just this, a work of the imagination. It is a piece of speculation, which many would see as a step too far. However, so long as caution is maintained, such imaginative understandings may be instructive for ongoing theological reflection.

Nonetheless, such developments are effectively seen as flights of fancy in the critique offered by Maurice Wiles in his classic essay 'Some Reflections on the Origins of the Doctrine of the Trinity'.[27]

> Attempts in the modern period [. . .] to provide *ex post facto* justifications for the doctrine of the Trinity out of the church's early experience are in Wiles' view fatally flawed: we find in the ante-Nicene Fathers, he shows, neither any consistent allocation of different *activities* to the three 'persons', nor (the epistemological correlate of this) any distinctive set of *experiences* associated with each of the three.[28]

The critique which Wiles offers is compounded by the doctrine that *ad extra* the action of God is undivided, in the sense that it would seem that the threefoldness is indiscernible *ad extra*, i.e., in the economy. Sarah Coakley seeks to address the flaws which Wiles discerns in the construction of the doctrine of the Trinity in the patristic period. In particular, she seeks to rehabilitate the appeal to 'religious experience' made by the Fathers for the context of the present day.[29] It seems to me that the ability to make an epistemological appeal to experience, be that witnessed in Scripture, tradition or lived context, is vital for theological reflection as such and, in particular, for the doctrine of the Trinity. The criteria for doing so can be illusive and difficult to substantiate or agree. If the endeavour to craft a doctrine of the Trinity is to be ongoing, the attempt to agree such criteria has to be made. One thing is certain: that the doctrine of the undivided divine action requires a nuanced reception and interpretation if it is not to be an insurmountable problem. The experience of the gift-giving of the Holy Spirit in present-day charismatic renewal may prove highly illustrative of an encounter with 'one' of the 'three' in which one can yet argue that the divine intentionality and activity remains undivided *ad extra*. In other words, the reception of the charismatic gifts may suggest an encounter evidential of the divine three, and yet, despite its specificity, does not necessarily undermine the unity of the divine will and being.

TRINITY: IMMANENT AND ECONOMIC

This third analysis will examine the implications of the axiomatic claim articulated by Rahner that, 'The "economic" Trinity is the "immanent" Trinity and the "immanent" Trinity is the "economic" Trinity.' In what ways does this conceptual framework impact on the theological epistemology of revelation? Rahner's axiom goes to the heart of the question concerning the relationship between the encounter with God in the economy of salvation and speculation about God *in se*. Not only are there questions about how God is known in the economy, but there are also questions about whether there is knowledge of God *in se*. Two areas of discourse that relate to these questions have been examined already in this chapter and in Chapter 2. I have explored the differences between the Thomist and Palamite theological constructs in relation to the knowledge of God *in se* and also the questions relating to the undivided action of God *ad extra*. In this section, I shall analyse the claim that 'the immanent Trinity is the economic Trinity' and 'the economic Trinity is the immanent Trinity'. It is evident that the earliest writers who reflected on the threefoldness of God did so on the basis of what they understood was encountered in the economy. Theirs is an 'economic' understanding of God as threefold. God is understood as Trinity as revealed and encountered in the activities and events of creating and redeeming. As reflection continues and becomes more nuanced, and as the impact of what is understood as heterodox is felt, the question emerges: was God triune before the activities of creating and redeeming? In other words, is God *in se* to be understood as triune? Is there an 'immanent Trinity' as well as an 'economic Trinity'?

Discourse concerning the relationship between the economic and the immanent Trinity has been a firm feature of Trinitarian reflection since the emergence of Nicene orthodoxy in the fourth century, based as it was upon the claim of the *homoousion* of Father, Son and Holy Spirit, which is a claim about the inner reality of the Godhead. For instance, by the time of the High Middle Ages, Thomas Aquinas took the inner Trinitarian relations as a given. During the twentieth century, the relationship between the economic and the immanent Trinity became a touchstone of the renewal of Trinitarian discourse, as is witnessed in the writings of both Barth and Rahner. It is generally agreed that while Barth and Rahner share a common understanding of the Godhead which is rooted in the Hegelian concept of the absolute subject and a common concern to express the divine personhood in terms which they understand relate to the modern Western notion of a person, they hold divergent views of the conceptuality of the relationship between the economic and the immanent Trinity. Trinitarian theological reflection suggests that the threefoldness of the Godhead is what is encountered in the human experience of the divine (self-)revelation.[30] The relationship between the experience of God in the economy and the knowledge of the divine interior life is something which is determined by the particular concept of divine self-revelation employed by Barth or Rahner. Rahner argues that the mystery of the Trinitarian Godhead is a mystery of *salvation*. His construction of the divine self-giving in salvation and revelation entails the axiomatic claim that: 'The "economic" Trinity is the "immanent" Trinity and the "immanent" Trinity is the "economic" Trinity.'[31] Rahner envisages the divine revelation as a real *self-communication*.[32] The hypostases of the Son and the Holy Spirit are understood to be really given and received in this communication; nonetheless, it is also Rahner's view that God remains sovereign and incomprehensible in this self-giving. There is no distinction to be drawn between the revealed Trinitarian God, known in the economy of salvation, and the interior eternal life of the Godhead. Barth, on the other hand, does draw such a distinction:

it is not just good sense but absolutely essential that along with all older theology we make a deliberate and sharp distinction between the Trinity of God as we may know it in the Word of God revealed, written and proclaimed, and God's immanent Trinity, i.e., between 'God in Himself' and 'God for us,' between the 'eternal history of God' and His temporal acts. In so doing we must always bear in mind that the 'God for us' does not arise as a matter of course out of the 'God in Himself,' that it is not true as a state of God which we can fix and assert on the basis of the concept of man participating in His revelation, but that it is true as an act of God, as a step which God takes towards man and by which man becomes the man that participates in His revelation. This becoming on man's part is conditioned from without, by God, whereas God in making the step by which the whole correlation is first fashioned is not conditioned from without, by man.[33]

The distinction Barth draws between the economic and the immanent Trinity rests upon his understanding that the divine self-revelation is an act of free choice, rooted in the divine sovereignty. To make a direct identification between God given in that revelation and God *in se* would, in Barth's view, lead to there being an element of necessity in the divine acts of creation and self-revelation. In other words, God would not be God without creating and redeeming the cosmos. Barth is, therefore, at pains to draw a distinction between the economic and immanent Trinity, in order to remove any dependency or necessity in God's relationship to the creation.[34] Implicit in the distinction which Barth draws, is a rejection of the kind of conceptuality of the relationship between the economic and the immanent Trinity in Rahner's understanding. From Barth's perspective, Rahner has allowed the eternal life of the Godhead to be conditioned by the need to relate to the created order, compromising divine freedom and sovereignty and a traditional understanding of the ultimacy of the divine.

The identification of the economic with the immanent Trinity made by Rahner is also called into question by Jürgen Moltmann and Paul Molnar. Moltmann criticizes Rahner's notion of divine self-communication. He argues that Rahner is dependent upon the 'reflection trinity of the absolute subject',[35] which means that the classic understanding of the Trinity and of the experience of the threefoldness of the Godhead is made superfluous. Moltmann argues that the consequences of Rahner's concept of divine self-communication mean that 'not only is the Trinitarian differentiation in God surrendered; the distinction between God and the world is in danger of being lost too.'[36] Molnar also contends that Rahner's identification of the economic with the immanent Trinity brings with it the problems of necessity. He also rejects the proposal made by T. F. Torrance and Eberhard Jüngel that Rahner's understanding might be reconciled with Barth's view.[37] 'While Torrance sees Rahner's axiom as a way of avoiding any separation of the immanent and economic Trinity, the question raised here is whether there can be a "rapprochement" between Barth's method and Rahner's without introducing the necessities of creation into the Godhead'.[38]

What is at stake here is a crucial epistemological debate about the relationship between the encounter with the Divine Three in the economy and speculation about the inner life of God. While Barth and Rahner work from similar pre-understandings, they arrive at very different conclusions about the construal of the Godhead. As noted already, they are both undoubtedly influenced by the Hegelian notion of the reflection subject, and, on this basis, they use similar terminology to express the Divine Threefoldness. Nonetheless, there is an important difference between the ways in which Barth and Rahner conceive of the relation between the economy and the inner divine life. The importance of this distinction is often lost or ignored by those who commentate on Barth or Rahner.[39] One way in which to characterize this distinction might be to suggest that while Rahner works from an understanding of the divine self-communication as a sacramental act of salvation, Barth understands divine self-revelation as an epistemological act. This is a significant divergence that rests upon the construction of an epistemological framework by each in relation to different criteria. Barth finds it necessary to construct in relation to Kant's proscription of knowledge, while Rahner constructs on the basis of the possibility of a natural knowledge of God, through his appeal to mystery.

Torrance argues that the movement of thought between the immanent and economic Trinity may involve 'a logical necessity', but that this is not to be confused with any actual conditioning of the Godhead.[40] Molnar also argues that Moltmann's understanding of the immanent Trinity is deficient, despite his criticism of Rahner. Molnar's critique of Moltmann's understanding focuses upon the mutual conditioning between the human and the divine and, in particular, the projection of human love and suffering on to the Godhead. In addition, Molnar offers a critique of Pannenberg's understanding of the relation between God *in se*, and God for us. Molnar argues that the mythical status of Christ's pre-existence, which Pannenberg suggests in *Jesus: God and Man*,[41] removes any basis for a notion of a *real* immanent Trinity.[42] Molnar also criticizes Jüngel for his acceptance of Rahner's axiom and for the introduction of mutual conditioning into human–divine relations.[43] Furthermore, the eschatological understanding of the relation between the economic and immanent Trinity, which is found in Jenson, is also problematic for similar reasons. Jenson presents the action and revelation of God in the economy as the primary reality,

> the 'immanent' Trinity is simply the eschatological reality of the 'economic' [. . .] the Trinity is simply the Father and the man Jesus and their Spirit as the Spirit of the believing community. This 'economic' Trinity is *eschatologically* God 'himself,' an 'immanent' Trinity. And that assertion is no problem, for God *is* himself only eschatologically, since he is Spirit.[44]

This presents the same kind of difficulties as Moltmann's understanding of the Cross does.[45] For, if the reality of the Godhead is conditioned primarily by the economy, then it is inevitable that the questions of mutual conditioning and necessity should arise.

On the other hand, the relationality and communion of the immanent Trinity are understood by Schwöbel to provide the rootedness of the economic Trinity, without compromising the divine freedom and sovereignty.[46] While he argues that the traditional insight *opera trinitatis ad extra sunt indivisa* holds good for the action of God in the economy, he understands that

> God's relational being in the mutual communion of the persons of Father, Son and Spirit, whose relationship towards one another is constituted in forms of action particular to each person (*opera trinitatis ad intra sunt divisa*) is the condition for the possibility of the unitary intention which regulates God's action in the divine economy. [. . .] The doctrine of the immanent Trinity as the expression of the eternal personal communion of Father, Son and Spirit explains why God's relationship to humanity in the divine economy is a personal relationship although the personal being of God is not constituted in the personal relationship of the creator to the personal creatures.[47]

Schwöbel demonstrates that the relationality of the Godhead may be understood in terms of the social model of the Trinity, without collapsing the distinction between the economic and immanent Trinity through any mutual conditioning between the human and the divine. Rahner's axiom that the economic Trinity is the immanent Trinity and that the immanent Trinity is the economic Trinity is evidently not without its problems. The axiom was an attempt on Rahner's part to bring Trinitarian reflection back from the irrelevance of a speculative discourse into the mainstream life of the Church. It has become clear that his axiom needs to be qualified or perhaps made even more radical in its claims. Rahner sought to introduce a discourse into Roman Catholic theology that was more firmly rooted in a Trinitarian model. In other words, he sought a model which was not shaped by Thomas Aquinas' appeal to the primacy of the one God over against the triune God. Equally, he perceived the need to move discourse on from a focus on the intricacies of the internal divine relations and to begin reflection from the economy in order to establish the relevance of the doctrine for the Church. The axiom is, therefore, to be understood in the light of this as an attempt to ground Trinitarian reflection in the economy of salvation, so that the missions of Son and the Holy Spirit are seen as that which undergirds all Christian experience and reflection and so influences the crafting of all doctrine. If Rahner's endeavour is to be reappropriated today, his understanding of a focus on the economy may need to be qualified with a clearer understanding of God's freedom in relation to the cosmos, of the kenotic implications of the incarnation and the outpouring of Holy Spirit and the avoidance of any sense of necessity in the enactment and being of the Trinity, which is the danger implicit in Rahner's dependency on Hegel in his Trinitarian construction. Alternatively, following a more radical line of thought, the axiom might be reinterpreted in terms of a pre-Nicene understanding in which the immanent is understood only as relating to what is experienced in the economy. Such a stance might involve the following readjustments: first, on the basis of Rahner's soteriological principle, God's being would itself be understood as a saving activity; second, the events of the incarnation of God in Christ and the outpouring of the Holy Spirit would be understood in dialogical relation to God the Father; third, there would be an understanding of relationality and personhood, which saw human personhood and ecclesial life as grounded in the divine nature revealed in the economy, with each human being understood as created in the *imago dei*.[48]

The epistemological implications of the identification are sophisticated and complex. On the one hand, the identification can offer the reassurance that what is encountered and experienced in the economy is the 'real God' and not some transient or capricious aspect of the divine. It is in this regard that Rahner's axiom is most convincing, in the sense that the human encounter is with God, God who is truth and goodness as well as loving and saving. In other words, the axiom infers that a God who is truth and goodness can only make known what is true of God *in se*, in the act of self-disclosure. But it is important to remember where Rahner begins his construction of epistemology: i.e., the human encounter with mystery. It is one thing to say that God is really encountered and known in the economy of salvation and in the events of revelation. It is another to claim an identification of the economic and immanent Trinities arising from the interpretation of the events of revelation as threefold. In order for the axiom to be watertight, one has to accept that there is *a priori* 'knowledge' that the God who is revealed is both three and one. For the axiomatic identification of the economic and immanent Trinity to 'work', it is necessary to accept another axiomatic claim, that is, an expectation to encounter the Divine Three in the economy. This is, of course, what Nicene orthodoxy claims, expects and intends. These two axioms taken together are a reminder that the basis for the epistemological claims made in Trinitarian theological reflection is fragile. Those claims need to be expressed with modesty and reticence, in the apophatic tradition, in recognition of the limitations of human language and in acknowledgement of divine mystery.

EVENT CONCEPTUALITY

This fourth and final analysis will focus on the noetic and ontic implications of event conceptuality. In what ways does the appropriation of an event conceptuality enable the believing ecclesial community to know and receive the reality which the doctrine of the Trinity is understood to symbolize? From the outset of this guide, I have been seeking to suggest that there needs to be an ongoing question concerning the outcome of Trinitarian theological reflection. Is the expected outcome a fully fledged ontology of divine relationality? Or is such an expectation too advanced? Does reflection on the doctrine of the Trinity suggest a more cautious, less ambitious outcome? Rather than seeking to construct an ontology of relationality, perhaps a hermeneutic of relationality recognizes more clearly the inadequacies of human language and concepts in the face of the *mysterium tremendum*. Offering a hermeneutic of relationality is not a path of avoidance. This does not suggest either that ontology is unimportant or, indeed, that it is avoidable. But it does suggest that the outcome of reflection on the doctrine of the Trinity is always provisional, that ontological conclusions are always going to be speculative and suggestive. Alain Badiou's proposals for event strike me as particularly pertinent as a metaphor for constructing an epistemological framework for the doctrine of the Trinity. Badiou has argued that 'event' is the rupturing of ontology, through which the subject finds his or her realization and reconciliation with truth.[49] This is not the place for a detailed analysis of Badiou's conceptuality.[50] His vision of event over against a received understanding of ontology, it seems to me, sits well with the endeavour of theologians such as Barth and Zizioulas, who attempt to craft an understanding of the divine being in terms of 'event' in order to challenge received understandings of ontology within the Christian tradition and beyond it in wider philosophical discourse.

The appeal to a conceptuality of divine revelation itself understood as event raises a number of epistemological questions in terms of constructing a doctrine of the Trinity. In so far as revelation is understood as divine 'self-revelation', it may be inferred that the event(s) of revelation have something to say about God's being. So, a first concern with event conceptuality relates to ontology; a second concern relates to the question 'How is it possible for the divine being as event to be known?' Understandings of an undivided action in the economy, and an axiomatic understanding of the relationship of the economic to the immanent Trinity impact considerably on the construction of an event-based ontology, as well as the creation of an event-based epistemological framework. The starting place for the construction of such event-based understandings is in the economy, in the experience of Jesus of Nazareth and the Day of Pentecost, the Eucharist and the Christian life. It is in the encounter with a threefoldness in the economy that there emerges an appeal to event as the means by which to structure the doctrine of the Trinity in relation to ontology and epistemology. The inference of event from the encounters in the economy has been so constructed by some theologians as to suggest that the divine being is an acting, moving being, rather than a being in ultimate repose. It has been argued that this is a better expression of the living, acting God to whom the Hebrew Bible bears witness, than the solitary, still God of Platonism. Undoubtedly, this caricature is an oversimplification and should not be taken too seriously. However, the challenge to the thought of a Platonist thinker such as Plotinus, in the Christian theological appeal to movement (*kinesis*) and action (*energeia*) should not be underestimated.

Many writers have appealed to a notion of event or act in order to communicate something of the Divine Being, as revealed in the economy and, on occasion, *in se*. For example, Maximos the Confessor appealed to triadic formulations that used the language of activity, which, in some sense, imply 'happening' in order to reflect upon the being of God. In the twentieth century, Karl Barth used the language of 'God's being as event,'[51] while Zizioulas writes of God's being in terms of 'an event of communion'.[52] In these instances, it is not only ontological claims that are being made, but epistemological claims are also inherent in them, because they have the appearance of suggesting that the divine event is something which happens in the economy, in the human encounter with the divine. In other words, event conceptuality is being used to describe a process of knowing as well as of designating the Divine Being.

The tradition of a dynamic or energetic understanding of the Divine Being can be traced to a number of patristic sources. Gregory of Nyssa[53] appeals to an understanding of the divine in terms of *energeia*, which is developed later in the works of Maximos the Confessor, in relation to the triad of: *ousia–dynamis–energeia*.[54] This triad can be understood in the following general terms: 'A being (*ousia*) is capable of doing something (*dynamis*), and does it (*energeia*).'[55] The general concept might then be applied in particular to the divine being: 'God by his Nature (οὐσία) is; and is omnipotent and therefore has the capacity (δύναμις) for all act; and is perfect and so brings all act to perfection (ἐνέργεια).[56]

The crafting together of these three categories: *ousia, dynamis* and *energeia* offers the basis for a dynamic concept of the Divine Being. The balance between being and activity, and between the capacity for action and the perfection of activity, provides the basis of conceiving of the Godhead in terms of both being and becoming. Maximos develops this notion of becoming in relation to the contingent world and explicates it in terms of a contingent triad: becoming, movement and rest (*genesis–kinesis–stasis*): 'contingent becoming and eternal being, begins from God, takes place within him as his *dynamis*, [is] sustained by him at every point, and returns to him in the end. Contingent becoming lies, as it were, at the heart of eternal Being'.[57]

Such a concept opens up the possibility of an alternative to the Aristotelian notion of *actus purus*, which implies a static perfection rather than dynamic activity. The Divine Being is understood no longer in terms of the strictures of classical philosophy of antiquity. Christian theological reflection leads to novel understandings of being and divinity, in which 'becoming' and movement are core concepts. These in turn reflect their origin in the economy of salvation or revelation. It becomes clear that the appeal to a relational understanding of God, who is understood to be 'an event of communion', arises from the economy of ecclesial experience. The noetic and ontic implications of the Godhead understood in terms of communion and relationality arise from reflection on the lived experience of Christian discipleship in the community of the Church.

The appeal to an event conceptuality for the understanding of the divine and ecclesial communion has been made in recent times in a variety of contexts. One such context is the report from the Roman Catholic/Orthodox bilateral dialogue of 1982, which appeals to the concept of the Eucharist as event, in which the Church, Christ and the Godhead are identified. The document states that, 'The sacrament of the event of Christ happens in the sacrament of the Eucharist. The sacrament which incorporates us fully into Christ.'[58] The document also makes the interesting claim that, 'Jesus the Saviour enters into the glory of the Father, and at the same time by the outpouring of the Spirit, enters into this world in his sacramental mode (*tropos*).'[59] On the basis of the concept of Christ's 'sacramental mode', the document goes on to argue that it is in the paschal event of the Eucharist that the Church truly becomes herself, her members are grafted into Christ through the work of the Spirit, and the Church as a whole is caught up in the mystery of divinization. Thus, the document makes the claim that Trinitarian theological reflection is rooted in the experience of the Eucharist.

When the Church celebrates the Eucharist, she realizes, 'that which she is', the Body of Christ [1 Cor. 10.17]. By Baptism and Chrismation, in effect, the members of Christ are joined [together] by the Spirit, grafted onto Christ. But the Eucharist, the paschal event causes the Church to develop. The Church becomes what she is called to be in Baptism and Chrismation. By the communion of the Body and Blood of Christ, the faithful believe in this mystical divinization, which achieves their dwelling in the Father, and the Son by the Spirit.[60]

This example of an instance in which the Eucharist is understood in terms of event, with reference to the Trinity, raises the question: What is the content of such a conceptuality? In order to attempt to answer this question, I shall examine more closely Zizioulas's appeal to 'an event of communion'.

The event conceptuality of which Zizioulas writes opens up the possibility of situating the discussion of his appeal to God understood in terms of an event of *koinonia* in the realm of what Caputo calls 'radical hermeneutics'. In the quest to defend a 'hermeneutic of relationality' rather than an ontology, John Caputo gives a timely reminder that, 'This new hermeneutics would not try to make things look easy, to put the best face on existence, but rather to recapture the hardness of life before metaphysics showed us a fast way out the back door of flux.'[61] In the project to deconstruct the metaphysics of presence, *kinesis* is to be read back into *ousia*, in order to face up to time and flux, without an appeal to Greek recollection.[62] If the appeal to *koinonia* as event is to be sustained, a move towards a metaphysics of presence, enfolded in an ontology of relationality needs to be resisted. If the appeal to an event conceptuality of *koinonia* is an attempt to recognize *kinesis* (movement) in *ousia* (being), then 'an event of communion' will be understood as a looking forwards (i.e., repetition), rather than backwards (i.e., recollection). Caputo goes on to argue for the recognition that 'Repetition [. . .] is not repetition of the same, but a creative production which pushes ahead, which produces *as* it repeats'.[63] Caputo, in company with Derrida, warns against the easy achievement of the outcome of adopting an event conceptuality. Hegel, Heidegger and Gadamer are all criticized for their persistent inability to overcome recollection and presence. Caputo writes (referring initially to Gadamer):

> Even though it contains a useful critique of 'method,' the question of 'truth' in *Truth and Method* remains within the metaphysics of truth. Constantin warned us about those friends of the flux who make a lot of noise about becoming, when what they have up their sleeve all along is the noiseless hush of *Aufhebung*.[64]

In his recent work, *The Weakness of God*,[65] Caputo writes of 'event', in particular in terms of the name of God as an event. He sets out eight characteristics of this event, beginning with the idea that 'The event is the open-ended promise contained within a name, but a promise that the name can neither contain nor deliver.'[66] The notion of promise may be understood in that 'every event occurs against a horizon of expectation that it breaches'.[67] An event is an excess, an overflow, a surprise, an uncontainable incoming (*l'invention*), an irruption, a gift beyond economy, 'something that cannot be constricted to either the ontic or ontological order at all'.[68] If Zizioulas's phrase 'an event of communion' were to be construed in relation to Caputo's notion of event, it would mean that 'communion' is no longer an appeal to a metaphysics of presence but an expectation of what Derrida would understand as 'the impossible'. Such conceptualities bring new insights to the construal of communion divine and ecclesial. Caputo expands upon the conceptuality of event with reference to the thought of Derrida on the impossible:

> The event begins *by* the impossible [. . .] By that he means that the event is moved and driven by the desire for the *gift* beyond economy, for the *justice* beyond the law, for the *hospitality* beyond proprietorship, for *forgiveness* beyond getting even, for the coming of the *tout autre* beyond the presence of the same . . .[69]

It is necessary to be clear that for Derrida it would be 'idolatry to think that anything *present* can embody the *tout autre*, or claim to be the visible form in history, the instantiation and actualization of *the* impossible'.[70] However, one way in which Derrida does envisage the 'impossible' is in terms of the 'gift'.

During the latter years of the twentieth century and into the twenty-first, 'gift' has been explored by philosophers and theologians as a possible alternative to the received ways of understanding 'being'. Their discourse stands alongside the appeal to event or, possibly, as a complement to it. Jacques Derrida and Jean-Luc Marion have been drawn into this discourse in particular, as both seek to explicate 'gift' in terms of their critique of the Modern or Enlightenment construction of knowledge in which in their view there are too many limits. 'Gift' is a giving that transgresses all the impossibilities which the Enlightenment created. For Derrida, it is the 'impossible',[71] which never arrives, for 'the moment of the gift is instantly destroyed by exposure to the light of givenness'.[72] For

Marion, too, the gift is also about the overcoming of too many limits.[73]

> The challenge of this *new* phenomenology, which would let that which gives itself be given from itself, not merely within the limits of reason alone (Kant), not merely 'within the limits in which it is given,' which is the limit that Husserl put upon the principle of all principles, but to go to the limit of what gives itself without limits, to prepare oneself for the possibility of the impossible.[74]

Marion crafts 'gift and 'event' together, which suggests that the 'impossible' has a greater scope for being realized than in the sense of Derrida.

> [The] event of saturating givenness, an event of donative excess or of gifting which so catches up both giver and recipient in its dazzling dynamics that they are not to be regarded as the causal agents of the gift but rather as the scene of its impossible gifting or self-giving.[75]

Use of 'gift' in philosophy as a means of reunderstanding 'being' or as a means of transgressing the possibilities of the 'modern' has also been the focus of theological discourse. John Milbank, in particular, has sought to employ the idea of 'gift' in his endeavour to reform 'being' language. Milbank has sought to use 'gift' in order to speak of God as being beyond created being. God as 'gift' implies that the giver is greater than the gift of being given to beings. Milbank is highly critical of both Derrida and Marion and rejects any sense that the gift is finally 'impossible'.[76] The theological discourse concerning 'gift' has also sought to engage specific writers in a discussion with Derrida and Marion. For example, Brian V. Johnstone seeks to draw Derrida and Marion into dialogue with Aquinas,[77] and Morwenna Ludlow makes a parallel attempt with Gregory of Nyssa and also draws upon the work of Milbank.[78] 'Gift' has become a central concept in the discussion of the questions of the being of and human knowing of God. I shall return to the topic of 'gift' in the final chapter.

During the course of the development of doctrine in the Christian tradition, there have been a number of attempts to understand the being of God in terms of an event conceptuality. On the whole, the being of God has typically been understood in terms of changelessness or of an eternal and perfect rest, even when that has been expressed as *actus purus*. The appeal to an event conceptuality has been much more prevalent during the course of the twentieth century. This is in part due to the influence of Hegelian metaphysics but also has its roots in the questioning of concepts of being to be found, for example, in the works of Kierkegaard.[79] Barth used the framework of an event conceptuality to construct his understanding of structure of revelation, which, in turn, becomes the basis for his understanding of God as an act or event. Other writers have interpreted revelation and salvation history in terms of the 'Christ Event'. There has been a trend towards the interpretation of the encounter with the divine in the economy in terms of 'event', which has led to event-based constructions of the doctrines of revelation and the Trinity, so that God *in se* is also understood in terms of event. This has meant a considerable change in the tradition in relation to the construction of ontology and epistemology. It is against this background that Zizioulas made his appeal to 'an event of communion'.

The kinetic understanding of communion and relationality that Zizioulas sets out in this phrase is fundamental to his claims for a radical reconstruction of ontology. Being and communion happen. They happen, in his understanding, because God the Father chooses in freedom to beget the Son and breathe out the Holy Spirit. As this stands, his claim is a highly speculative construct of the inner divine life. However, it may also be possible to structure communion in terms of event from the encounter with the Divine Three in the economy. The appeal to event in terms of 'the impossible' is problematic because in Derrida's understanding the incoming of the impossible never arrives. So, if an appeal to event in terms of 'the impossible' is to be made, it will need to be as a metaphor. The events of revelation, the earthly ministry of Christ and the giving of the Holy Spirit at Pentecost are generally understood in the tradition to be 'historical'. The foundational revelation in Christ and Spirit has already happened: it is in the past. However, the outcome and implications of those events could be understood in terms of a metaphorical use of 'the impossible'. It is usual to understand the outcome of the events of salvation in eschatological terms. The redemption and sanctification to which revelation bears witness will only be realized fully in *ta eschata*. The implications of the encounter with the Divine Three in the economy of salvation and also in the experience of worship, understood in terms of the divine communion and tri-unity might also be interpreted in terms of the metaphor of 'the impossible' as set out above. Divine revelation and human encounter with the divine may be understood in terms of gift, justice, hospitality, forgiveness and space for the other. Such an understanding leads into the discussion of communion, otherness and the Church in the final chapter.

In this chapter, I have analysed four conceptual frameworks which shape the formation of the doctrine of the Trinity: the construction of epistemology and revelation; the undivided divine activity *ad extra*; the axiomatic claims made for the immanent and economic Trinity; and event conceptuality. In the case of each of the first three frameworks, it is evident that there are elements of cognitive claims in the formulation of these structures that contribute to the doctrine of the Trinity. But it is also the case that there are elements which are founded upon experience. In each instance, there is a possibility of understanding that to which the frameworks point in experiential-expressive terms. So I would suggest that there is a *via media* to be found between the cognitive and the expressive (aesthetic) in the separate frameworks as well as in the overall construction of a doctrine of the Trinity. Thus Del Colle's claim that divine revelation is of God *in se*, or that Trinitarian language is the triadic representation of God in history according to the receptive capacity of the human subject and nothing more,[80] is brought into question. The cumulative effect of the analysis of these frameworks suggests that the understanding of God *in se* relates to the structures which are used to receive, know and interpret the human encounter with mystery. The analysis of these frameworks demonstrates that the reception, knowledge and interpretation of that encounter is complex and nuanced. The appeal to event conceptuality adds another layer of structure to those processes, but I would suggest it does so on the basis of the reality of the happeningness of the encounter. Event conceptuality is not foreign to the encounter, but expresses it directly. It has the potential to earth speculation on the inner divine life in the experience of the human encounter with the Divine Three. A metaphorical appeal to 'the impossible' may further assist the functionality of Trinitarian reflection by recalling it to issues of justice, inclusion and salvation.

SUGGESTED READING

D. W. Hardy, 'The English Tradition of Interpretation and the Reception of Schleiermacher and Barth in England', in O. J. Duke and R. F. Streetman (eds), *Barth and Schleiermacher: Beyond the Impasse?* (Philadelphia, Pa.: Fortress Press, 1988), pp. 138–62.

K. Tanner, *Jesus, Humanity and the Trinity: A Brief Systematic Theology* (Edinburgh: T. & T. Clark, 2001).

M. Wiles, 'Some Reflections on the Origins of the Doctrine of the Trinity', in *Working Papers in Doctrine* (London: SCM, 1976), pp. 1–17.

K. Rahner, *The Trinity* (London: Burns and Oates, 1970).

J. D. Caputo, *The Weakness of God: A Theology of the Event* (Bloomington, Ind.: Indiana University Press, 2006).

J. D. Caputo and M. J. Scanlon (eds), *God, the Gift and Postmodernism* (Bloomington, Ind.: Indiana University Press, 1999).

A. Badiou, *Being and Event* (London and New York: Continuum, 2005).

CHAPTER 5

TRINITY

THE OTHER AND THE CHURCH

In this concluding chapter, the focus moves beyond issues relating strictly to the doctrine of the Trinity to a focus on areas where the relevance of the doctrine may be tested. As noted in the previous chapter, questions of the revelation and experience of God in the economy relate in particular to the context of the believing community. It is the relationship or identification of that community with the divine that I shall now seek to investigate. As a preliminary to this, I shall first address an area of concern closely related to Trinitarian discourse today. This concern is the place of 'the Other' in theological reflection on the doctrine of the Trinity. Concern for the Other and the relationship between triune God and the Christian community of the Church are both closely related to the appeal made to communion (*koinonia*). A relational understanding of the Godhead constructed around the category of communion raises questions of whether there can be space for the Other within such conceptuality. There are parallel concerns over models of the Church which are built around *communio* ecclesiology. These concerns raise crucial questions about the applicability or relevance of the doctrine of the Trinity. If, as Pecknold has suggested, the functionality of the doctrine is a proper development, then it would be unfortunate if that functionality were to founder on the rock of alterity.

THE DOCTRINE OF THE TRINITY AND THE OTHER

The question about the relationship of Trinitarian reflection to the Other emerges in the present day against a background in current philosophical discourse concerning alterity, diversity and difference which arose from concern with the marginalized and the horrors of the 'civilized' West manifest in the Holocaust and other parallel events in the twentieth century. Such theological discourse concerning the Other may relate to intra-Christian and extra-Christian relations and dialogue. The Other may be seen in terms of 'the different' as in a stranger or foreigner, whom 'we' might welcome or reject. How are such instances of difference inscribed in language? One answer might be 'in spaces of relation' such as ethnicity, city, state, nation. Another might be in terms of the opposition of friend against foe (terrorist). This, in turn, leads to the drawing of borders or boundaries and begs questions of how the Other is to be treated or assimilated. I want to suggest that the question of the relationship of Trinitarian reflection to the Other also needs to be asked in terms of 'the spaces of relation' for the Other; particularly against the background of a theology of communion and relationality, which has been criticized for its hegemonic potential for eliminating 'Otherness'. So, there are questions to be asked at a number of levels or in a variety of areas: e.g., epistemological, hermeneutical and ontological concerning the relationship of the doctrine the Trinity and the Other.

In terms of a broader philosophical and political context of the discussion of the Other, Derrida and Habermas have argued for a need to leave behind nation-states and to pursue the possibility of transforming classical international law into a new cosmopolitan order. This order would rest upon an understanding of hospitality, which would replace enmity. This hospitality would not be a new form of philanthropy but would be based upon the right to share the earth's surface, becoming members of a universal cosmopolitan community. Here then is the challenge for theologians in their crafting of understandings of the Trinity. It is a challenge to all forms of sectarianism and exclusivism and to any conceptuality of the divine that produces division and conflict.

It is appropriate at this juncture to mention the deconstruction of the concept of community made by Derrida. Through an interpretation of a possible etymology of community, in which he suggests that part of the word relates to the origin of 'munitions', he argues that community as a defensive and enclosed concept is in need of deconstruction.[1] A reclamation of 'community' as a less defensive and more open concept might be made on the basis of an appeal to hospitality and alterity. Such an approach raises the issue of the appeal to 'communion' vis-à-vis the Other in Trinitarian reflection. So, a further question emerges: in 'an event of communion', what place is there for the Other? Caputo suggests that such a question is unavoidable, as he reflects that

Lévinas's idea is to rethink the religious in terms of our obligation to the Other, not in terms of becoming happy, and to rethink God, not by way of a renewed experience of the truth of Being, but by getting beyond the anonymity of Being and experiencing the God whose withdrawal from the world leaves a divine trace on the face of the stranger.[2]

If the question of the Other is to be taken seriously in relation to the doctrines of God and the Church based upon an appeal to *koinonia*, a more fundamental question emerges: How is alterity of the Other to be understood? Reflecting upon internal difference, Deleuze has argued that it is to be distinguished from *contradiction, alterity* and *negation*. Deleuze appeals to Bergson's theory and method of difference, which he distinguishes from that of Plato or Hegel's dialectic, understood in terms of internal difference.[3] Bergson rejects the internal dynamics of Plato and Hegel's thought, which he argues understands alterity in terms of contradiction. Rather, alterity is to be understood in terms of difference, which is external. In the light of this, it is important to examine the alterity of the Other in relation to the characteristics of *koinonia*. In the construction of a 'hermeneutic of relationality', it would be necessary to ask how the alterity of the Other might be factored into the 'structure' of communion. Such a process raises issues concerning power relations. Derrida argues that in the usual reality of hospitality, the host remains in control and retains property. Thus, in hospitality and hosting, some hostility is always to be found.[4] Derrida does not suggest that this is a final outcome: rather, hospitality is also an instance of 'the impossible'. There is a need to push against 'the limit'; hospitality is always to come.[5] The 'limit' suggests the dynamics of the economy of giving and receiving, including the debt of gratitude and the felt need to reciprocate. For Derrida, only the in-breaking of 'the impossible' can overcome such dynamics. For community to emerge that is unfettered by the dynamics of the economy of credit and debt of hospitality, there needs to be 'an exposure to "*tout autre*" that escapes or resists community'.[6]

Is it possible to conceive of a structure for *koinonia* that expresses these understandings of hospitality and *tout autre*? The classic statement of the doctrine of the Trinity is constructed around notions of the monarchy of the Father and of the begetting of the Son and the breathing out of the Spirit. Such classic concepts might be employed in a reconstruction of the concept of *perichoresis* in which the monarchy, begetting and breathing out are each seen as examples of pushing against the 'limit', the limit of traditional monist ontology. In the perichoretic dance monarchy, begetting and breathing out might also be understood as signs of transgressing of the economy of giving and receiving, through which hospitality and the 'impossible' characterize not only God *in se* but also the encounter with mystery in the economy of revelation and salvation. The construction of an understanding of the divine communion or community has been attempted in a variety of ways in the course of the tradition. Ralph Del Colle has argued that the development of 'a virtual Trinitarian metaphysics' in the work of Thomas Aquinas,[7] may be understood to have an understanding of the place of alterity or diversity within it. 'The relation of the other (*ad alium*) for example, the Father actively generates the Son, and the Son is passively generated by the Father, is coincident with subsistence in oneself (*in se*).'[8] And, as Aquinas himself argues,

The idea of relation, necessarily means regard of one to another, according as one is relatively opposed to another. So as in God there is a real relation (1), there must also be a real opposition. The very nature of relative opposition includes distinction. Hence, there must be real distinction in God, not, indeed, according to that which is absolute – namely, essence, wherein there is supreme unity and simplicity – but according to that which is relative.[9]

Aquinas has structured space for the otherness of the different persons within the common divine nature. The language of *tout autre* has populated Trinitarian thought in such writers as Karl Barth, Jürgen Moltmann and Eberhard Jüngel.[10] Barth, for instance, argues that God reveals himself 'in the form of something He Himself is not'.[11] The reiteration or repetition of the divine (*Wiederholung Gottes*) in this conceptuality begs many questions, which I cannot pursue in this guide. What is crucial for an understanding of *koinonia* is whether the divine self-revelation is simply that: the reiteration of the divine or absolute '*Ich*'? Is this an example of the influence of Hegel's concept of *Aufhebung*? Hegel's own understanding of *Aufhebung* – annihilation, invalidation and also preservation – means that in annihilation there is also preservation: preservation of an absolute *Ich*. In seeking to identify 'the spaces of relation' for the Other in terms of the doctrine of the Trinity, the preservation of an absolute *Ich*, it would seem, does not permit space for radical difference or diversity. A Hegelian model of divine reiteration is insufficient in the endeavour to conceptualize what the doctrine of the Trinity might mean in terms of relating to the Other. Is it possible to construct an alternative conceptual framework that provides space for alterity within the Godhead understood in terms of communion? Could such a framework comprehend alterity in terms of externality? Such an alternative might be found in the concept of sophiology, developed by Bulgakov and others, which was explored briefly in Chapter 3.

ZIZIOULAS: COMMUNION AND OTHERNESS

The development of a conceptual framework that includes both alterity and communion is likely to be complex and intricate. The construction of a framework around the classic statement of the doctrine of the Trinity may be a useful tool by which to test the outcomes of John Zizioulas's endeavour to craft an ontology of otherness. The relationship between communion and otherness and, by implication between the Trinity and the Other has been explored by John Zizioulas in a collection of essays published under that title, as well as an article, also of the same title originally published in 1994.[12] Zizioulas has sought to engage in discourse concerning the Other, aware of the homogenizing and potentially hegemonic tendencies of an all-embracing communion ontology and ecclesiology. Indeed, his ongoing concern for the relationship between 'the One and the Many' may be interpreted as a manifestation of this concern with the Other. It is in the newly published essay, 'On Being Other: Towards an Ontology of Otherness', that Zizioulas provides the most extensive reflection on the Other. Zizioulas begins by asking, 'What can we learn about communion and otherness from study of the Trinity? First, *otherness is constitutive of unity*. God is not first One and then Three, but simultaneously One and Three.'[13] On the basis of his construction of Trinitarian theology, Zizioulas understands that otherness is not additional to the doctrine of the Trinity but inherent in it. 'Study of the Trinity reveals that otherness is *absolute*. The Father, the Son and the Holy Spirit are absolutely different (*diaphora*), none of them being subject to confusion with the other two.'[14] It becomes evident that this study remains unreconstructed in regard to its rhetoric against Augustine and in its defence of a traditional Eastern understanding of the Paternal *arche*:

God's oneness or unity is not safeguarded by the unity of substance, as St. Augustine and other western theologians have argued, but by the *monarchia* of the Father. It is also expressed through the unbreakable *koinonia* (community) that exists between the three Persons, which means that otherness is not a threat to unity but the *sine qua non* of unity.[15]

The being of God as Trinity and communion is then held out as both a model and the ontological reality of otherness and the space for the Other.

There is no other model for the proper relation between communion and otherness either for the Church or for the human being than the Trinitarian God. If the Church wants to be faithful to her true self, she must try to mirror the communion and otherness that exists in the Triune God. The same is true of the human being as the 'image of God.'[16]

Crucially, Zizioulas also argues that the construction of a space for the Other, by the Holy Spirit, is within his conceptuality of 'an event of communion'.

The Holy Spirit is associated, among other things, with *koinonia* [2 Cor. 13.13] and the entrance of the last days into history [Acts 2.17–18], that is *eschatology*. When the Holy Spirit blows, he creates not good individual Christians, individual 'saints', but an event of communion which transforms everything the Spirit touches into a *relational* being. In this case the Other becomes an ontological part of one's identity. The Holy Spirit deindividualizes and personalizes beings wherever he operates.[17]

This passage perhaps tends to confirm the critics' view that an appeal to communion is likely to condense the alterity of the Other into a pervasive homogeneity. However, Zizioulas is careful to argue for the distinctiveness of the individual Other, at least in terms of ecclesial communion.

The eschatological dimension, on the other hand, of the presence and activity of the Holy Spirit affects deeply the identity of the Other: it is not on the basis of one's past or present that we should identify and accept him or her but on the basis of one's future.

And, since the future lies only in the hands of God, our approach to the Other must be free from passing judgement on him. In the Holy Spirit, every other is a potential saint, even if he appears be a sinner.[18]

Perhaps the main problem with these passages is the eliding of the discussion of divine and ecclesial communion and, thus, a lack of a clear and necessary differentiation between the place of the Other within divine communion, and the alterity of individuals within the fellowship of the Church, or human society at large.

While Zizioulas is explicit in his intentions to relate his argument concerning otherness to the patristic period, his desire to read twentieth-century philosophy in the light of his interpretation of patristic sources is problematic in the sense that each source is, on the whole, treated as though it were acontextual. In particular, I feel that the question of the influence of Heidegger upon Zizioulas is something that remains to be clarified.[19] In relation to late-twentieth-century philosophy, what he himself calls 'postmodernism', Zizioulas demonstrates a careful reading of these writers. Finding in some of their ideas elements of a shared concern: e.g., in *Communion and Otherness*, Zizioulas shares with Derrida the desire to liberate philosophy from the Greek domination of the Same to the One, which is seen to be based on an assumption that ontology and comprehension are tied together.[20] Indeed, Zizioulas declares that an aim of the essay is to question this assumption. However, despite accepting the distinction made by Maximos the Confessor between *diaphora* (difference) and *diairesis* (division) in terms of otherness, Zizioulas does not seem to find any usefulness in the appeal to 'difference' made by Derrida or Deleuze. Zizioulas is clear that there is a need to respect otherness, which he deems to be a central ethical principle, and argues that, 'The crucial question has to be not simply whether otherness is acceptable or desirable in our society – but whether it is a *sine qua non* condition for one's very being and for the being of all that exists.'[21] However, Zizioulas does not engage with the underlying assumptions of those who have developed the concepts of difference and *tout autre*, that is to say with issues such as pluralism and cultural diversity. His essay remains primarily at a theoretical level, which tends to remove contemporary concerns for otherness from its purview. Also, while it is clear that Zizioulas perceives that postmodern philosophy is primarily a matter of method, he sidesteps any engagement with contemporary philosophy on that basis.[22] I suggest that if theologians are to engage with postmodern or deconstructive philosophy, they need to do so on the basis of this very matter of method. Indeed, the postmodern method of 'reflexivity' raises many crucial questions for any understanding of the otherness of the Other.[23] So, what are the core preconceptions and values which Zizioulas espouses in his construction of an ontology of otherness? He claims that the essay is an analysis of patristic interest in otherness. He roots his discourse about otherness in an appeal to the notion of *creatio ex nihilo*; this appeal resonates strongly with the understanding of Oliver Davies to which I shall return below. He clearly identifies the values of otherness and freedom with this doctrine of creation and, in doing so, sets his face against what he labels as 'substantialism' or the appeal to substance as the origin of being. This understanding is connected to his interpretation of the Eastern concept of the divine *monarchia* rooted in the person of the Father. Allied to these preconceptions, Zizioulas clearly values the understanding that human beings are created in *imago dei*, which he identifies with freedom as well as rationality. The Fall of Adam has a crucial bearing on the interpretation of the human situation. 'The rejection of God by Adam signified the rejection of otherness as constitutive of being. By claiming to be God, Adam rejected the Other as constitutive of his being and declared himself to be the ultimate explanation of his existence.'[24] As a consequence, the 'Self' has ontological priority over the Other; in other words, otherness and communion are dislocated. This also establishes Zizioulas's argument in relation to biological death and the need for liberation from this in resurrection as a precondition for the coincidence of otherness and communion in the *eschata* and in ontology. In the assemblage of these values and preconceptions, Zizioulas sets out his understanding of the constitutive character of the Other in ontology.[25]

Despite his claim that the essay is an analysis of patristic interest in otherness, Maximos the Confessor is the one patristic source with whom Zizioulas engages in any detail. In particular, he highlights the distinction which Maximos draws between *logos* (reason) and *tropos* (mode) of a human being. From this distinction, he extrapolates the possibility for communion. 'Substance is relational not in itself but in and through and because of the "mode of being" it possesses.'[26] Human being is said to be 'tropical', i.e., personal and hypostatic. This 'tropical' element of the person allows for freedom – freedom for the Other – and, for 'an ontology of love: in which freedom and otherness can be conceived as indispensable and fundamental existential realities without the intervention of separateness, distance or even nothingness, or a rejection of ontology, as so much so-called postmodernity assumes to be necessary in dealing with the subject of otherness'.[27] Zizioulas also makes appeal to the work of Emmanuel Levinas, quite simply because, in his view, Levinas comes closest to a patristic understanding of the Other; albeit that Levinas rejects any ontological interpretation. Zizioulas argues that for Levinas the Other is not constituted by the Self, nor by relationality as such, but by absolute alterity, which cannot be derived, engendered or constituted on the basis of anything other than itself. Levinas rejects communion; for him, sameness and the general leads to the subjection of otherness to unity. This produces the inference that nothingness is the relationship between Others, for Levinas insists on separation and distance as the alternative to that of relationship. This leads Zizioulas to make one of the most interesting and insightful claims in the whole essay: he argues that the crucial difference between patristic and postmodern conceptions of otherness lies in 'filling the gap' between particulars. There is, he argues, a movement of constant departure from one to another in the name of the Other. Patristic and postmodern writers share this understanding of constant new beginnings, he argues: 'but whereas for postmodernism alterity involves negation, rupture and "leaving behind", for patristic thought the "new" relates to the "old" in a *positive* way'.[28] While postmodern suspicion of coincidence of otherness and communion as a totalizing reduction (and even violence) led Levinas and others to reject relational otherness, Zizioulas argues that communion does not produce sameness, because the relations between the particulars (persons) are not substantial but personal or tropical.

Zizioulas's appeal to the concept of *creatio ex nihilo* is echoed by Oliver Davies in his examination of ontology and of the place for the Other.[29] Davies sets out four possibilities for an understanding of being. The first type of ontology he describes focuses on being itself, rather than on the self and the Other, and stresses being as a unity or totality. It tends to reduce the self and the many others to the same, which Davies attributes to the thought of Heidegger. A third type gives priority to the self. In this case, the Other is set apart as separate and yet risks being absorbed into the self in the process of thought, akin to the concepts of Descartes and Kant. The fourth type understands that ontology begins from the separate other. The other imposes itself on the self. It is the second type of ontology to which Davies appeals. This is rooted in

the Judeo-Christian belief in creation *ex nihilo*, here being stands over against nothingness; being itself is a gift, originally a gift from God. Being, so understood, is inherently relational, and the relationship itself is personal in origin. In this way of thinking, the self and the Other, which both receive the gift of being, are inextricably related to each other, in receiving, with their being, the capacity to give to others. The 'sameness' expressed in the (analogical) notion of being, does not obliterate the difference between the self and the Other, nor the difference between the self and the Other, and the transcendent other, God, who is the source of the gift of being.[30]

Davies' understanding of an ontology constructed in relation to *creatio ex nihilo* provides a bridge between Zizioulas's understanding of communion and the Other and understandings of the 'gift', in particular of Milbank's construal of the divine gift. (See Chapter 4.) From this emerges a nexus of concepts that draw together a conceptuality of being neither homogenizing nor hegemonic, with the conceptuality of 'gift', which allows for difference between the self and the Other.

In his articulation of the issue of what lies between particular persons or Others, Zizioulas offers an answer to the critique that the appeal to communion eliminates otherness through its homogenizing and hegemonic tendencies. Zizioulas's construction of the 'gap' between Others has created the space for the Other within the structure of communion. In this sense, Zizioulas's construction of an ontology of otherness does bear comparison with my suggestion for the reconceptualization of the classic ingredients of the doctrine of the Trinity, in the metaphor of a perichoretic dance that pushes against the 'limit' towards 'impossible' hospitality and gift-giving, allowing space for the Other. Zizioulas's understanding of the 'gap' between persons, and my own exploration of a novel metaphorical understanding of *perichoresis*, may be seen as further examples of the functionality of the doctrine of the Trinity in relation to alterity. Paul Fiddes, in his construal of the concept of *perichoresis*, also suggests that there is space in the divine dance. First, he argues that 'the Holy Spirit continually "opens up" the divine space into new dimensions of love'.[31] Then, drawing on von Balthasar's picture of 'distances' in God, he interprets these 'as spaces within and between the interweaving currents of relational love in God – spaces in the dance of *perichoresis*'.[32] Once again, the potential for homogeneity is counteracted, and the spaces of love may be interpreted as spaces within a framework built on the vision of pushing against the 'limit' of traditional ontology and transgressing of the economy of giving and receiving, toward the 'impossible' gift-giving as the ground of space for the Other.

TRINITY, COMMUNION AND ECCLESIOLOGY

The question of the space for the Other is not simply a question about the communion of the Divine Three. The tendency perceived by some towards homogeneity and hegemony in the appeal to communion is a matter not only for consideration in the construction of the doctrine of the Trinity but also of the doctrine of the Church. The conceptualization of the relationship between God and the Church has been a matter of sharp controversy during the history of the Christian tradition. Issues of the power and authority of the Church were matters of deep-seated conflict at the time of the Reformation. The Reformers were highly critical of the ways in which the Church and the Kingdom, and clerical and divine authority, had become identified with each other during the course of the Middle Ages. The expression of power in medieval Christendom was often experienced in terms of exclusion. The dispute between the Roman Catholic and Eastern Orthodox churches has also been focused on issues of authority and jurisdiction in terms of the papal primacy and the relationship between the local and universal manifestations of the Church. Beneath these disputes were different conceptions of the Body of Christ and of the relationship of the One to the Many. The revival of interest in the doctrine of the Trinity during the course of the twentieth century brought with it an appeal to *koinonia*, which has been explored in relation to God *in se* and the Church. The rediscovery of the place of communion within the Tradition promised to open up a way through the old disputes. In the light of such expectations, Susan Wood has addressed the issue that ecumenical dialogues fail to address how communion 'is effected'.[33] She makes the assumption that agreement that the divine being as Trinity, 'is communion' is uncontested and at least to some extent self-evident. It seems to me that this is not uncontested and self-evident. Rather, part of the reason that churches have found it difficult to articulate the effecting of communion or to practise it in relation to the advancement of the ecumenical endeavour is precisely because what divine *koinonia* means is not clear-cut, and, therefore, what ecclesial *koinonia* may be is also problematic.

In seeking to situate the discussion of the relationship between the doctrines of the Trinity and the Church, and between divine and ecclesial communion, I will mention briefly three documents of ecumenical dialogue that identify Church and Trinity. The first is a Roman Catholic–Orthodox dialogue which dates to 1982, *Le Mystère de l'église et de l'eucharistie à la lumière de mystère de la Sainte Trinité* (*The Mystery of the Church and the Eucharist in the Light of the Mystery of the Holy Trinity*).[34] This document situates the relation between the Trinity and the Church in terms of the Eucharist, using such concepts as 'event' and Christ's 'sacramental *tropos*' to conceptualize the identification of the Church with the divine.[35] I have already referred to this document in Chapter 4. A second document is *The Church of the Triune God*, an Anglican–Orthodox statement from 2006,[36] in which a close identification of Church and Trinity is set out: 'the communion of the Persons of the Holy Trinity creates, structures and expounds the mystery of the communion experienced in the Church'.[37] This leads to the claim that, by the indwelling grace of the Holy Spirit, the Church is created to be an image of the life of communion of the Triune God. Finally, in the Faith and Order document *The Nature and Mission of the Church*, also from 2006, there are several claims made concerning the identification of Church and Trinity.[38] In this first claim, the Church relates to the divine in dialogical terms: 'The Church is the communion of those who, by means of their encounter with the Word, stand in a living relationship with God, who speaks to them and calls forth their trustful response; it is the communion of the faithful'.[39]

In this subsequent passage, the ontological identification between Church and Trinity is made explicit:

> The Church is not merely the sum of individual believers in communion with God, nor primarily the mutual communion of individual believers among themselves. It is their common partaking in the life of God [2 Pet. 1.4], who as Trinity, is source and focus of all communion. Thus the Church is both a divine and a human reality.[40]

In these three documents, it can be seen that the conceptualization of the identification of Church and Trinity can encompass a wide variety of categories and understandings. These raise questions: about the appeal to metaphysical frameworks and to analogy; about doctrines such as theosis and participation in the divine; about Eucharistic ecclesiology and core metaphors such as the Body of Christ.

In order to investigate the ways in which the identification of Church and Trinity has been framed, I shall continue with an analysis of the ecclesiology to be found in several theologians, mainly from the twentieth century. I hope by this means to set out a broad variety of understandings that illuminate each other and manifest their strengths and limitations, as a preliminary to a more searching interrogation of the Trinity–Church relation, before moving on to examine the space for the Other in this relation.

The Roman Catholic theologian Jean-Marie R. Tillard, a leading ecumenist, sought to be formulate an irenic ecclesiology, rooted in a concept of 'the Church' as a communion of local churches.[41] He roots his conceptuality of communion in the event of Pentecost and in an appeal to an understanding of a close relation between the metaphor of the Body of Christ and the phenomena of the Church and the Eucharist. The Church of God is to be understood as a communion of communions – a communion of local churches, gathered by the Holy Spirit, on the basis of baptism and the Eucharist:

> This existence as *communion* constitutes its essence. And the relationship to *communion* with the Father, Son and Spirit shows its deep-rootedness, even in the eternal reality of the mystery of God.[42]

This framing of the identification of Church and Trinity is rooted in an appeal to the economy of salvation and ecclesial experience from which is inferred the grounding of the Church in the life of God *in se*.

Leonardo Boff appeals to context and history as the basis for the identification of the Church with the triune life *in se*.[43] He argues that the communion among Father, Son and Spirit that constitutes the one God is a mystery of inclusion and that 'The three divine Persons open to the outside and invite human beings and the entire universe to share in their community and their life.' Furthermore, 'The presence of Trinitarian communion in history makes it possible for the barriers that turn difference into inequality and discrimination to be overcome.'[44] And, 'The communion of the Divine Three offers a source of inspiration.'[45] For Boff, the doctrine of the Trinity is the pattern for a programme of liberation and transformation for society and Church. The identification of Trinity–Church is something almost tangible and certainly, in his view, historical. He reiterates this claim as follows: 'We believe that in [the Church] the substance of the incarnation is continued in history; through Christ and the Holy Spirit, God is definitively close to each of us and within human history. This mystery becomes embodied in history, because it is organized in groups and communities'.[46]

The explicit appeal to human history in this passage leads me to reflect how dependent Boff is on the philosophy of Hegel at this point. This is perhaps inevitable as Hegel is *the* modern philosopher to espouse and value context. Such an appeal is not without its problems, and I shall return to these below. It is interesting to note that at least to some extent that there is an overlap here between the views of Boff and Zizioulas in the thought that the divine communion can be perceived as manifest in the fabric of 'ordinary' society and communities.

From another perspective, Alan Torrance argues for an *analogia communionis*, through which he attempts to set out the foundations of an identity between Church and Trinity on the basis of the divine self-communication: 'The triune grounds of divine communication repose on a communion intrinsic to the Trinity as this creates and sustains communion with God and with one another which is intrinsic to the very being of the New Humanity'.[47]

It seems to me that this easily remains a circular argument and requires a clearer reference to the 'world of particulars' of the economy, in order for this to have meaning outside of itself. If the appeal to an *analogia communionis* could be clearly related to the economy, then this might offer a useful way forward in seeking to conceptualize the Trinity/Church identity.

Recently, Andrew Louth has worked on the ecclesiological understandings to be found in the writings of Maximos the Confessor.[48] In particular, Louth discerns that Maximos suggests that the Church may be understood as an 'image and type of God' by imitating and representing God's activity (*energeia*). 'It is in this way that the holy Church of God will be shown to be working for us the same effects as God, in the same way as an image reflects its archetype.'[49] This identification of Trinity–Church in terms of 'image' is a strong trajectory in modern Orthodox writings and is often found in Orthodox bilateral ecumenical dialogue statements. However, it is not always clear what conceptuality or metaphysical framework is implied or required in this contemporary ecumenical appeal to 'image' in ecumenical dialogue.

Zizioulas is one of those Orthodox writers who employs the language of 'image' in his construction of the Trinity–Church identity,[50] but he complements this with a conceptuality of event. He argues that, 'True being comes only from the free person, from the person who loves freely – that is, who freely affirms his being, his identity, by means of an event of communion with other persons.'[51] Both ecclesiology and ontology are imagined in terms of an 'event of communion'. This is qualified by his understanding that between the being of God and human being there is a gulf of 'creaturehood'. The being of each human person is 'given' to him or her. The event of communion is possible between human persons, in the form of love or social or political life. Such 'natural' expressions of freedom are relative, because human being is 'given'. This clearly resonates with the conceptuality of 'gift'. Zizioulas argues that absolute freedom requires a 'new birth', a birth from above, which he identifies with baptism and the phrase 'ecclesial *hypostasis*'. It is through baptism that the individual human being finds true personhood or 'ecclesial being'. '[I]t is precisely the ecclesial being which "hypostasizes" the person according to God's way of being. That is what makes the Church the image of the Triune God'.[52]

Zizioulas echoes Boff's view that the divine communion may be found and experienced in the 'ordinary' communities of everyday life, but he also sees the limitations of these expressions and points to the need for an 'absolute' expression of communion in 'ecclesial being'. While Zizioulas may have seen the limitations of the Hegelian structure of Boff's appeal to history, his own appeal to an absolute 'ecclesial being' or 'ecclesial *hypostasis*' is not without its problems, not least in terms of an articulation of ecclesial reality in terms of the Other.[53]

An alternative construction of the identification of Church and Trinity may be found in the works of Hans Küng on the Church.[54] Küng grounds his construction on the notion of the Church as *ekklesia* (i.e., called out), an understanding that echoes the works of both Karl Barth and John Meyendorff. In his discussion of Councils, *Synod* in Greek and *Concilium* in Latin,[55] he notes that *concilium* comes from the same root as *ekklesia*.[56] In Barth's understanding, the Church is God's convocation, from the Latin *convocare* 'to call together'. These formulations suggest that there is a dialogical structure to the divine–human, Trinity–Church relation.

In *The Church*, Küng argues that the Church as communion be understood in two senses: that of fellowship in Christ and with other Christians. He identifies Christ and the Church in terms of the body metaphor. This he roots in an understanding of the living and efficacious presence of Christ in the present, especially in the congregation's experience of worship. He is keen to emphasize the reality of Christ beyond the Church. He appeals in particular to the model of the body of Christ in which Christ is the head of body, to suggest that Christ relates to the world as well as the Church. But, most importantly, he rejects any notion that the Church is a 'divine–human' reality. He argues that there is no hypostatic union between Christ and the Church. Rather, the Church is a fellowship of believers 'in Christ', and that 'this relationship of faith is never altered'.[57] Küng's construction of the Trinity–Church identity is more restrained in the expression of its claims, which suggests a different kind of identity from that constructed around an appeal to 'icon', or the Eucharist.

Of the theologians discussed so far, Miroslav Volf is the one who raises explicit questions about the conceptuality and expression of Trinity–Church identity.[58] He asks what correspondence is there between ecclesial and Trinitarian communion, where are such correspondences to be found, and what are the limits to such analogical thinking? In response, he seeks to sketch out the Trinitarian foundation of a non-individualistic Protestant ecclesiology. He argues, as others have done before him, that the creature can never correspond to the Creator. Yet, in created reality, he suggests that there must still be broken creaturely correspondence to the mystery of triunity. Such correspondence is to be rooted in an eschatological conceptuality that the world should be indwelt by the divine Trinity, i.e., the world will come to correspond to God.[59] Having begun in reticence, he goes on to argue that as the divine and ecclesial communion correspond to each other through baptism, so the churches are imprinted with the image of the triune God through baptism. The churches share in a communion that is ontological because it is soteriological.[60] Volf raises important questions, which are crucial for an understanding of the Trinity–Church identity and, in particular, for an understanding of that identity in relation to the Other. However, Volf's answers to the questions he raises are themselves infected with the problematic he criticizes.

By way of concluding this investigation of different approaches to the Trinity–Church identity, I want to take up the argument set out by John Behr, concerning the problematic of divine–ecclesial communion.[61] Behr presents a review of the use of *koinonia* in the conceptualization of the Trinity–Church identity and concludes that, 'In this approach, the *koinonia* of the three Persons of the Holy Trinity, the very being of God, is taken as the paradigm of the *koinonia* that constitutes the being of the ecclesial body, the Church.'[62] The Church as 'communion' is said to reflect God's being as communion, a communion that will be revealed fully (only) in the Kingdom of God. He perceives that such understandings of ecclesiology fit with what is broadly understood as Eucharistic Ecclesiology, i.e., 'it is in the sacrament of eucharist, the event of communion *par excellence*, that the Church realizes her true being, manifesting already, here and now, the Kingdom which is yet to come.'[63] His response to this conceiving of the Trinity–Church identity is remarkable and perceptive. He questions the way in which Trinity *and* Church are juxtaposed. While what is said of the Church is based upon what is said of the Trinity, the effect of the 'and' is to separate Church from Trinity as a distinct entity that reflects the divine being. He argues that communion ecclesiology understands the Church to be parallel to the 'immanent Trinity'. That is to say, it is the three Persons in communion, the one God as a relational being that the Church is said to 'reflect'. 'This results in a horizontal notion of communion, or perhaps better parallel "communions," without being clear about how the two intersect.'[64]

Behr goes on to argue that through his rejection of any sociological understanding of relationality, Zizioulas has jettisoned any possibility of starting with the human experience of relating to others, and so rejects any appeal to experience in the construction of the doctrine of the Trinity. Rather, faith begins with the belief that God is 'very *koinonia*'. Behr identifies the problematic of the *a priori* characterization of the Trinity as a communion of three Persons, in that this approach does not make adequate allowance for the 'economic' reality upon which Trinitarian theology is based. While Zizioulas may stress that the Church is not any kind of Platonic 'image' of the Trinity, nonetheless he can assert that 'Church as communion reflects God's being as communion';[65] thus Behr argues that the Trinity *and* Church remain unconnected.

In order to find an alternative way of conceiving the Trinity–Church identity, Behr appeals to the work of Bruce Marshall, who focuses on three scriptural images of the Church: the people of God, the body of Christ and the temple of the Spirit. Behr argues that this way of looking at the Trinitarian being of the Church integrates it directly and intimately to the relationship between Father, Son and Spirit, and also attaches the Church to each of the Persons, while not undermining the notion of the unity of the divine action *ad extra*. The Church is conceived in terms of communion; but as a communion *with* God – as Body of Christ, anointed by the Spirit and calling upon Abba Father.

Behr's questions are very important for the future of discourse concerning the conceptualization of the Trinity–Church identity; and his focus on the 'and' that polarizes Trinity over against Church as separate entities is crucial; his appeal to the conclusions of Marshall are, for me, less convincing. What does it mean to say that the Church is a communion 'with God' any more than the Church as a communion reflects the communion which God is? The possibility of collapsing the Church into the divine, prevalent in Behr's construction is surely to be avoided: Küng's warning that there is no hypostatic union between the divine and the Church needs to be heeded.

An alternative way of conceiving the Trinity–Church identity may possibly be found in the notion that the Eucharist-event can be understood as a hermeneutical framework. Jean-Luc Marion has suggested that a Eucharistic hermeneutic could be crafted by using the journey to Emmaus as a paradigm. In the breaking of bread, there was both 'recognition' and 'their eyes were opened'. 'The Eucharist accomplishes, as its central moment, the hermeneutic.'[66] Smit argues that the hermeneutical possibility is rooted in an exchange which he identifies with the celebration of the Eucharist. 'The community itself takes part in this hermeneutic only as far as it lets itself be gathered and converted by Christ, that is, as far as it lets itself be sacramentally interpreted by the incarnate Word.'[67] This Eucharistic interpretative framework may provide a useful basis upon which to construct the Trinity–Church identity, and I will return to this at the conclusion of the chapter. An appeal to a Eucharistic ecclesiology is rooted in the experience of worship and in the economy of revelation and salvation, providing a useful grounding for Trinitarian theological reflection. A radical conceptuality of Church–Eucharist which is attributed to Augustine of Hippo has been espoused widely during the twentieth century. Nicolas Afanassieff is credited with the terminology: 'Eucharistic Ecclesiology',[68] and this was also taken up by Henri de Lubac.[69] The understanding that 'the Eucharist makes the Church; and the Church makes the Eucharist'[70] may be interpreted at various levels. First, it can be understood in terms of the phenomena involved: (a) the liturgical text and action of the Eucharistic ritual and (b) the community gathered to enact the liturgy. Second, it may be understood in terms of the metaphor of the Body of Christ, in terms of (a) the designation of the community and (b) of the sacramental elements themselves. Third, it may be understood in metaphysical terms: i.e., in terms of substance, nature, presence, *koinonia*, the one and the many. To these I would add a fourth understanding: that of event conceptuality. The community gathers and celebrates the liturgy, which, in Zizioulas's phrase, is a 'communion-event'. Such is the persuasiveness of this conceptuality that Joseph Ratzinger wrote, 'The Church is the celebration of the Eucharist; the Eucharist is the Church; they do not simply stand side by side; they are one and the same; it is from there that everything else radiates'.[71] Marc Ouellet makes even stronger claims of such a Eucharistic ecclesiology, when he writes,

The mystery of the Incarnation comes to completion in the Eucharist, in the moment that the communion in Jesus' paschal sacrifice brings the inner unity of the divine Persons into the hearts of believers. This Trinitarian unity becomes not only open and accessible to them, but truly communicated and received in communion.[72]

Lest it be thought that such a conceptuality were unchallenged, it is good to be reminded of Karl Barth's rejection of any such undifferentiated understanding of Church/Eucharist/God. Barth's understanding is that while God freely enters into communion with men and women, there is no synthesis with them or bread and wine.[73] Eucharistic ecclesiology may provide a good starting place for reflection in present experience and the economy of salvation, but how the structure built upon this starting place is put together needs to be given careful consideration, particularly in the light of the provisos of Küng, Behr and Barth.

THE CHURCH AND THE OTHER

As well as considering the identification of Trinity–Church per se, it is also important to consider the doctrines of the Trinity and the

Church in light of the present-day context of pluralism in the West. Does the construction of the doctrines of the Trinity and of the Church allow space for the Other? And in the various structures of Trinity–Church identity is there space for the Other? Among those who promoted an appeal to relationality, Colin E. Gunton argued that 'A perichoretic unity is a unity of a plural rather than unitary kind.'[74] He develops an understanding of the different roles of the Son and the Spirit; attributing rationality to the Son and freedom to the Spirit, which Dan Hardy and David Ford have called 'non-order'.[75] 'What becomes conceivable as a result of such a development is an understanding of particularity which guards against the pressure to homogeneity that is implied in modern relativism and pluralism.'[76] Gunton sets out an understanding that 'Being is diversity within unity.'[77] He expounds this conceptuality further, 'God appears to be conceived neither as a collectivity nor as an individual, but as a communion, a unity of persons in relation.'[78] Within such a conceptuality, he argues that there is space for the Other, i.e., a 'communion-in-otherness'.[79]

It is one thing to construct an understanding of relationality, which has space for the Other – indeed even an ontology of 'communion-in-otherness' – but it is another to craft a structure that has place for those who may be considered 'radically Other' in regard to the communion of the Church: i.e., the heretic, the excommunicate and those who do not confess Christ as Lord and Saviour. Küng argues that the Church has to find space for the heretic and no longer pursue the role of Inquisitor. He argues eloquently that as Christ's love is boundless, no one may be excluded, not even one's enemies.[80] Understandings of the Eucharist which include space for the Other are to be found in the writings of Tissa Balasuriya, Timothy Gorringe and Anne Primavesi and Jennifer Henderson.[81] There are, of course, alternative voices, which argue that although the Eucharist is to be understood as making an eschatological community, this does not sanction intercommunion with the schismatic or heretic. The Eucharist is not a means of achieving unity. 'The Eucharist is not a means to an end; it is the end itself foretasted.'[82] From a similar perspective, there are those who argue that the reception of Holy Communion is related to an understanding of true or right belief. Andrew Louth argues that in the understanding of Maximos the Confessor, communion is only genuine communion if it is communion in the truth.[83] It is difficult to see where space for the Other is to be found in such understandings of the eucharistic community of the Church.

Not only are 'other' Christians excluded but so also are the (non-) religious Others. The place of the heretic, the schismatic, the excommunicate and the (non-)religious Other in relation to the Eucharist and the Church raises profound questions about exclusion and inclusion and the status of those 'outside' and about space for the Other. How can the Church respond to demands for tolerance and hospitality? Can the Church facilitate participation and reciprocity in a universal cosmopolitan community? One way in which to answer these questions would be to posit an understanding of certain concepts and realities as 'trancendentals'. Hardy argued that 'sociality' should be understood as a transcendental in his essay *Created and Redeemed Sociality*.[84] Gunton distanced himself from this understanding, arguing that an ontological conceptuality of relationality did not make 'sociality' a transcendental.

> Communion is being in relation, in which there is due recognition of both particularity and relationality. But that does not make sociality a transcendental, [. . .] It is a doctrine of the personal, and leaves unresolved the question of the relation of human society to the material context within which it takes shape. It is therefore ideal rather than transcendental.[85]

Kant's understanding of 'transcendental' as 'that which provides the possibility of experience' may resonate more nearly with Hardy's concept of 'sociality' than an 'ideal' understanding with its resonances of perfection. There may be a possibility of forging a link between Gunton's understanding of sociality and relationality, as an ideal, and Habermas' concept of speech acts releasing 'ideality' and in this way overcoming the utopian connotations of the appeal to the 'ideal'. Habermas makes his claim for 'ideal speech communities' on the basis of 'the relation of human society to the material context within which it takes shape', understood in terms of a rigorous understanding of human communication.[86] In these constructs, community and sociality are rooted in a dialogical understanding of the human person, which sits in the tradition of Aristotle and modern writers such as Macmurray and McFadyen, which I discussed in Chapter 3. Kant argued for the particular status of categories of relation, as I have argued elsewhere.[87] For Kant, such categories are, 'pure concepts of the understanding which apply *a priori* to objects of intuition in general',[88] and the category of community (reciprocity between agent and patient) 'is not conceivable as holding between things each of which, through its subsistence, stands in complete isolation'.[89] In Kant's view, the isolated subsistence of the individual thing is transcended by its relationality in 'community'. Hardy argued that, 'transcendentals should be understood as the basis for the real', which are to be understood as 'necessary notes of being' and 'the presupposed basis for the establishment of knowledge through argument and agreement'.[90] Habermas' conceptuality of the 'ideal speech community' lends support to Hardy's appeal for sociality to be understood as a transcendental.

On the basis that 'sociality' may be understood as a transcendental, and that the Church is an expression of sociality, it might be argued that the Church could facilitate participation in a universal cosmopolitan community. However, serious questions are raised by the fractured reality of the Church and the ongoing exclusion of the heretic, the schismatic, the excommunicate and the (non-)religious Other. In seeking to respond to demands for tolerance and hospitality, the pursuit of Church unity becomes a priority in the quest to allow the claims of sociality understood as a transcendental to be lived out. The construction of the Trinity–Church identity in relation to the question of space for the Other is not only a theoretical concern but is imperative for the churches' realization of their participation in the divine communion in and for the cosmos.

EUCHARIST-EVENT AS LOCUS FOR CONSTRUCTING TRINITY–CHURCH IDENTITY

In conclusion, I want to suggest that the Trinity–Church identity may be constructed in relation to Caputo's understanding of event as incoming of 'the impossible', which may also be construed in terms of the discourse on 'gift'. Caputo argues that 'every event occurs against a horizon of expectation that it breaches'.[91] An event is an excess, an overflow, a surprise, an uncontainable incoming (*l'invention*), an irruption, a gift beyond economy, 'something that cannot be constricted to either the ontic or ontological order at all'.[92] This conceptuality of event interprets *kinesis*, in terms of gift, justice, hospitality and forgiveness, which gives content to an understanding of what is to be understood in terms of the outcome of the divine gifting of *koinonia*. Such understandings of an irruption of 'the impossible', which Caputo puts forward, might be understood as a metaphor for the Eucharist. On the basis of this metaphorical understanding of the Eucharist as an eschatological instance of 'the impossible', I will seek to set out a conceptual framework for the Trinity–Church identity and for the construction of a hermeneutics of relationality, which has space for the Other.

A first element in the conceptual framework rests upon Jean-Luc Marion's paradigmatic use of the journey to Emmaus. On this basis, the dynamic movement (*kinesis*) of the Eucharist making the Church may be understood as a communion-event in which a hermeneutic of relationality is not only crafted but in a sense realized, akin to Marion's Emmaus paradigm. The event of Christ's self-offering to the Father on the Cross is that which interprets the Church as the Body of Christ in the Eucharist, in Word and Sacrament. The interplay between Eucharist and Church in terms of the metaphor of the Body of Christ brings about an identity which is rooted in the phenomena of community and ritual, and in the intentionality of a synergy of wills. On this basis, the communion-event may be understood as a ritual and communal event in which the relationality of the community is interpreted in terms of the metaphor of the Body of Christ, which is both one and many (1 Cor. 10.17). Furthermore, the communion-event may be interpreted in broader Christological terms as a synergy of wills between Christ and the members of his Body, which instantiates a relationality of communion and the emergence of divinization which is intentional, moral and virtuous rather than an ontological merging of human and divine.

A second element rests upon a combining of an appeal to the notion of event in both Caputo and Badiou, with an understanding of the divine as gift, or gifting. The communion-event of the Eucharist understood within an eschatological metaphysical framework might be seen in metaphorical terms as a foretaste of the 'impossible' gift. The 'presence' of Christ also understood in eschatological terms as *parousia* (arrival) might be interpreted as a metaphor for an irruption of the future into the present as well as a rupturing of the received understanding of *ousia*. The *parousia* of Christ in the communion-event of the Eucharist ruptures accepted understandings of ontology and allows the subject to emerge: the subject of Christ whose Body is both one and many. If the Eucharist were to be seen as a metaphor for an 'irruption' of 'the impossible', it could form the basis of the structure of communion not only in terms of the Trinity–Church identity but also in terms of the space for the Other.

Such an understanding would require a radical re-evaluation of the understandings of the Church as community in terms of the postmodern take on hospitality and inclusion. A final element would be an appeal to the economy of salvation and the world of particulars. The radical relationality of the Eucharistic community, structured around the metaphor of 'the impossible', would emerge from the particulars of the event, an event in which the members of the Body would be companions (from *con pane*, i.e., with bread: companions are those who share bread together) with Christ and with each other, in the fellowship of the Holy Spirit. Each member of the Body would become in Zizioulas's words a 'eucharistic *hypostasis*' with his or her 'roots in the future and [. . .] branches in the present'.[93] The core particulars of the communion-event, the anamnesis of Christ and the epiclesis of the Holy Spirit, draw the Church into the perichoretic divine dance that pushes against the 'limit' towards 'impossible' hospitality and gift-giving, allowing space for the Other. As the Eucharist makes the Church, the Church encounters the Divine Three and enters into communion with them. In the action of the communion-event of the Eucharist, the Church as Body of Christ is revealed as and becomes 'relational'. On the basis of the Emmaus paradigm set out by Marion, I would argue that there is no *deus absconditus* lurking behind this action, but, rather, what is known in the economy of the communion-event is be understood to refer to the immanent life of the divine.

The structure of the Trinity–Church identity raises many questions, not least concerning the space for the Other. I believe that it is possible to structure the concept of communion in ways which are open to the concerns of contemporary philosophy and the pluralist reality of contemporary Western societies. On the basis of Davies' appeal to *creatio ex nihilo* as the basis for ontology, Hardy's understanding of sociality as a transcendental and Marion's Emmaus paradigm, it may be possible to construct doctrines of the Trinity and the Church that allow the structure of the Trinity–Church identity to hold together radical alterity with an understanding of communion, which is neither homogenizing nor hegemonic. On such a basis, the functionality of the doctrine of the Trinity could be claimed not only for the churches and for their ecumenical endeavour but also for human societies in general in the search for a universal cosmopolitan community.

SUGGESTED READING

J. D. Zizioulas, *Communion and Otherness: Further Studies in Personhood and the Church*, ed. Paul McPartlan (London: T. & T. Clark, 2006).

O. Davies, *A Theology of Compassion* (London: SCM Press, 2001).

Faith and Order Commission, *The Nature and Mission of the Church*, Faith and Order Document No. 198 (Geneva: World Council of Churches, 2005).

J. Behr, 'The Trinitarian Being of the Church', *St Vladimir's Theological Quarterly*, 48 (1) (2004): 67–88.

D. W. Hardy, 'Created and Redeemed Sociality', in C. E. Gunton and D. W. Hardy, *On Being the Church: Essays on the Christian Community* (Edinburgh: T. & T. Clark, 1989), pp. 21–47.

AFTERWORD

In this guide, I have sought to provide access to sources, to interpretative moments, to the means of expression and symbolization, to epistemological questions and to the application of the doctrine of the Trinity in terms of the Other and the Church. There are certainly other fields of enquiry which could have been pursued, such as the discourse concerning the Trinity and pluralism and non-Christian traditions. As I look back over the guide, I am aware of two medieval responses to the doctrine of the Trinity. The first relates to Bernard of Clairvaux, one of the founders of the Cistercian reform of Benedictine monasticism. As a sign that the doctrine of the Trinity was both problematic and yet also a profound mystery, Bernard forbade preaching on Trinity Sunday within the Cistercian order, an injunction which I understand was only changed as a result of the reforms made following the Second Vatican Council. A recognition that the doctrine of the Trinity emerges from the human encounter with mystery is also something for each and every student of the doctrine to bear in mind. The second example relates to Thomas Aquinas. In this instance, he reflected on all his writings, but I would suggest that the doctrine of God as Trinity is core to those writings. A year before his death, Thomas had some kind of mystical experience that led him to cease his writing. He is attributed with the following quotation: 'All that I have written appears to be as much straw after the things that have been revealed to me.' Again, this reminds all engaged in reflection on the doctrine of the Trinity that human words are always going to be inadequate for the endeavour.

In conclusion, I cite the opening clauses of the 'Athanasian Creed' which evokes the limits of language and the sense of mystery, as well as the existential dimensions of believing in the Trinity:

Quicunque Vult, commonly called the Creed of Saint Athanasius[1]

Whosoever will be saved: before all things it is necessary that he
  hold the Catholick Faith.

Which Faith except every one do keep whole and undefiled:
  without doubt he shall perish everlastingly.

And the Catholick Faith is this:

That we worship one God in Trinity, and Trinity in Unity;

Neither confounding the Persons: nor dividing the substance.

For there is one Person of the Father, another of the Son: and
  another of the Holy Ghost.

But the Godhead of the Father, of the Son, and of the Holy
  Ghost, is all one: the Glory equal, the Majesty co-eternal.

Such as the Father is, such is the Son: and such is the Holy Ghost.

The Father uncreate, the Son uncreate: and the Holy Ghost
  uncreate.

The Father incomprehensible, the Son incomprehensible: and the
  Holy Ghost incomprehensible.

The Father eternal, the Son eternal: and the Holy Ghost eternal.

And yet they are not three eternals: but one eternal.

As also there are not three incomprehensibles, nor three
  uncreated: but one uncreated, and one incomprehensible.

NOTES

INTRODUCTION

1 British Council of Churches, *The Forgotten Trinity* (London: British Council of Churches, 1989).

2 British Council of Churches, *The Forgotten Trinity*, Vol. I, p. 1.

3 See, for example, D. MacKinnon, 'The Relation of the Doctrines of the Incarnation and the Trinity', in R. McKinney (ed.), *Creation, Christ and Culture: Studies in Honour of T. F. Torrance* (Edinburgh: T. & T. Clark, 1976), pp. 92–107, p. 104.

4 L. Hurtado, *One God, One Lord: Early Christian Devotion and Ancient Jewish Monotheism* (Philadelphia, Pa.: Fortress Press, 1976), p. 741.

5 F. Schleiermacher, *The Christian Faith* (Edinburgh: T. & T. Clark, 1928), p. 741.

6 C. Welch, 'Faith and Reason: In Relation to the Doctrine of the Trinity', *Journal of Bible and Religion* 16 (1) (1948), pp. 21–9; 21.

7 P. Tillich, *Systematic Theology* (London: SCM Press, 1951), Vol. I, p. 228.

8 M. R. Barnes, 'Rereading Augustine's Theology of the Trinity', in S. T. Davis, D. Kendall and G. O'Collins (eds), *The Trinity: An Interdisciplinary Symposium on the Trinity* (Oxford: Oxford University Press, 1999), pp. 145–76.

9 G. Lindbeck, *The Nature of Doctrine: Religion and Theology in a Postliberal Age* (London: SPCK, 1984).

10 G. Kaufmann, *The Theological Imagination* (Philadelphia, Pa.: Westminster Press, 1981).

11 For example, P. W. Butin, *The Trinity* (Louisville, Ky.: Geneva Press, 2001); M. J. Erickson, *Making Sense of the Trinity: Three Crucial Questions* (Grand Rapids, Mich.: Baker Books, 2000); A. McGrath, *Understanding the Trinity* (Eastbourne: Kingsway Publications, 1987).

I WHY 'THE TRINITY' AT ALL?

1 See G. Lindbeck, *The Nature of Doctrine: Religion and Theology in a Postliberal Age* (London: SPCK, 1985).

NOTES

2 For example, M. Foucault, *Discipline and Punish: The Birth of the Prison* (London: Allen Lane, 1977).
3 A. Harnack, *Lehrbuch in der Dogmengeschichte*, 4th edn (Freiburg: J. C. B. Mohr, 1909), Vol. I, p. 90.
4 For example, C. Welch, 'Faith and Reason: In Relation to the Doctrine of the Trinity', *Journal of Bible and Religion* 16 (1) (1948): 21–9; p. 21.
5 The personification of wisdom may be found in the Hebrew Bible and Septuagint: e.g., Prov. 8; Wis. 6; Eccl. 15.
6 Baptism of Jesus: Mt. 3.13–4.1.; Mk 1.9–12; Lk. 3.21–2; Jn 1.29–34. It is not clear whether the latter infers that Jesus was baptised.
7 Transfiguration of Jesus: Mt. 17.1–6; Mk 9.2–7; Lk. 9.28–36.
8 For example, Jn 14, 15, 16.
9 For example, Jn 17.3, 14.6; also 1 Cor. 15.24, Mk 10.18, 14.36, 15.34.
10 J. de Satgé, *Mary and the Christian Gospel* (London: SPCK, 1976), p. 25.
11 For example, G. Lampe, *God as Spirit* (Oxford: Clarendon Press, 1977).
12 See J. D. G. Dunn, '1 Corinthians 15.45: Last Adam, Life-giving Spirit', in B. Lindars and S. S. Smalley (eds), *Christ and the Spirit in the New Testament* (Cambridge: Cambridge University Press, 1973), pp. 127–42.
13 For example, Rom. 15.30; 2 Thess. 2.13; 1 Cor. 2.12, 6.11; Gal. 3.1–5.
14 See Origen, *Contra Celsum* 5.22; Gregory of Nyssa, *On the Hexaemeron*, P.G. 44, 73C; Maximos the Confessor, *Ambigua*, 7, MPG 91: 1081C.
15 For example, A. K. Gabriel, 'Pneumatological Perspectives for a Theology of Nature: The Holy Spirit in Relation to Ecology and Technology', *Journal of Pentecostal Theology* 15 (2) (2007): 195–212.
16 The appeal to the 'Gospel Sacraments' made here does, of course, raise issues concerning the expectations of those traditions such as the Society of Friends and Salvationists, which do not celebrate the sacraments.
17 J.-L. Marion, *God without Being: Hors-Texte* (Chicago, Ill. and London: University of Chicago Press, 1991), Chapter 5.
18 For example, G. Wainwright, *Doxology: The Praise of God in Worship, Doctrine and Life* (London: Epworth Press, 1980); D. Ford and D. W. Hardy, *Jubilate: Theology in Praise* (London: Darton, Longman and Todd, 1984); R. Gresser, 'The Need for and the Use of Doxological Language in Theology', *Quodlibet Journal* 6 (1) (2004). Available online at <http://www.Quodlibet.net> (accessed 1 March 2008).
19 Basil of Caesarea, *De spiritu sancto*, Chapter 10.
20 J. Pelikan, *Christianity and Classical Culture: The Metamorphosis of Natural Theology in the Christian Encounter with Hellenism* (New Haven, Conn.: Yale University Press, 1993), p. 234.
21 Pelikan, *Christianity and Classical Culture*, p. 300.
22 Gregory Nazianzen, 'The Fifth Theological Oration: On the Holy Spirit', in P. Schaff and H. Wace (eds), *Nicene and Post-Nicene Fathers* (Peabody, Mass.: Hendrickson, 1994), Vol. VII, Second series, pp. 318–28; p. 327.
23 Basil of Caesarea, *De spiritu sancto*, Chapter 29 (73).
24 For example, 'The Westminster Directory of the Public Worship of God', in R. C. D. Jasper and G. J. Cuming (eds), *Prayers of the Eucharist: Early and Reformed* (New York: Pueblo Publishing Company, 1987),

148

p. 268; R. Baxter, 'The Reformation of the Liturgy 1661', in Jasper and Cuming, *Prayers of the Eucharist*, p. 275.

25 For example, a Trinitarian structure can be found in the Eucharistic Prayer of the 1982 Liturgy of the Scottish Episcopal Church.

26 For example, M. Foucault, *Les Mots et les choses* (Paris: Gallimard, 1966), published in English as *The Order of Things* (London: Tavistock Publications, 1970); see also J. Bernauer and J. Carrette (eds), *Michel Foucault and Theology* (Aldershot: Ashgate, 2004).

27 Pseudo-Dionysius, *The Divine Names*, 13.3 MPG 3 (980D–981A).

28 For example, Basil of Caesarea, *Letter*, 234 MPG 32.

29 See B. McGinn, *The Mystical Thought of Meister Eckhart: The Man from whom God Hid Nothing* (New York, The Crossroad Publishing Company, 2004), Chapter 5 'The Metaphysics of Flow'.

30 P. L. Reynolds, '*Bullitio* and the God beyond God: Meister Eckharts' Trinitarian Theology, Part I: The Inner Life of God', *New Blackfriars* 70 (April) (1989): 169–81, p. 169; see also 'Part II: Distinctionless Godhead and Trinitarian God', *New Blackfriars* 70 (May) (1989): 235–44.

31 See P. M. Collins, *Christian Inculturation in India* (Aldershot: Ashgate, 2007), pp. 132–7.

32 R. Otto, *The Idea of the Holy* (London: Oxford University Press, 1977), pp. 12–13.

33 I. T. Ramsey, *Models for Divine Activity* (London: SCM Press, 1973), p. 4.

34 Ramsey, *Models for Divine Activity*, p. 37.

35 Ramsey, *Models for Divine Activity*, pp. 48–51.

36 K. Rahner, *Foundations of Christian Faith: An Introduction to the Idea of Christianity* (London: Darton, Longman and Todd, 1978).

37 Rahner, *Foundations of Christian Faith*, Chapter 2.

38 J. Macquarrie, *The Principles of Christian Theology* (London, SCM Press, 1977), pp. 87–8.

39 J. Derrida, *The Gift of Death* (Chicago, Ill.: University of Chicago Press, 1995); J.-L. Marion, *Reduction and Givenness: Investigations of Husserl, Heidegger and Phenomenology* (Evanston, Ill.: Northwestern University Press, 1998) and *Toward a Phenomenology of Givenness* (Stanford, Calif.: Stanford University Press, 2002); J. Milbank, 'Can a Gift Be Given? Prolegomena to a Future Trinitarian Metaphysic', *Modern Theology* 11 (1) (1995): 119–61 and *Being Reconciled: Ontology and Pardon* (London: Routledge, 2003).

40 C. Welch, 'Faith and Reason', p. 22.

41 Welch, 'Faith and Reason', p. 25.

42 Welch, 'Faith and Reason', p. 23; also, Augustine of Hippo, *De trinitate*, Books I, II, IV.

43 Aquinas, *Summa theologiae*, Ia. Q.43.

44 J. D. Zizioulas, *Being as Communion: Studies in Personhood and Church* (London: Darton, Longman and Todd, 1985), p. 15.

45 R. Del Colle, 'The Triune God', in C. E. Gunton (ed.) *The Cambridge Companion to Christian Doctrine* (Cambridge: Cambridge University Press, 1997), p. 136.

2 MOMENTS OF INTERPRETATION

1 For example, D. Brown, *The Divine Trinity* (London: Duckworth, 1985).

2 The Constitution of the World Council of Churches indicates that membership is on the basis of the confession of a faith in God the Trinity, Father, Son and Holy Spirit. For example, I Basis; and Rules: I Membership: 3. Criteria (a) 4. The church recognizes the presence and activity of Christ and the Holy Spirit outside its own boundaries and prays for the gift of God's wisdom to all in the awareness that other member churches also believe in the Holy Trinity and the saving grace of God.

3 The collective phrase the 'Cappadocian Fathers' is often used to indicate Basil the Great (of Caesarea), his brother Gregory of Nyssa and their friend Gregory Nazianzen. The formation and theological development of Basil and his brother Gregory was fostered by their sister Macrina, who clearly had a strong influence upon them. Some scholarly opinion would also include Didymus the Blind and Epiphanius of Salamis among this grouping.

4 T. de Régnon, *Études de théologie positive sur la Sainte Trinité*, 3 vols (Paris: Retaux, 1892–8).

5 V. Lossky, *The Mystical Theology of the Eastern Church* (Cambridge: James Clarke & Co. Ltd, 1957), Chapter 3, especially pp. 56–8.

6 For example, see A. Louth, 'Unity and Diversity in the Church of the Fourth Century', in E. Ferguson (ed.) *Doctrinal Diversity: Recent Studies in Early Christianity: A Collection of Scholarly Essays* (London: Garland, 1999), Vol. IV, pp. 1–18.

7 L. Boff, *Trinity and Society* (Maryknoll, NY: Orbis, 1988), p. 9.

8 Boff, *Trinity and Society*, p. 118.

9 Boff, *Trinity and Society*, p. 119.

10 See J. Moltmann, *The Trinity and the Kingdom of God: The Doctrine of God* (London: SCM, 1981); C. Mowry LaCugna, *God for Us: The Trinity and the Christian Life* (New York: HarperCollins, 1991); M. Volf, *After Our Likeness: The Church as the Image of the Trinity* (Cambridge and Grand Rapids, Mich.: Eerdmans, 1998).

11 S. J. Grenz, *The Social God and the Relational Self* (Louisville, Ky.: Westminster John Knox Press, 2001), p. 5.

12 F. LeRon Shults, *Reforming Theological Anthropology: After the Philosophical Turn to Relationality* (Cambridge and Grand Rapids, Mich.: Eerdmans, 2003).

13 C. Schwöbel and C. E. Gunton (eds), *Persons, Divine and Human: King's College Essays in Theological Anthropology* (Edinburgh: T. & T. Clark, 1991); C. Schwöbel (ed.), *Trinitarian Theology Today: Essays on Divine Being and Act* (Edinburgh: T. & T. Clark, 1995); C. Schwöbel, *Gott in Beziehung: Studien zur Dogmatik* (Tübingen: Mohr Siebeck, 2002).

14 Shults, *Reforming Theological Anthropology*.

15 Moltmann, *The Trinity and the Kingdom of God*.

16 Boff, *Trinity and Society*.

17 R. W. Jenson, *The Triune Identity: God According to the Gospel* (Philadelphia, Pa.: Fortress Press, 1982).

18 J. D. Zizioulas, *Being as Communion: Studies in Personhood and Church* (London: Darton, Longman and Todd, 1985).
19 R. J. Feenstra and C. Plantinga, Jr. (eds), *Trinity, Incarnation and Atonement: Philosophical and Theological Essays* (Notre Dame, Ind.: University of Notre Dame Press, 1989).
20 LaCugna, *God for Us*.
21 C. E. Gunton, *The One, the Three and the Many: God, Creation and the Culture of Modernity* (Cambridge: Cambridge University Press, 1993).
22 J. D. Zizioulas, 'Human Capacity and Human Incapacity: A Theological Exploration of Personhood', *Scottish Journal of Theology* 28 (1975): 401–48.
23 See Zizioulas, 'Human Capacity and Human Incapacity', p. 408, footnote 1; namely, M. Buber, *I and Thou* (Edinburgh: T. & T. Clark, 1970); J. Macmurray, *The Form of the* Personal, Vol. II: *Persons in Relation* (London: Faber and Faber, 1961); W. Pannenberg, 'Person', in H. F. V. Campenhausen, E. Dinkler, G. Gloege, K. E. Logstrup and K. Galling (eds), *Religion in Geschichte und Gegenwart*, 3rd edn (Tubingen: J. C. B. Mohr, 1957), pp. 230–5; D. Jenkins, *The Glory of Man* (London: SCM Press, 1967), *What is Man?* (London: SCM Press, 1970) and *Living with Questions* (London: SCM Press, 1969).
24 Zizioulas, 'Human Capacity and Human Incapacity', p. 408.
25 See C. Yannaras, *The Ontological Content of the Theological Notion of Person* (Athens: University of Salonika, 1970) (in Greek).
26 N. A. Nissiotis, 'The Importance of the Doctrine of the Trinity for Church Life and Theology', in A. J. Philippou (ed.), *The Orthodox Ethos* (Oxford: Holywell Press, 1964).
27 De Régnon, *Études de théologie positive sur la Sainte Trinité*.
28 J. R. Illingworth, *Personality Human and Divine* (London and New York: Macmillan, 1894).
29 L. S. Thornton, 'The Christian Conception of God', in E. G. Selwyn (ed.), *Essays Catholic and Critical* (London: SPCK, 1926), pp. 121–50.
30 *Lumen Gentium* (1964) paragraphs: 4, 7, 8, 9, 13, 14, 15, 18, 21, 22, 24, 25, 28, 29, 41, 49, 50, 51.
31 L. Lochet, 'Charité fraternelle et vie trinitaire', *Nouvelle Revue Theologique* 78 (2) (1956): 113–34.
32 B. Fraigneau-Julien, 'Réflexion sur la signification religieuse du mystère de la Sainte Trinité', *Nouvelle Revue Theologique* 87 (7) (1965): 673–87.
33 K. Hemmerle, *Thesen zu einer trinitarischen Ontologie* (Freiburg: Johannes Verlag Einsiedeln, 1992).
34 M. J. Scheeben, *Handbuch der katholischen Dogmatik*, Vol. IV (Freiburg im Breisgau: Herder, 1948).
35 T. d'Eypernon, *Le Mystère primordial: la trinité dans sa vivante image* (Brussels and Paris: L'Éditions Universelle/Desclée de Brouwer, 1946).
36 Other significant contributions to this landscape are: L. Hodgson, *The Doctrine of the Trinity* (New York: Charles Scribner's Sons, 1944); C. Welch, *In This Name: The Doctrine of the Trinity in Contemporary Theology* (New York: Charles Scribner's Sons, 1952); E. J. Fortman, *The Triune God: A Historical Study of the Doctrine of the Trinity* (Philadelphia, Pa.: Westminster, 1972); W. Hill, *The Three-Personed God: The*

NOTES

Trinity as a Mystery of Salvation (Washington, DC: Catholic University of America Press, 1982); W. Kasper, *The God of Jesus Christ* (London: SCM, 1984); D. Brown, *The Divine Trinity* (La Salle, Ill.: Open Court, 1985); J. Bracken, *The Triune Symbol: Persons, Process and Community* (Lanham, Md.: University Press of America, 1985); J. J. O'Donnell, *The Mystery of the Triune God* (London: Sheed and Ward, 1988); E. Johnson, *SHE WHO IS: The Mystery of God in Feminist Theological Discourse* (New York: Crossroad, 1992).

37 D. S. Cunningham, *These Three Are One: The Practice of Trinitarian Theology* (Oxford: Blackwell, 1998).
38 P. S. Fiddes, *Participating in God: A Pastoral Doctrine of the Trinity* (London: Darton, Longman and Todd, 2000).
39 J. Milbank and C. Pickstock, *Truth in Aquinas* (London: Routledge, 2001).
40 S. J. Grenz, *The Social God and the Relational Self* (Louisville, Ky.: Westminster John Knox Press, 2001).
41 P. L. Metzer (ed.), *Trinitarian Soundings in Systematic Theology* (London and New York: Continuum, 2005).
42 Shults, *Reforming Theological Anthropology*, p. 32.
43 S. Grant, *Sankaracarya's Concept of Relation* (Delhi: Motilal Banarsidass Publishers, 1999), p. 1. See also J. Locke, *An Essay Concerning Human Understanding* (London and New York: Dent and Dutton, 1972), Vol. I; and I. Kant, *Critique of Pure Reason* (London: MacMillan, 1933), pp. 111–15.
44 *Unto the Churches of Christ Everywhere*, Encyclical of the Ecumenical Patriarchate, 1920.
45 O. Tomkins, *The Wholeness of the Church* (London: SCM, 1949), p. 71.
46 Commission on Faith and Order, World Council of Churches, *One Lord, One Baptism*, Paper No. 29 (London: SCM, 1960), pp. 13–14.
47 M. Tanner, 'Opening Remarks', in T. F. Best and G. Gassmann (eds), *On the Way to Fuller Koinonia*, Faith and Order Paper No. 166 (Geneva: World Council of Churches, 1994).
48 J. D. Zizioulas (ed.) P. McPartlan (see p. 186), *Communion and Otherness: Further Studies in Personhood and the Church* (London: T. & T. Clark, 2006), p. 34.
49 J. L. Gresham, 'The Social Model of the Trinity and Its Critics', *Scottish Journal of Theology* 46 (3) (1993): 325–43.
50 K. Kilby, 'Perichoresis and Projection: Problems with Social Doctrines of the Trinity', *New Blackfriars* (October) (2000): 432–45; S. Coakley, ' "Persons" in the "Social" Doctrine of the Trinity: A Critique of Current Analytic Discussion', in S. T. Davis, D. Kendall and G. O'Collins (eds), *The Trinity: An Interdisciplinary Symposium on the Trinity* (New York and Oxford: Oxford University Press, 1999), pp. 123–44; M. R. Barnes, 'Rereading Augustine's Theology of the Trinity', in Davis et al., *The Trinity*, pp. 145–77; R. Williams, 'The Paradoxes of Self-Knowledge in the *De trinitate*', in J. T. Lienhard, E. C. Muller and R. J. Teske (eds), *Collectanea Augustiniana, Augustine: Presbyter Factus Sum* (New York: Peter Lang Publishing Inc., 1993), pp. 121–34; L. Ayres, *Nicaea and its Legacy: An Approach to Fourth-Century Trinitarian Thought* (Oxford:

Oxford University Press, 2004); L. Turcescu, 'Prosopon and Hypostasis in Basil of Caesarea's *Against Eunomius and the Epistles*', *Vigiliae Christianae* 51 (4) (1997): 374–95, ' "Person" Versus "Individual"', and Other Modern Misreadings of Gregory of Nyssa', in S. Coakley (ed.), *Re-Thinking Gregory of Nyssa* (Malden, Mass. and Oxford: Blackwell, 2003), pp. 97–109, *Gregory of Nyssa and the Concept of Divine Persons* (New York and Oxford: Oxford University Press, 2005).

51 Coakley, ' "Persons" in the "Social" Doctrine of the Trinity', p. 129.
52 Coakley, ' "Persons" in the "Social" Doctrine of the Trinity', p. 137.
53 See Lossky, *The Mystical Theology of the Eastern Church*, Chapter 3, especially pp. 56–8.
54 De Régnon, *Études de thèologie positive sur la Sainte Trinité*.
55 See Note 6, p. 150.
56 J. G. F. Wilks, 'The Trinitarian Ontology of John Zizioulas', *Vox Evangelica*, 25 (1995): 63–88.
57 R. M. Fermer, 'The Limits of Trinitarian Theology as a Methodological Paradigm', *Neue Zeitschrift für Systematische Theologie und Religionsphilosophie* 41 (2) (1999): 158–86.
58 Fermer, 'The Limits of Trinitarian Theology', p. 174.
59 A. Meredith, *The Cappadocians* (Crestwood, NY: St Vladimir's Seminary Press, 2000).
60 N. Lash, *Believing Three Ways in One God: A Reading of the Apostles' Creed* (London: SCM, 2002), p. 32.
61 S. Coakley, 'Why Three? Some Further Reflections on the Origins of the Doctrine of the Trinity', in S. Coakley and D. A. Pailin (eds), *The Making and Remaking of Christian Doctrine: Essays in Honour of Maurice Wiles* (Oxford: Clarendon Press, 1993), pp. 29–56; p. 35.
62 J. Mackey, 'Are There Christian Alternatives to Trinitarian Thinking?', in J. M. Byrne (ed.), *The Christian Understanding of God Today* (Dublin: The Columba Press, 1993), p. 67.
63 Mackey, 'Are There Christian Alternatives?', p. 68.
64 Mackey, 'Are There Christian Alternatives?', p. 74.
65 Fermer, 'The Limits of Trinitarian Theology', p. 173.
66 N. Metzler, 'The Trinity in Contemporary Theology: Questioning the Social Doctrine of the Trinity', *Concordia Theological Quarterly* 67 (2003): 270-88; p. 284.
67 K. Barth, *Church Dogmatics* I.1 (Edinburgh: T. & T. Clark, 1975), pp. 333, 382; K. Rahner, *The Trinity* (London: Burns and Oates, 1970), p. 22.
68 L. Krempel, *La Doctrine de la relation chez Saint Thomas* (Paris: Librairie Philosophique J. Vrin, 1952), Chapter 1.
69 Cunningham, *These Three Are One*, p. 9.
70 J. Milbank, 'Theology without Substance: Christianity, Signs, Origins', *Literature and Theology* 2 (1) (1988): 1–17 and 2 (2): 131–52; J.-L. Marion, *God without Being: Hors-Texte* (Chicago, Ill.: Chicago University Press, 1991).
71 For example, Moltmann, *The Trinity and the Kingdom of God*, pp. 174–6; L. Boff, *Holy Trinity, Perfect Community* (Maryknoll, NY: Orbis Books, 2000), pp. 14–16; Gunton, *The One, the Three and the Many*, pp. 163–6; LaCugna, *God for Us*, pp. 270–8; Fiddes, *Participating in God*, passim.

NOTES

72 J. Zimmermann, *Recovering Theological Hermeneutics: An Incarna-tional–Trinitarian Theory of Interpretation* (Grand Rapids, Mich.: Baker Academic, 2004).
73 Zimmermann, *Recovering Theological Hermeneutics*, p. 283.
74 D. Bonhoeffer, *Sanctorum communio* (London: Collins, 1963), p. 40.
75 J. Galot, *Who Is Christ? A Theology of the Incarnation* (Chicago, Ill. and Rome: Franciscan Herald Press and Gregorian University Press, 1980), pp. 305–13.
76 Coakley, *Why Three?*, pp. 31–9.
77 R. Williams, *On Christian Theology* (Malden, Mass. and Oxford: Black-well, 2000), p. 161.
78 Coakley, *Why Three?*, p. 34; Williams, *On Christian Theology*, p. 160.
79 A. J. Torrance, *Persons in Communion: Trinitarian Description and Human Participation* (Edinburgh: T. & T. Clark, 1996), p. 4.
80 Schwöbel and Gunton, *Persons, Divine and Human*, p. 10.
81 See Dionysius Petavius, *Theologicorum dogmatum* (Paris, 1644–50), Vol. II, Book 3, Chapters 3–11.
82 P. Melanchthon, *Loci communes rerum theologicarum seu hypotyposes theologicae* (Wittenberg and Basel, 1521): 'since to know Christ means to know his benefits and not, as they [the scholastics] teach, to reflect upon his natures and the modes of his incarnation. For unless you know why Christ put on flesh and was nailed to the cross, what good will it do you to know merely the history about him?. [. . .] Christ was given us as a remedy and, to use the language of Scripture, a saving remedy. It is therefore proper that we know Christ in another way than that which the scholastics have set forth'.
83 P. Bayle, *Commentaire philosophique sur ces paroles de Jesus-Christ: Con-trains les d'entrer: oir l'on prouve par plusieurs raisons demonstratives qu'il n'ya a rien de plus abominable que de faire des conversions par la con-trainte, et ou l'on rifute tous les sophismes des convertisseurs a contrainte et l'apologie que St. Auaustin a faite des persecutions*, trans. J. Fox de Bruggs par M. J. F. (Cantorbery: Thomas Litwel). The first and second parts appeared in 1686 and the third in 1687.
84 B. S. Tinsley, 'Sozzini's Ghost: Pierre Bayle and Socinian Toleration', *Journal of the History of Ideas*, 57 (4) (1996): 609.
85 See D. Waterland, 'Vindication of Christ's Divinity' (1719) in *The Works*, ed. W. Van Mildert (Oxford: The University Press, 1843), Vol. III.
86 J. H. Newman, *The Arians of the Fourth Century* (1833; Leominster and Notre Dame, Ind.: Gracewing and University of Notre Dame Press, 2001). The Introduction is by Rowan Williams.
87 I. Newton, 'De Athanasio, & Antonio', in *Theological Notebook*, 1684–1690.
88 E. Gibbon, *The History of the Decline and Fall of the Roman Empire* (1776–1789) (London: J. M. Dent and Son Limited, Everyman edition, 1910). Petavius is cited in Vols. II and V.
89 See Barth, *Church Dogmatics*, pp. 353–68; W. Pannenberg, *Systematic Theology* (Edinburgh: T. & T. Clark, 1991), Vol. I, pp. 325–6; R. W. Jenson, *Systematic Theology* (New York and Oxford: Oxford University

Press, 1997), Vol. I, Chapter 6; D. Brown, *The Divine Trinity* (London: Duckworth, 1985).

90 C. E. Braaten and R. W. Jenson (eds), *Christian Dogmatics*, 2 vols (Philadelphia, Pa.: Fortress Press, 1984).

91 T. Paine, *The Age of Reason* (1795); F. Schleiermacher, *The Christian Faith* (Edinburgh: T. & T. Clark, 1928), pp. 377–424; A. Ritschl, *Justification and Reconciliation* (Edinburgh: T. & T. Clark, 1900), p. 386; A. Harnack, *What is Christianity?* (London: Williams and Norgate, 1901), pp. 124–46.

92 J. Hick (ed.), *The Myth of God Incarnate* (London: SCM Press, 1977).

93 R. Williams, 'Introduction', in Newman, *The Arians of the Fourth Century*, p. xli.

94 Williams, 'Introduction', p. xlii.

95 In monarchianism, Sabellianism and modalism, it was understood that the Heavenly Father, Resurrected Son and Holy Spirit were different modes or aspects of one God in human perception, rather than three distinct persons *in se*. Patripassianism, a form of modalism, understood that the Father, in the mode of the Son, was crucified and suffered death on the cross.

96 J. H. Newman, *An Essay on the Development of Christian Doctrine* (Garden City, NY: Doubleday/Image, 1960), Chapter 4, section 3 subsection 4.

97 C. C. Pecknold, 'How Augustine Used the Trinity: Functionalism and the Development of Doctrine', *Anglican Theological Review* (winter) (2003): 127–42, Note 8, p. 130.

98 B. Lonergan, *The Way to Nicea: The Dialectical Development of Trinitarian Theology* (Philadelphia, Pa.: Westminster, 1976), p. 136.

99 Pecknold, 'How Augustine Used the Trinity', Note 10, p. 130; and Lonergan, *The Way to Nicea*, p. 137.

100 Lonergan, *The Way to Nicea*, p. 7.

101 Pecknold, 'How Augustine Used the Trinity', p.131.

102 Pecknold, 'How Augustine Used the Trinity', p.131.

103 Pecknold, 'How Augustine Used the Trinity', p. 132.

104 Pecknold, 'How Augustine Used the Trinity', Note 24, p. 136: The notion of 'function' I am using is somewhat akin to the dictionary definition that attaches the word to 'usage' and sees such 'uses' and 'functions' contributing 'to the development or maintenance of a larger whole'. It is also akin, then, to the philosophy of design called 'functionalism'. As in architectural 'functionalism', where it is held that 'form should be adapted to use' both in material and structure, my argument shows that this has happened naturally, that is to say, organically, during the course of doctrinal development. But more generally, and more pervasively, the notion of 'function' has been shaped by the American pragmatists whose central idea (similar to Wittgenstein and J. L. Austin) was that ideas were tools to be used.

105 R. A. Markus, *Saeculum: History and Society in the Theology of St. Augustine*, (Cambridge: Cambridge University Press, 1988) p. 67.

106 Markus, *Saeculum*, p. 67.

107 Pecknold, 'How Augustine Used the Trinity', p. 138.

3 EXPRESSING THE INEXPRESSIBLE?

1 For example, Philo of Alexandria, *De opificio mundi*, 24; *De plantatione*, 9–10.
2 Theophilus of Antioch, *Apologia ad Autolycum*, Chapter 10.
3 Irenaeus, *Adversus Haereses*, Book IV, Preface (4).
4 See Tertullian, *Adversus Praxeam*, 2.
5 C. Welch, 'Faith and Reason: In Relation to the Doctrine of the Trinity', *Journal of Bible and Religion* 16 (1) (1948), 26; Tertullian, *Adversus Praxeam*, 2.
6 Origen, *De principiis*, Book 1, Chapter 2 (3).
7 Origen, *De principiis*, Book 1.
8 G. L. Prestige, *God in Patristic Thought*, 2nd edn (London, SPCK, 1952), pp. 197–201.
9 Eusebius, *Praeparatio Evangelica*, xi. 21. 6f. MPG 21; Origen, *Contra Celsum*, vi. 64 MPG 11.
10 Tertullian, *Adversus Praxeam*, 9 MPL 2.
11 Tertullian, *Adversus Nationes*, ii.2 MPL 2.
12 Origen, *Contra Celsum*, vi. 64 MPG 11 (this is akin to Plato's understanding of the Form of the Good).
13 Origen, *In Johannem*, fr. 37 MPG 14.
14 Boethius, *De trinitate*, iii, 1–5, MPL 64 and *Contra Eutychem*, 111.4–5, MPL 64; cf. Aquinas, *Summa theologiae*, Ia 29.I.
15 Richard of St Victor, *De trinitate*, IV, 22.8.
16 R. Williams, 'The Paradoxes of Self-Knowledge in the *De Trinitate*,', in J. T. Lienhard, E. G. Muller, and R. J. Teske (eds), *Collectanea Augustiniana, Augustine: Presbyter Factus Sum* (New York: Peter Lang, 1993), pp. 121–34.
17 Augustine, *De trinitate*, Books V, VI and esp. VII.
18 Augustine, *De trinitate*, VII, 1.2.
19 Augustine, *De trinitate* VII, 11.
20 The Holy Spirit is understood to be 'breathed forth'. The Greek words most often used prefer to mission (being sent) *ekpempsis*, or procession: *ekporeusis;* the Latin *spiratio* refers to the breathing forth.
21 R. Del Colle, 'The Triune God', in C. E. Gunton, (ed.) *The Cambridge Companion to Christian Doctrine* (Cambridge: Cambridge University Press, 1997), p. 131.
22 Del Colle, 'The Triune God', p. 132.
23 Del Colle, 'The Triune God'.
24 C. C. Pecknold, 'How Augustine Used the Trinity: Functionalism and the Development of Doctrine', *Anglican Theological Review*, 2003 (winter), 127–42; also M. T. Clark, '*De Trinitate*', in E. Stump and N. Kretzmann (eds), *The Cambridge Companion to Augustine* (Cambridge: Cambridge University Press, 2001), pp. 91–102; p. 91.
25 A. I. McFadyen, *The Call to Personhood: A Christian Theory of the Individual in Social Relationships* (Cambridge: Cambridge University Press, 1990), pp. 9f.
26 J. Macmurray, *Persons in Relation* (London: Faber and Faber, 1961), p. 178.

27 W. Kasper, *The God of Jesus Christ* (New York: Crossroad, 1984), p. 290.
28 J. Ratzinger, 'Zum Personverständnis in der Theologie', in *Dogma und Verkündigung* (Munich and Freiburg: Wewel, 1973), pp. 205–23; p. 206 n.97.
29 J. Auer, *Person: Ein Schlüssel zum christlichen Mysterium* (Regensburg: Verlag Friedrich Pustet, 1979).
30 A. Wilder, 'Community of Persons in the Thought of Karol Wojtyla', *Angelicum* (1979), pp. 211–44.
31 L. B. Porter, 'On Keeping "Persons" in the Trinity: A Linguistic Approach to Trinitarian Thought', *Theological Studies*, 41 (3) (1980): 530–48.
32 Porter, 'On Keeping "Persons" in the Trinity', p. 548.
33 J. D. Zizioulas, *Being as Communion: Studies in Personhood and Church* (London: Darton, Longman and Todd, 1985). See also: C. Mowry LaCugna, 'The Relational God: Aquinas and Beyond', *Theological Studies*, 46 (4) (1985): 647–63; J. Ratzinger, 'Concerning the Notion of Person in Theology', *Communio: International Catholic Review*, 17 (autumn) (1990): 439–54; K. L. Schmitz, 'The Geography of the Human Person', *Communio: International Catholic Review*, 13 (spring) (1986): 27–48.
34 H. Urs von Balthasar, 'On the Concept of Person', *Communio: International Catholic Review*, 13 (spring) (1986): 18–26.
35 See D. Parfit, *Reasons and Persons* (Oxford: Oxford University Press, 1984); M. Carrithers, S. Collins and S. Lukes (eds), *The Category of the Person: Anthropology, Philosophy, History* (Cambridge: Cambridge University Press, 1985); C. Taylor, *Sources of the Self: The Making of Modern Identity* (Cambridge, Mass.: Harvard University Press, 1989); J. Foster, *The Immaterial Self: A Defence of the Cartesian Dualist Conception of the Mind* (London and New York: Routledge, 1991).
36 See Wilder, 'Community of Persons', p. 221.
37 Wilder, 'Community of Persons', pp. 222, 223.
38 For example, A. N. Whitehead, *The Adventure of Ideas* (New York: Free Press, 1967), p. 169; *Process and Reality: An Essay in Cosmology* (Cambridge: Cambridge University Press, 1929); C. Hartshorne, *The Divine Relativity: A Social Conception of God* (New Haven, Conn.: Yale University Press, 1964); J. Cobb, *A Christian Natural Theology* (Philadelphia, Pa.: Westminster, 1965), pp. 188–92.
39 J. A. Bracken, 'Subsistent Relation: Mediating Concept for a New Synthesis?', *Journal of Religion*, 64 (2) (1984): 188–204; p. 193.
40 Bracken, 'Subsistent Relation', p. 194.
41 R. A. Connor, 'The Person as Resonating Existential', *American Catholic Philosophical Quarterly*, 66 (1) (1992): 39–56; p. 56.
42 Connor, 'The Person as Resonating Existential', p. 56.
43 See also J. S. Grabowski, 'Person: Substance and Relation', *Communio: International Catholic Review*, 22 (spring) (1995): 139–63.
44 Ratzinger, *Zum Personverständnis in der Theologie*, p. 211.
45 Ratzinger, 'Concerning the Notion of Person in Theology', 444.
46 D. Parfit, *Reasons and Persons* (Oxford: Clarendon Press, 1984); Gunton

comments that in spite of his reductionism, Parfit's views are still individualistic: C. E. Gunton, *The Promise of Trinitarian Theology*, 2nd edn
(London: T. & T. Clark, 1997), p. 88.

47 J. Moltmann, *The Trinity and the Kingdom of God: The Doctrine of God*
(London: SCM, 1980, 1981), Chapter V, passim.

48 J. Bracken, *The Triune Symbol: Persons, Process and Community*
(Lanham, Md.: University Press of America, 1985).

49 L. S. Thornton, 'The Christian Conception of God', in E. G. Selwyn
(ed.), *Essays Catholic and Critical* (London: SPCK, 1926), pp. 139–45.

50 Thornton, 'The Christian Conception of God', p. 140. Thornton's
argument is in line with the classic statement of divine agency : *opera
trinitatis ad extra sunt indivisa.*

51 See Thornton, 'The Christian Conception of God', p. 140.

52 Rahner, *The Trinity*, p. 106, see also Thornton, 'The Christian Conception of God', p. 144.

53 Rahner, *The Trinity*, p. 109.

54 Rahner, *The Trinity*, pp. 109–10.

55 See C. Welch, *The Trinity in Contemporary Theology* (London: SCM
Press, 1953), pp. 97–9, and pp. 252–72.

56 F. Bourassa, *Personne et conscience en theologie trinitaire, Gregorianum*
LV (1974), p. 709; translated and cited by J. J. O'Donnell, *The Mystery of
the Triune God* (London: Sheed and Ward, 1988), p. 111.

57 Karl Barth, *Church Dogmatics* (Edinburgh: T. & T. Clark, 1975), 1.1,
p. 355.

58 Barth, *Church Dogmatics*, 1.1, p. 357.

59 Barth, *Church Dogmatics*, 1.1, p. 359. See also *Church Dogmatics*, 1.1,
p. 469, where Barth rules out the possibility that the Holy Spirit could in
any sense be deemed to be a 'person'.

60 Barth, *Church Dogmatics*, 1.1, p. 359. See also Cappadocian Fathers viz.,
Basil, *De sancto spiritu* 46, 43, 44, *Epistula* 189.7, *Contra Sabellium* 6;
Gregory of Nyssa, *Contra Eunomium*, 1; and John of Damascus, *De fide
orthodoxa*, 1.8. The editors of the second English edition of the first part
of the first volume of the *Church Dogmatics* interpret this appeal as a
clear statement of Barth's intention to use a term which has a Cappadocian pedigree. *Church Dogmatics*, 1.1, p. viii.

61 T. F. Torrance argues that the use of *tropos hyparxeos* in the *Church
Dogmatics* places Barth's view of personhood within the tradition which
may be traced back to the Cappadocians via Calvin and Richard of
St Victor.

62 Prestige, *God in Patristic Thought*, p. 245.

63 Prestige, *God in Patristic Thought*. It has been argued that this is the very
understanding implicit in the Greek Fathers' understanding of *hypostasis*. Orphanos explains this implicit understanding in some detail, 'The
earlier Greek Fathers – particularly after the Cappadocians clearly distinguished between οὐσία and ὑπόστασις, common or natural, and
individual or hypostatic properties, which are not interchangeable or
confounded – steadfastly argued that the Father is the principle, cause
and fountain-head of deity. Thus, the Father, deriving his being
from himself, brings forth from his essence, but on the capacity of his

hypostatic property, the Son by way of generation, and the Holy Spirit by way of procession. He confers to them his whole essence but he does not communicate to them his hypostatic property of begetting and proceeding'. M. A. Orphanos, 'The Procession of the Holy Spirit According to Certain Later Greek Fathers', in L. Vischer (ed.), *Spirit of God, Spirit of Christ, Ecumenical Reflections on the Filioque Controversy*, Faith and Order Paper 103 (London and Geneva: World Council of Churches, 1981), p. 42f.

64 Prestige, *God in Patristic Thought*, p. 249.
65 Barth, *Church Dogmatics*, 1.1, p. 299.
66 Barth, *Church Dogmatics*, 1.1, pp. 299, 355 and 366.
67 Barth, *Church Dogmatics*, 1.1, p. 360. Here Barth cites B. Bartmann, *Lehrbuch der Dogmatik* (Freiburg: Verlag Herder, 1928), Vol. I, p. 169.
68 Barth, *Church Dogmatics*, 1.1, p. 382.
69 Barth, *Church Dogmatics*, 1.1, p. 361.
70 Barth, *Church Dogmatics*, 1.1, p. 364.
71 See Barth, *Church Dogmatics*, 1.1, p. 355.
72 Moltmann, *The Trinity and the Kingdom of God*, pp. 140–4.
73 Kasper, *The God of Jesus Christ*, pp. 287f.
74 C. E. Gunton, *The One, the Three and the Many: God, Creation and the Culture of Modernity* (Cambridge: Cambridge University Press, 1993), p. 191.
75 J. D. Zizioulas, 'On Being a Person: Towards an Ontology of Personhood', in C. Schwöbel and C. E. Gunton (eds), *Persons, Human and Divine* (Edinburgh: T. & T. Clark, 1991), pp. 33–46; p. 33.
76 Zizioulas, 'On Being a Person', p. 34.
77 Zizioulas, 'On Being a Person'.
78 Zizioulas, 'On Being a Person'.
79 J. D. Zizioulas, *Being as Communion, Studies in Personhood and the Church* (London: Darton, Longman and Todd, 1985), p. 18.
80 See Zizioulas, *Being as Communion*, p. 36.
81 Zizioulas, *Being as Communion*, p. 39.
82 That is, *tropos hyparxeos*: see St Basil *Letter* 38.2 and Gregory of Nyssa, *Against Eunomius* 1; also see Zizioulas, *Being as Communion*, p. 41, footnote 36.
83 Zizioulas, *Being as Communion*, p. 41.
84 J. D. Zizioulas, 'The Ontology of Personhood: The British Council of Churches', in Alasdair I. C. Heron (ed.), *The Forgotten Trinity. 3, a Selection of Papers Presented to the BCC Study Commission on Trinitarian Doctrine Today* (London: BCC/CCBI, 1991).
85 A. de Halleux, ' "Hypostase" et "Personne" dans la formation de dogme trinitaire (ca 375–381)', *Revue d'Histoire Ecclesiastique*, 79 (1984): 313–69, 625–70; p. 663.
86 A. de Halleux, 'Personnalisme ou essentialisme trinitaire chez les Pères cappadociens?' *Revue Théologique de Louvain*, 17 (1986): 143–4.
87 De Halleux, 'Personnalisme', p. 265.
88 N. Metzler, 'The Trinity in Contemporary Theology: Questioning the Social Trinity', *Concordia Theological Quarterly*, 67 (3) (2003): 270–87.

NOTES

89 Metzler, 'The Trinity in Contemporary Theology', p. 284.
90 L. Turcescu, 'Prosopon and Hypostasis in Basil of Caesarea's Against Eunomius and the Epistles', *Vigiliae Christianae*, 51 (4) (1997): 374–95; ' "Person" Versus "Individual", and Other Modern Misreadings of Gregory of Nyssa', in Sarah Coakley (ed.) *Re-Thinking Gregory of Nyssa* (Malden, Mass. and Oxford: Blackwell, 2003); *Gregory of Nyssa and the Concept of Divine Persons* (Oxford: Oxford University Press, 2005).
91 Turcescu, 'Prosopon and Hypostasis', p. 98.
92 Zizioulas, *Being as Communion*, p. 16.
93 Letter 38 is attributed by some scholars to Gregory of Nyssa.
94 Basil of Caesarea, *Letter* 38.4, MPG 32; 332. a. 17f. English translation taken from: *St Basil: Letters and Selected Works, A Select Library of Nicene and Post-Nicene Fathers of the Christian Church*, 2nd series, ed. H. Wace and P. Schaff, vii, (Oxford and New York, 1895), p. 139. ἀλλά τίνα συνεχή καί ἀδιασπαστον κοινωνίαν ἐν αὐτοῖς θεωρεισθαι.
95 Basil of Caesarea, *Letter* 38.4. ὥσπερ ἐν αἰνιγμάτι καινήν καί παράδοχον διάκρισιν τε συνήμμενην, καί διά κεκριμένην συναφείαν.
96 Zizioulas, *Being as Communion*, p. 17.
97 Zizioulas, *Being as Communion*, p. 17.
98 Zizioulas, *Being as Communion*, p. 17.
99 Zizioulas, *Being as Communion*, p. 18.
100 Zizioulas, *Being as Communion*, p. 43.
101 Zizioulas, *Being as Communion*, p. 44.
102 See Moltmann, *Trinity and the Kingdom of God*, pp. 174–6; L. Boff, *Holy Trinity, Perfect Community* (Maryknoll, NY: Orbis Books, 2000), pp. 14–16; P. S. Fiddes, *Participating in God: A Pastoral Doctrine of the Trinity* (London: Darton, Longman and Todd, 2000), pp. 71–81; D. S. Cunningham, *These Three Are One: The Practice of Trinitarian Theology* (Oxford: Blackwell, 1998), pp. 176–86 and C. Mowry LaCugna, *God for Us: The Trinity and the Christian Life* (New York: HarperCollins, 1991), pp. 270–8.
103 Pecknold, 'How Augustine Used the Trinity'.
104 Aquinas, *Summa theologiae*, Ia. 42, 5, where he reflects upon Jn 14.11, and concludes the Father and Son mutually indwell one another on the understanding of a single shared essence.
105 For example, Gregory of Nazianzus, *Epistula*, 101.6, (MPG 37). There is evidence in the *Scholia*, F.149 (MPG 36, 911) to suggest that Gregory knew the term from Anaxagoras (c.500–c.427 BC). In the *Scholia*, Gregory acknowledges the understanding of Empedocles and Anaxagoras that 'there is a portion of everything in everything'. Anaxagoras argues that the emergence of order in natural substances is the result of the rotation (*periochoresis*) initiated by Mind; see G. S. Kirk and J. E. Raven, *The Presocratic Philosophers: A Critical History with a Selection of Texts* (Cambridge: Cambridge University Press, 1960), pp. 372f. It is from this passage that Gregory quotes. See also A. Grillmeier, *Christ in Christian Tradition*, trans. J. Bowden. Vol. I: *From the Apostolic Age to*

Chalcedon (London: Mowbrays, 1975), p. 511, who argues that Nestorius also understood that there was an interpenetration (*perichoresis*) of the two *prosopa* in Christ. Also, Prestige, *God in Patristic Thought*, p. 293, who suggests that the first instance of the use of the noun *perichoresis* in patristic usage, is in the writings of Maximus the Confessor, *Questiones ad Thalassium* 59, 202 B, *Corpus Christianorum, Series Graeca*, Vols. 7 and 22, (Louvain: Brepols, 1980 and 1990).

106 John of Damascus, *De fide orthodoxa*, I.8 MPG 94, 829 A. Large sections of *De fide orthodoxa* are the work of an unknown author (usually known as pseudo-Cyril) writing at the beginning of the eighth century, which were simply taken over by John. Prestige argues that we owe the term *perichoresis* to him rather than to John of Damascus himself. See Prestige, *God in Patristic Thought*, p. 284.

107 Athenagoras, *Supplicatio pro Christianis*, 10 MPG 6. See also Irenaeus, *Adversus Haerases*, 3.6.2 MPG 7, Dionysius of Rome, *Letter to Dionysius of Alexandria*, in J. Neuner and J. Dupuis (eds), *The Christian Faith, in the Doctrinal Documents of the Catholic Church*, 4th edn (London: Collins, 1983), pp. 98–9; p. 99; Athanasius, *De decretis nicaenae synodi* 26, MPG 25, 461–6; Hilary, *De trinitate*, 3.4, 4.10 MPL 10.

108 Jn 14.10, 11 (RSV). Also, Jn 10.30, 'I and the Father are one'; 17.21, 'even as thou, Father, art in me, and I in thee'.

109 See Athanasius, *Ad Serapionem*, 3.4, 4.4, 4.12. MPG 25.

110 Basil, *De spiritu sancto*, 63 MPG 32, 184 B.

111 Hilary, *De trinitate*, 3.1, 3.2, 3.4, 9.69 MPL 10.

112 Gregory of Nyssa, *Adversus Arium et Sabellium*, 12, MPG 45, 1297 B–D. It is noteworthy that Gregory cites Jn 14.11 as the scriptural basis for what he is arguing.

113 John of Damascus, *De fide orthodoxa*, I.8.

114 John of Damascus wrote his *De fide orthodoxa* as an apologetic defence of Christian monotheism in the context of living in a Muslim context in eighth-century Damascus.

115 John of Damascus, *De fide orthodoxa*, I.8, MPG 94, 828 C, trans. V. Lossky, *The Mystical Theology of the Eastern Church* (Cambridge and London: James Clarke & Co. Ltd, 1957), p. 54. Εν γαρ εκαστον αυτων εχει προς το ετερον, ουχ ηττον η προς εαυτον.

116 See Aquinas, *Summa theologiae*, Ia 42, 5.

117 See W. Newton Clarke, *Christian Theology in Outline* (New York: C. Scribner's Sons, 1898), p. 149, who may be described as a neo-Ritschlian.

118 For example, J. Macquarrie, *Principles of Christian Theology* (London: SCM Press, 1977), p. 194.

119 L. S. Thornton, 'The Christian Conception of God', in E. G. Selwyn (ed.), *Essays Catholic and Critical* (London: SPCK, 1926), pp. 123–50; p. 145.

120 See Y. M. J. Congar, *I Believe in the Holy Spirit*, trans. David Smith. Vol. III: *The River of the Water of Life (Rev 22.1) Flows in the East and in the West* (London: Chapman, 1983), p. 37, and British Council of Churches, *The Forgotten Trinity* (London: British Council of Churches, 1989), Vol. I, p. 21.

121 A. I. McFadyen, *The Call to Personhood: A Christian Theory of the*

Individual in Social Relationships (Cambridge: Cambridge University Press, 1990), p. 29.

122 Barth, *Church Dogmatics*, 1.1, p. 370.

123 Barth, *Church Dogmatics*.

124 For example, Barth, *Church Dogmatics*, 1.1, p. 360.

125 See A. J. Torrance, *Persons in Communion* (Edinburgh: T. & T. Clark, 1996), p. 254.

126 Torrance, *Persons in Communion*. p. 254.

127 Torrance, *Persons in Communion*. p. 254.

128 Barth, *Church Dogmatics*, 1.1, p. 487.

129 Moltmann, *The Trinity and the Kingdom of God*, p. 245, footnote 73. This comment is offered in particular as a critique of the work of H. Mühlen, *Der Heilige Geist als Person* (Munster: Verlag Aschendorff, 1963), Section 5, pp. 100–69. Moltmann also argues that any Helegian based doctrine of the Trinity cannot do justice to the conceptuality of *perichoresis*. See Moltmann, *The Trinity and the Kingdom of God*, p. 175.

130 Barth, *Church Dogmatics*, 1.1, p. 487.

131 Barth, *Church Dogmatics*, 1.1, p. 338.

132 A. I. C. Heron, *The Holy Spirit* (Philadelphia, Pa.: Westminster John Knox Press, 1984), p. 164.

133 Moltmann, *The Trinity and the Kingdom of God*, p. 174.

134 Moltmann, *The Trinity and the Kingdom of God*, p. 176.

135 Boff, *Holy Trinity, Perfect Community*, p. 14.

136 Boff, *Holy Trinity, Perfect Community*, p. 15.

137 Boff, *Holy Trinity, Perfect Community*.

138 F. Capra, *Tao of Physics: An Exploration of the Parallels Between Modern Physics and Eastern Mysticism* (Berkeley, Calif.: Shambhala Publications, 1975).

139 LaCugna, *God for Us*, p. 272.

140 LaCugna, *God for Us*, p. 274.

141 The most famous image of the dancing Shiva, the Lord Nataraja, is to be found in the Shrine of the temple at Chidambaram, Tamil Nadu.

142 Cunningham, *These Three are One*, pp. 177–81.

143 Fiddes, *Participating in God*, p. 73.

144 Fiddes, *Participating in God*, p. 77.

145 Fiddes, *Participating in God*, pp. 242–3.

146 For example, J. Moltmann, *The Crucified God: the Cross of Christ as the Foundation and Criticism of Christian Theology* (London: SCM Press, 1974), p. 241; and H. Urs von Balthasar, *Mysterium Paschale* (Edinburgh: T. & T. Clark, 1990); *Theo-Drama: Theological Dramatic Theory*, Vol. IV (San Francisco, Calif.: Ignatius Press, 1988).

147 For example, 1 Cor. 1.24 and 30.

148 C. Mowry LaCugna, 'God in Communion with Us: The Trinity', in C. Mowry LaCugna (ed.), *Freeing Theology: The Essentials of Theology in Feminist Perspective* (New York: Harper Collins, 1993), pp. 83–114.

149 M. Daly, 'After the Death of God the Father', *Commonweal*, March 12, 1971, pp. 7–11.

150 Daly, 'After the Death of God the Father'.
151 See, for example, the argument in T. W. Jennings, Jr., *Beyond Theism* (New York: Oxford University Press, 1985).
152 R. L. Maddox, 'Wesleyan Theology and the Christian Feminist Critique', *Wesleyan Theological Journal*, 22 (1987): 101–11.
153 For example, C. Gilligan, *In a Different Voice* (Cambridge, Mass.: Harvard University Press, 1982).
154 Maddox, 'Wesleyan Theology'.
155 D. Neal, 'Out of the Uterus of the Father: A Study in Patriarchy and Symbolization of Christian Theology', *Feminist Theology*, 13 (September) (1996): 8–30.
156 Moltmann, *The Trinity and the Kingdom of God*, p. 165; Council of Toledo 675, J. Denzinger, *Enchiridion Symbolorum*, 26th edn (Freiburg: Herder, 1947), no. 276.
157 Neal, 'Out of the Uterus of the Father', p. 19.
158 Neal, 'Out of the Uterus of the Father', p. 27.
159 G. D'Costa, *Sexing the Trinity: Gender, Culture and the Divine* (London; SCM Press, 2000).
160 S. Bulgakov, *The Wisdom of God: A Brief Summary of Sophiology* (New York: Paisley Press, 1937; see also R. Williams, *Sergii Bulgakov: Towards a Russian Political Theology* (Edinburgh: T. & T. Clark, 1999).
161 V. Soloviev, 'Three Meetings', a poem in *Poems of Sophia*, trans. B. Jakim and L. Magnus (New Haven, Conn.: Variable Press, 1996) and *Lectures on Divine Humanity (God Manhood)*, trans. B. Jakim (Herndon, Va.: Lindisfarne Books, 1995).
162 V. Lossky, *The Mystical Theology of the Eastern Church* (Cambridge: James Clarke, 1957), p. 62.
163 See A. Nichols, 'Wisdom from Above? The Sophiology of Father Sergius Bulgakov', *New Blackfriars*, 2004, 85 (1000), 598–613.
164 Nichols, 'Wisdom from Above?', p. 609.
165 Nichols, 'Wisdom from Above?', p. 609.
166 *The Church of the Triune God, The Cyprus Agreed Statement of the International Commission for Anglican–Orthodox Theological Dialogue 2006*, London: The Anglican Communion Office, 2006, section 36.
167 See R. W. Jenson, 'The Father, He . . .,' in A. J. Kimel (ed.), *Speaking the Christian God: The Holy Trinity and the Challenge of Feminism* (Grand Rapids, Mich.: Eerdmans, 1992), pp. 95–109.
168 T. F. Torrance, 'The Christian Apprehension of God the Father', in A. F. Kimel (ed.), *Speaking the Christian God: The Holy Trinity and the Challenge of Feminism* (Grand Rapids, Mich.: Eerdmans and Leominster: Gracewing, 1992), pp. 120–43.
169 Torrance, 'The Christian Apprehension of God the Father'.
170 J. A. DiNoia, 'Knowing and Naming the Triune God: The Grammar of Trinitarian Confession', in A. F. Kimel (ed.), *Speaking the Christian God: The Holy Trinity and the Challenge of Feminism* (Grand Rapids, Mich.: Eerdmans and Leominster: Gracewing, c.1992).
171 DiNoia, 'Knowing and Naming the Triune God'.
172 K. Barth, *The Word of God and the Word of Man* (London: Hodder and Stoughton, 1928).

173 J. M. Sosckice, *Metaphor and Religious Language* (Oxford: Oxford University Press, 1985).

4 THE RECEPTION OF REVELATION

1 R. Del Colle, 'The Triune God', in C. E. Gunton (ed.), *The Cambridge Companion to Christian Doctrine* (Cambridge: Cambridge University Press, 1997), p. 136.
2 G. Lindbeck, *The Nature of Doctrine: Religion and Theology in a Post-liberal Age* (London: SPCK, 1984), Chapter 1.
3 K. Rahner, *The Trinity* (London: Burns and Oates, 1970), p. 22.
4 P. Melanchthon, *Loci communes rerum theologicarum seu hypotyposes theologicae* (Wittenberg and Basel, 1521).
5 I. Kant, *Critique of Pure Reason* (London: J. M. Dent, 1993).
6 A. Harnack, *What is Christianity?* (London: Williams and Norgate, 1901), pp. 124–46.
7 G. W. F. Hegel, *Phenomenology of Geist (Spirit)* (Oxford: Oxford University Press, 1977).
8 For example, K. Barth, *Church Dogmatics* (Edinburgh: T. & T. Clark, 1975), 1.1, and J. Moltmann, *The Trinity and the Kingdom of God: The Doctrine of God* (London: SCM, 1981).
9 See D. W. Hardy, 'The English Tradition of Interpretation and the Reception of Schleiermacher and Barth in England', in O. J. Duke and R. F. Streetman (eds), *Barth and Schleiermacher: Beyond the Impasse?* (Philadelphia, Pa.: Fortress Press, 1988), pp. 138–62.
10 F. Schleiermacher, *The Christian Faith* (Edinburgh: T. & T. Clark, 1928), pp. 739–51.
11 Barth, *Church Dogmatics*, 1.1.
12 Schleiermacher, *The Christian Faith*, pp. 739–51.
13 Schleiermacher, *The Christian Faith*, pp. 741–2.
14 Barth, *Church Dogmatics*, 1.1 Preface, p. xiii.
15 Barth, *Church Dogmatics*, 1.1, p. 299.
16 For example, M. Luther, *Lectures on the Psalms* (*Dictata*, 1513–16), *D. Martin Luthers Werke, Kritische Gesamtausgabe* (Weimar: Verlag Hermann Böhlausn Nochfolger, 1883–   ), 3.124.29.
17 For example, P. Tillich, *The Courage to Be* (London; Fontana, 1962), p. 177.
18 Barth, *Church Dogmatics*, 1.2, pp. 203–79.
19 K. Tanner, *Jesus, Humanity and the Trinity: A Brief Systematic Theology* (Edinburgh: T. & T. Clark, 2001).
20 Barth, *Church Dogmatics*, 4.1. p. 192: If in faith in Jesus Christ we are ready to learn, to be told, what Godhead, or the divine nature is, we are confronted with the revelation, of what is and always will be a mystery, and indeed a mystery which offends. The mystery reveals to us that for God it is just as natural to be lowly as it is to be high, to be near as it is to be far, to be little, as it is to be great, to be aboard as to be at home.
21 See Gregory of Nyssa, *To Ablabius: That There Are Not Three Gods (Ad Ablabium)*; G. C. Stead, 'Why Not Three Gods? The Logic of Gregory of Nyssa's Trinitarian Doctrine', in H. R. Drobner and C. Klock (eds),

Studien zu Gregor von Nyssa und der christlichen Spätantike (Leiden: E. J. Brill, 1990), pp. 149–63; T. W. Bartel, 'Could There Be More Than One Almighty?', *Religious Studies* 29 (4) (1993): 465–95; P. van Inwagen, 'And Yet They Are Not Three Gods but One God', in T. V. Morris (ed.), *Philosophy and Christian Faith* (Notre Dame, Ind.: University of Notre Dame Press, 1988), pp. 241–78.

22 For example, Augustine, *De trinitate*, I.4.7 and I.5.8.
23 S. T. Davis, 'Periochetic Monotheism', in M. Y. Stewart (ed.), *The Trinity: East/West Dialogue* (Dordrecht: Kluwer Academic Publishers, 2003), p. 44.
24 See H. Denzinger, *Enchiridion Symbolorum*, 26th edn (Freiburg: Herder, 1947), sections 491, 535, 571, 618.
25 D. Bradshaw, *Aristotle East and West: Metaphysics and the Division of Christendom* (Cambridge: Cambridge University Press, 2004), p. 155.
26 Davis, 'Periochetic Monotheism', p. 44.
27 M. Wiles, 'Some Reflections on the Origins of the Doctrine of the Trinity', in *Working Papers in Doctrine* (London: SCM, 1976).
28 S. Coakley, 'Why Three? Some Further Reflections on the Origins of the Doctrine of the Trinity', in S. Coakley and D. A. Pailin (eds), *The Making and Remaking of Christian Doctrine: Essays in Honour of Maurice Wiles* (Oxford: Clarendon Press, 1993), pp. 29–56; p. 29.
29 Coakley, 'Why Three?'.
30 See L. S. Thornton, 'The Christian Conception of God', in E. G. Selwyn (ed.), *Essays Catholic and Critical* (London, 1926), pp. 123–50; p. 144; also Rahner, *The Trinity*, p. 106.
31 Rahner, *The Trinity*, p. 22.
32 Rahner, *The Trinity*, p. 36.
33 Barth, *Church Dogmatics*, 1.1, p. 172; see also *Church Dogmatics*, 1.1, pp. 479, 481, 484. There are instances where Barth is inclined to blur the sharp distinction between the economic and immanent Trinity, e.g., *Church Dogmatics*, 2.1, p. 274, 3.1, p. 51 and 4.1, pp. 200f. However, these instances should not be taken as definitive, in the light of Barth's clear disavowal of necessity in the human–divine relationship.
34 See T. Bradshaw, *Trinity and Ontology: A Comparative Study of Karl Barth and Wolfhart Pannenberg* (Edinburgh: Rutherford, 1988), p. 312, where he argues that Barth does not draw a clear distinction between the immanent and economic Trinity. Bradshaw writes, 'This is because even that distinction must be a distinction within a relation. [. . .] Barth uses a double-edged method when he takes up that of "free relation and differentiation," or rather when this method compels itself because it is a reflection of God's essence.' Bradshaw's argument comes close to the suggestion that the relationality of the divine essence is a relationality that requires a relationship with the creation.
35 Moltmann, *The Trinity and the Kingdom of God*, p. 147. The phrase 'reflection trinity' refers to the structure of the absolute subject, usually in Idealism. In other words, however the reiteration or repetition of the absolute subject may be conceived, it refers to a single subject, rather than to actual differentiation.
36 Moltmann, *The Trinity and the Kingdom of God*, p. 148.

NOTES

37 P. D. Molnar, 'The Function of the Immanent Trinity in the Theology of
    Karl Barth: Implications for Today', *Scottish Journal of Theology* 42
    (1989): 367–99; see in particular pp. 367 and 370 for the critique of
    Torrance and Jüngel.
38 Molnar, 'The Function of the Immanent Trinity', p. 367.
    See also T. F. Torrance, 'Towards an Ecumenical Consensus on the Trin-
    ity', in *Trinitarian Perspectives: Toward Doctrinal Agreement* (Edin-
    burgh: T. & T. Clark, 1994), pp. 77–102; pp. 79f.
39 For example, Torrance, 'Towards an Ecumenical Consensus', and E.
    Jüngel, *God as the Mystery of the World: On the Foundation of the
    Theology of the Crucified One in the Dispute Between Theism and Athe-
    ism* (Edinburgh: T. & T. Clark, 1983), p. 369f.
40 Torrance, 'Towards an Ecumenical Consensus', pp. 79f.
41 W. Pannenberg, *Jesus: God and Man* (London: SCM Press, 1958),
    pp. 34–5.
42 Molnar, 'The Function of the Immanent Trinity', in particular p. 390.
43 Molnar, 'The Function of the Immanent Trinity', in particular pp. 397f.
44 R. W. Jenson, *The Triune Identity: God According to the Gospel* (Phila-
    delphia, Pa.: Fortress Press, 1982), pp. 140–1.
45 See J. Moltmann, *The Crucified God: The Cross of Christ as the Founda-
    tion and Criticism of Christian Theology* (London: SCM Press, 1974).
46 C. Schwöbel, *God: Action and Revelation* (Kampen: Kok Pharos, 1992),
    p. 43.
47 Schwöbel, *God: Action and Revelation*.
48 R. Del Colle, 'The Triune God', in C. E. Gunton (ed.), *The Cambridge
    Companion to Christian Doctrine* (Cambridge: Cambridge University
    Press, 1997), pp. 137–8.
49 A. Badiou, *Being and Event* (London and New York: Continuum, 2005).
50 See J. Barker, *Alain Badiou: A Critical Introduction* (London and
    Sterling, Va.: Pluto Press, 2002).
51 Barth, *Church Dogmatics*, 1.1.
52 J. D. Zizioulas, *Being as Communion: Studies in Personhood and Church*
    (London: Darton, Longman and Todd, 1985), pp. 15, 17.
53 Gregory of Nyssa, *Contra eunomius*, 1.19 MPG 45.
54 Maximos the Confessor, *Ambigua ad Ioannem*, MPG 91, 1217 CD, and
    Theol. et Oecon. Centuria, I.1–4 MPG 90 1084 AC; see also Gregory of
    Nyssa, *Contra eunomius*, 1.19 MPG 45.
55 A. H. Armstrong (ed.), *The Cambridge History of Later Greek and Early
    Medieval Philosophy* (Cambridge: Cambridge University Press, 1967),
    p. 493.
56 Armstrong, *Later Greek and Early Medieval Philosophy*, p. 493.
57 Armstrong, *Later Greek and Early Medieval Philosophy*, p. 496.
58 *Le Mystère de l'église et de l'eucharistie à la lumière de mystère de la
    Sainte Trinité* Commission mixte catholique–orthodoxe pour le dia-
    logue theologique (1982) (Mesnil Saint-Loup: Éditions du Livre Ouvert,
    1994), p. 18. Translation my own: '*Le sacrement de l'événement du Christ
    passé ainsi dans le sacrement de l'Eucharistie. Sacrement qui nous incor-
    pore pleinement au Christ*'.
59 *Le Mystère de l'église et de l'eucharistie*, p. 20. '*Le Seigneur Jésus entre*

dans la gloire du Père et, en meme temps, par l'effusion de l'Esprit, dans son tropos sacramental en ce monde-ci.'

60 *Le Mystère de l'église et de l'eucharistie*, p. 22. *'Quand l'Église célèbre l'Eucharistie, elle realise "ce qu'elle est," Corps de Christ* [1 Cor. 10.17]. *Par le Baptême et la chrismation, en effet, les members du Christ sont joints par l'Esprit, greffés sur le Christ. Mais l'Eucharistie, l'événement pascal se dilate en Eglise. L'Eglise deviant ce qu'elle est appelée à être de par le baptême et la chrismation. Par le communion au Corps et au Sang du Christ, les fidèles croissant en cette divinisation mystérieuse qui accomplit leur demeure dans le Fils et le Père, par l'Esprit'.*

61 J. D. Caputo, *Radical Hermeneutics: Repetition, Deconstruction and the Hermeneutic Project* (Bloomington, Ind.: Indiana University Press, 1987), p. 1.

62 Caputo, *Radical Hermeneutics*, p. 2. See also S. Kierkegaard, *Repetition* (1843): *Kierkegaard's Writings*, Vol. VI: *'Fear and Trembling' and 'Repetition,'* ed. H. Hong and E. Hong (Princeton, NJ: Princeton University Press, 1983).

63 Caputo, *Radical Hermeneutics*, p. 3.

64 Caputo, *Radical Hermeneutics*, p. 6. *Aufhebung* may be understood as annihilation, invalidation and also preservation.

65 J. D. Caputo, *The Weakness of God: A Theology of the Event* (Bloomington, Ind.: Indiana University Press, 2006).

66 Caputo, *The Weakness of God*, p. 3.

67 Caputo, *The Weakness of God*, p. 4.

68 Caputo, *The Weakness of God*, p. 5.

69 Caputo, *The Weakness of God*, p. 111.

70 J. D. Caputo and M. J. Scanlon (eds), *God, the Gift and Postmodernism* (Bloomington, Ind.: Indiana University Press, 1999), p. 5.

71 J. Derrida, *The Gift of Death* (Chicago, Ill.: University of Chicago Press, 1995).

72 Caputo and Scanlon, *God, the Gift and Postmodernism*, p. 8.

73 See, J.-L. Marion, *Reduction and Givenness: Investigations of Husserl, Heidegger and Phenomenology* (Evanston, Ill.: Northwestern University Press, 1998); *Toward a Phenomenology of Givenness* (Stanford, Calif.: Stanford University Press, 2002).

74 Caputo and Scanlon, *God, the Gift and Postmodernism*, p. 7.

75 Caputo and Scanlon, *God, the Gift and Postmodernism*, p. 8.

76 For example, J. Milbank, 'Can a Gift Be Given? Prolegomena to a Future Trinitarian Metaphysic', *Modern Theology* 11 (1) (1995); *Being Reconciled: Ontology and Pardon* (London: Routledge, 2003).

77 B. V. Johnstone, 'The Ethics of the Gift: According to Aquinas, Derrida and Marion', *Australian EJournal of Theology*, 3 (August) (2004).

78 M. Ludlow, *Gregory of Nyssa, Ancient and (Post) Modern* (Oxford: Oxford University Press, 2007).

79 S. Kierkegaard, *Philosophical Fragments and Johannes Climacus*, ed. H. V. Hong and E. H. Hong (Princeton, NJ: Princeton University Press, 1985).

80 Del Colle, *The Triune God*, p. 136.

5 TRINITY

1 J. Derrida, *On the Name* (Stanford, Calif.: Stanford University Press, 1995), p. 46; *The Politics of Friendship* (London and New York: Verso, 1997), pp. 296–9.
2 J. D. Caputo (ed.), *The Religious* (Malden, Mass. and Oxford: Blackwell, 2002), p. 5.
3 G. Deleuze, 'Bergson's Conception of Difference', in J. Mullarkey (ed.), *The New Bergson* (Manchester: Manchester University Press, 1999), pp. 42–65; p. 49.
4 J. D. Caputo (ed.), *Deconstruction in a Nutshell: A Conversation with Jacques Derrida* (New York: Fordham University Press, 1997), p. 110; see, for example, J. Derrida, *Spectres of Marx* (London and New York: Routledge, 1993, 1994), p. 172.
5 See Caputo, *Deconstruction in a Nutshell*, p. 112.
6 Caputo, *Deconstruction in a Nutshell*, p. 124; see also J. D. Caputo and M. J. Scanlon (eds), *God, the Gift, and Postmodernism* (Bloomington, Ind.: Indiana University Press, 1999), p. 77; see, for example, J. Derrida, *Points . . . Interviews 1974–1994* (Stanford, Calif.: Stanford University Press, 1995), p. 355.
7 R. Del Colle, 'The Triune God', in C. E. Gunton (ed.), *The Cambridge Companion to Christian Doctrine* (Cambridge: Cambridge University Press, 1997), pp. 121–40; p. 132.
8 Del Colle, 'The Triune God'.
9 T. Aquinas, *Summa theologiae*, Ia.28.3; see also Ia.30.4 and 31.2.
10 K. Barth, *Church Dogmatics*, 1.1 (Edinburgh: T. & T. Clark, 1975), pp. 316, 364–6; J. Moltmann, *The Trinity and the Kingdom of God: The Doctrine of God* (London: SCM, 1981), pp. 162–70; E. Jüngel, *The Doctrine of the Trinity: God's Being is in Becoming* (Edinburgh: Scottish Academic Press, 1976), pp. 25–9.
11 Barth, *Church Dogmatics*, 1.1, p. 316.
12 J. D. Zizioulas, 'Communion and Otherness', Orthodox Peace Fellowship, Occasional Paper, 191 (1994); and *Communion and Otherness: Further Studies in Personhood and the Church*, ed. P. McPartlan (London: T. & T. Clark, 2006).
13 Zizioulas, *Communion and Otherness*, p. 5.
14 Zizioulas, *Communion and Otherness*.
15 Zizioulas, *Communion and Otherness*.
16 Zizioulas, *Communion and Otherness*, pp. 4f.
17 Zizioulas, *Communion and Otherness*, p. 6.
18 Zizioulas, *Communion and Otherness*.
19 For example, M. Lawrence, 'Theo-Ontology: Notes on the Implications of Zizoulas's Engagement with Heidegger', *Theandros* (Online Journal of Orthodox Christian Theology and Philosophy, 3 (2) (2005/2006). Available at <http://www.theandros.com/zizheidegger.html> (accessed 1 March 2008).
20 Zizioulas, *Communion and Otherness*, p. 44, footnote 86.
21 Zizioulas, *Communion and Otherness*, p. 14.

22 Zizioulas, *Communion and Otherness*, p. 52.
23 See H. Lawson, *Reflexivity: The Postmodern Predicament* (La Salle, Ill.: Open Court, 1985).
24 Zizioulas, *Communion and Otherness*, p. 43.
25 Zizioulas, *Communion and Otherness*, p. 48.
26 Zizioulas, *Communion and Otherness*, p. 25.
27 Zizioulas, *Communion and Otherness*, p. 26.
28 Zizioulas, *Communion and Otherness*, p. 54.
29 O. Davies, *A Theology of Compassion* (London: SCM Press, 2001), p. 49.
30 B. V. Johnstone, 'The Ethics of the Gift: According to Aquinas, Derrida and Marion', *Australian EJournal of Theology*, 3 (August) (2004). Available at <http://dlibrary.acu.edu.au/research/theology/ejournal/aejt_3/ Johnstone.htm> (accessed 1 March 2008).
31 P. Fiddes, *Participating in God: A Pastoral Doctrine of the Trinity* (London: Darton, Longman and Todd, 2000), p. 184.
32 Fiddes, *Participating in God*, p. 185.
33 S. Wood, 'Ecclesial Koinonia in Ecumenical Dialogues', *One in Christ*, 30 (2) (1994): 124–45.
34 *Le Mystère de l'église et de l'eucharistie à la lumière de mystère de la Sainte Trinité*, Commission mixte catholique-orthodoxe pour le dialogue theologique (1982) (Mesnil Saint-Loup: Éditions du Livre Ouvert, 1994).
35 *Le Mystère de l'église*, p. 22.
36 *The Church of the Triune God: The Cyprus Agreed Statement of the International Commission for Anglican–Orthodox Theological Dialogue 2006* (London: The Anglican Communion Office, 2006).
37 *The Church of the Triune God*, p. 13.
38 *The Nature and Mission of the Church*, Faith and Order Document No. 198 (Geneva: World Council of Churches, 2006).
39 *The Nature and Mission of the Church*, section 11.
40 *The Nature and Mission of the Church*, section 13.
41 J.-M. R. Tillard, *Church of Churches: The Ecclesiology of Communion* (Collegeville, Pa.: The Liturgical Press, 1992).
42 Tillard, *Church of Churches*, p. 29.
43 For example, L. Boff, *Holy Trinity, Perfect Community* (Maryknoll, NY: Orbis Books, 2000).
44 Boff, *Holy Trinity, Perfect Community*, p. 63.
45 Boff, *Holy Trinity, Perfect Community*, p. 64.
46 Boff, *Holy Trinity, Perfect Community*, p. 65.
47 A. J. Torrance, *Persons in Communion: Trinitarian Description and Human Participation* (Edinburgh: T. & T. Clark, 1996).
48 A. Louth, 'The Ecclesiology of Saint Maximos the Confessor', *International Journal for the Study of the Christian Church*, 4 (2) (2004): 109–20.
49 Maximos the Confessor, *Mystagogia*, MPG 91, Chapter 1; English translation from *Maximus Confessor: Selected Writings*, trans. G. C. Berthold (London: SPCK, 1985).
50 J. D. Zizioulas, *Being as Communion: Studies in Personhood and the Church* (London: Darton, Longman and Todd, 1985).
51 Zizioulas, *Being as Communion*, p. 18.

52 Zizioulas, *Being as Communion*, p. 19.
53 See Zizioulas, *Being as Communion*, p. 19.
54 See H. Küng, *Structures of the Church* (London: Burns & Oates, 1965), and *The Church* (London and Tunbridge Wells: Search Press, 1968).
55 *Concilium*, in Latin, first used by Tertullian.
56 Küng, *Structures of the Church*, p. 9.
57 Küng, *The Church*, p. 237.
58 M. Volf, *After Our Likeness: The Church as the Image of the Trinity* (Cambridge and Grand Rapids, Mich.: Eerdmans, 1998).
59 Volf, *After Our Likeness*, p. 192.
60 Volf, *After Our Likeness*.
61 J. Behr, 'The Trinitarian Being of the Church', *St Vladimir's Theological Quarterly*, 48 (1) (2004): 67–88.
62 Behr, 'The Trinitarian Being of the Church', p. 67.
63 Behr, 'The Trinitarian Being of the Church', p. 68.
64 Behr, 'The Trinitarian Being of the Church'.
65 Zizioulas, *Being as Communion*, p. 8.
66 J.-L. Marion, *God Without Being: Hors-Texte* (Chicago, Ill.: University of Chicago Press, 1992), p. 150. See also P.-B. Smit, 'The Bishop and His/Her Eucharistic Community: A Critique of Jean-Luc Marion's Eucharistic Hermeneutic', *Modern Theology*, 19 (1) (2003): 29–40.
67 Smit, *The Bishop and His/Her Eucharistic Community*, p. 33.
68 For example, N. Afanassieff, 'Una Sancta', *Irénikon*, 36 (1963): 436–75; p. 459.
69 H. de Lubac, *Corpus Mysticum: The Eucharist and the Church in the Middle Ages* (Notre Dame, Ind.: University of Notre Dame Press, 2007). First published in French, 1944.
70 P. McPartlan, *The Eucharist Makes the Church: Henri de Lubac and John Zizioulas in Dialogue* (Edinburgh: T. & T. Clark, 1993).
71 J. Ratzinger, *Principles of Catholic Theology* (San Francisco, Calif.: Ignatius, 1987), p. 53. The translation is amended to include the final clause, omitted in the English translation of *Theologische Prinzipienlehre* (Munich: Erich Wewel, 1982), p. 55; see P. McPartlan, 'Eucharist and Church, Clergy and Laity: Catholic and Orthodox Perspectives', *International Journal for the Study of the Christian Church*, 2 (1) (2002): 50–69; p. 50.
72 M. Ouellet, 'Trinity and Eucharist: A Covenantal Mystery', *International Catholic Review*, 27 (2) (2000): 262–83; p. 274.
73 P. D. Molnar, *Karl Barth and the Theology of the Lord's Supper: A Systematic Investigation* (New York: Peter Lang, 1996). Reviewed by W. P. McShea, *Theological Studies*, 58 (4) (1997): 740–1; p. 741.
74 C. E. Gunton, *The One, the Three and the Many: God, Creation and the Culture of Modernity* (Cambridge, Cambridge University Press, 1993), p. 212.
75 Gunton, *The One, the Three and the Many*.
76 Gunton, *The One, the Three and the Many*, p. 213.
77 Gunton, *The One, the Three and the Many*.
78 Gunton, *The One, the Three and the Many*, p. 215.
79 Gunton, *The One, the Three and the Many*, p. 216.

80 Küng, *The Church*, p. 252.
81 T. Balasuriya, *The Eucharist and Human Liberation* (London: SCM, 1979); T. Gorringe, *Love's Sign: Reflection on the Eucharist* (Madurai: Tamilnadu Theological Seminary, 1986); A. Primavesi and J. Henderson, *Our God Has No Favourites: A Liberation Theology of the Eucharist* (Tunbridge Wells: Burns & Oates/San José, Calif.: Resource Publications, 1989).
82 Ouellet, 'Trinity and Eucharist', p. 267.
83 Louth, 'The Ecclesiology of Saint Maximos the Confessor', p. 115.
84 D. W. Hardy, 'Created and Redeemed Sociality', in C. E. Gunton and D. W. Hardy, *On Being the Church: Essays on the Christian Community* (Edinburgh: T. & T. Clark, 1989), pp. 21–47.
85 Gunton, *The One, the Three and the Many*, p. 223.
86 Gunton, *The One, the Three and the Many*, p. 223.
87 See P. M. Collins, *Trinitarian Theology West and East: Karl Barth, the Cappadocian Fathers and John Zizioulas* (Oxford: Oxford University Press, 2001), pp. 187f.
88 I. Kant, *Critique of Pure Reason* (London: Macmillan, 1933), p. 113.
89 Kant, *Critique of Pure Reason*, p. 255.
90 Hardy, 'Created and Redeemed Sociality', p. 27; in support of his argument, Hardy quotes K.-O. Apel, *Towards a Transformation of Philosophy* (London: Routledge & Kegan Paul, 1980), p. 138.
91 J. D. Caputo, *The Weakness of God: A Theology of Event* (Bloomington, Ind.: Indiana University Press, 2006), p. 4.
92 Caputo, *The Weakness of God*, p. 5.
93 Zizioulas, *Being as Communion*, p. 59.

AFTERWORD

1 Text of the Athanasian Creed from the Book of Common Prayer (1662).

BIBLIOGRAPHY

Afanassieff, N., 'Una Sancta', *Irénikon*, 36 (1963): 436–75.
Anon., 'The Westminster Directory of the Public Worship of God', in R. C. D Jasper and G. J. Cuming (eds), *Prayers of the Eucharist: Early and Reformed* (New York: Pueblo, 1987), pp. 265–9.
Apel, K.-O., *Towards a Transformation of Philosophy* (London: Routledge & Kegan Paul, 1980).
Aquinas, T., *Summa Theologiae* (London: Blackfriars: Eyre and Spottiswoode, 1963–76).
Armstrong, A. H. (ed.), *The Cambridge History of Later Greek and Early Medieval Philosophy* (Cambridge: Cambridge University Press, 1967).
Athanasius, *Ad Serapionem*, MPG 25.
Athanasius, *De Decretis Nicaenae Synodi* MPG 25.
Athenagoras, *Supplicatio pro Christianis*, MPG 6.
Auer, J., *Person: Ein Schlüssel zum christlichen Mysterium* (Regensburg: Verlag Friedrich Pustet, 1979).
Augustine of Hippo, *De trinitate*.
Ayres, L., *Nicaea and its Legacy: An Approach to Fourth-Century Trinitarian Thought* (Oxford: Oxford University Press, 2004).
Badiou, A., *Being and Event* (London and New York: Continuum, 2005).
Balasuriya, T., *The Eucharist and Human Liberation* (London: SCM, 1979).
Balthasar, H. U. von, 'On the Concept of Person', *Communio: International Catholic Review*, 13 (spring) (1986): 18–26.
Balthasar, H. U. von, *Theo-Drama: Theological Dramatic Theory*, Vol. IV (San Francisco, Calif.: Ignatius Press, 1988).
Balthasar, H. U. von, *Mysterium Paschale* (Edinburgh: T. & T. Clark, 1990).
Barker, J., *Alain Badiou: A Critical Introduction* (London and Sterling, Va.: Pluto Press, 2002).
Barnes, M. R., 'Rereading Augustine's Theology of the Trinity', in Stephen T. Davis, Daniel Kendall, Gerald O'Collins (eds), *The Trinity: An Interdisciplinary Symposium on the Trinity* (New York: Oxford University Press, 1999), pp. 145–76.
Bartel, T. W., 'Could There Be More Than One Almighty?' *Religious Studies*, 29 (4) (1993): 465–95.
Barth, K., *The Word of God and the Word of Man* (London: Hodder and Stoughton, 1928).

Barth, K., *Church Dogmatics* (Edinburgh: T. & T. Clark, 1936–69).
Bartmann, B., *Lehrbuch der Dogmatik* (Freiburg: Verlag Herder Und Co., 1928), Vol. I.
Basil of Caesarea, *Contra Sabellium*, MPG 31.
Basil of Caesarea, *De spiritu sancto*, MPG 32.
Basil of Caesarea, *Letters*, MPG 32.
Baxter, R., *The Reformation of the Liturgy 1661*, in R. C. D. Jasper and G. J. Cuming (eds), *Prayers of the Eucharist* (New York: Pueblo Publishing Company, 1987), pp. 270–6.
Bayle, P., *Commentaire philosophique sur ces paroles de Jesus-Christ: Contrains les d'entrer: oir l'on prouve par plusieurs raisons demonstratives qu'il n'ya rien de plus abominable que de faire des conversions par la contrainte, et ou l'on rifute tous les sophismes des convertisseurs a contrainte et l'apologie que St. Auaustin a faite des persecutions*, trans. J. Fox de Bruggs (Cantorbery: Thomas Litwel). The first and second parts appeared in 1686 and the third in 1687.
Behr, J., 'The Trinitarian Being of the Church', *St Vladimir's Theological Quarterly*, 48 (1) (2004): 67–88.
Bernauer, J. and J. Carrette (eds), *Michel Foucault and Theology* (Aldershot: Ashgate, 2004).
Best, T. F. and G. Gassmann (eds), 'On the Way to Fuller Koinonia', Faith and Order Paper No. 166, Geneva: World Council of Churches, 1994.
Boethius, *Contra Eutychem*, MPL 64.
Boethius, *De trinitate*, MPL 64.
Boff, L., *Trinity and Society* (Maryknoll, NY: Orbis, 1988).
Boff, L., *Holy Trinity, Perfect Community* (Maryknoll, NY: Orbis, 2000).
Bonhoeffer, D., *Sanctorum Communio* (London: Collins, 1963).
Bourassa, F., *Personne et conscience en theologie trinitaire*, *Gregorianum*, 55 (1974): 471–93, 677–720.
Braaten, C. E. and R. W. Jenson (eds), *Christian Dogmatics*, 2 vols (Philadelphia, Pa.: Fortress Press, 1984).
Bracken, J. A., 'Subsistent Relation: Mediating Concept for a New Synthesis?' *Journal of Religion*, 64 (2) (1984): 188–204.
Bracken, J. A., *The Triune Symbol: Persons, Process and Community* (Lanham, Md.: University Press of America, 1985).
Bradshaw, D., *Aristotle East and West: Metaphysics and the Division of Christendom* (Cambridge: Cambridge University Press, 2004).
Bradshaw, T., *Trinity and Ontology: A Comparative Study of Karl Barth and Wolfhart Pannenberg* (Edinburgh: Rutherford, 1988).
British Council of Churches, *The Forgotten Trinity* (London: British Council of Churches, 1989), Vol. I.
Brown, D., *The Divine Trinity* (London: Duckworth, 1985).
Buber, M., *I and Thou* (Edinburgh: T. & T. Clark, 1970).
Bulgakov, S., *The Wisdom of God: A Brief Summary of Sophiology* (New York: Paisley Press, 1937).
Byrne, J. M. (ed.), *The Christian Understanding of God Today* (Dublin: The Columba Press, 1993).
Capra, F., *Tao of Physics: An Exploration of the Parallels Between Modern*

Physics and Eastern Mysticism (Berkeley, Calif.: Shambhala Publications, 1975).

Caputo, J. D., *Radical Hermeneutics: Repetition, Deconstruction and the Hermeneutic Project* (Bloomington, Ind.: Indiana University Press, 1987).

Caputo, J. D. (ed.), *Deconstruction in a Nutshell: A Conversation with Jacques Derrida* (New York: Fordham University Press, 1997).

Caputo, J. D. (ed.), *The Religious* (Malden, Mass. and Oxford: Blackwell, 2002).

Caputo, J. D., *The Weakness of God: A Theology of the Event* (Bloomington, Ind.: Indiana University Press, 2006).

Caputo, J. D. and M. J. Scanlon (eds), *God, the Gift, and Postmodernism* (Bloomington, Ind.: Indiana University Press, 1999).

Carrithers, M., S. Collins and S. Lukes (eds), *The Category of the Person: Anthropology, Philosophy, History* (Cambridge: Cambridge University Press, 1985).

Clark, M., *'De Trinitate'* in E. Stump and N. Kretzmann (eds), *The Cambridge Companion to Augustine* (Cambridge: Cambridge University Press, 2001), pp. 91–102.

Coakley, S., 'Why Three? Some Further Reflections on the Origins of the Doctrine of the Trinity', in S. Coakley and D. A. Pailin (eds), *The Making and Remaking of Christian Doctrine: Essays in Honour of Maurice Wiles* (Oxford: Clarendon Press, 1993), pp. 29–56.

Coakley, S., ' "Persons" in the "Social" Doctrine of the Trinity: A Critique of Current Analytic Discussion', in S. T. Davis, D. Kendall, G. O'Collins (eds), *The Trinity: An Interdisciplinary Symposium on the Trinity* (New York: Oxford University Press, 1999), pp. 123–44.

Coakley, S. and D. A. Pailin (eds), *The Making and Remaking of Christian Doctrine: Essays in Honour of Maurice Wiles* (Oxford: Clarendon Press, 1993).

Cobb, J., *A Christian Natural Theology* (Philadelphia, Pa.: Westminster, 1965).

Collins, P. M., *Trinitarian Theology West and East: Karl Barth, the Cappadocian Fathers and John Zizioulas* (Oxford: Oxford University Press, 2001).

Collins, P. M., *Christian Inculturation in India* (Aldershot: Ashgate, 2007).

Congar, Y., *I Believe in the Holy Spirit* (London and New York: Geoffrey Chapman and Seabury Press, 1983), Vol. III.

Connor, R. A., 'The Person as Resonating Existential', *American Catholic Philosophical Quarterly*, 66 (1) (1992): 39–56.

Cunningham, D. S., *These Three Are One: The Practice of Trinitarian Theology* (Oxford: Blackwell, 1998).

D'Costa, G., *Sexing the Trinity: Gender, Culture and the Divine* (London: SCM Press, 2000).

Daly, M., 'After the Death of God the Father', *Commonweal*, March 12, 1971, pp. 7–11.

Davis, S. T., 'Periochetic Monotheism' in M. Y. Stewart (ed.), *The Trinity: East/West Dialogue* (Dordrecht: Kluwer Academic Publishers, 2003), p. 44.

Davis, S. T., D. Kendall and G. O'Collins (eds), *The Trinity: An Inter-*

disciplinary Symposium on the Trinity (New York: Oxford University Press, 1999).

de Halleux, A., ' "Hypostase" et "Personne" dans la formation de dogme trinitaire (ca 375–381)', *Revue d'Histoire Ecclesiastique*, 79 (1984): 313–69, 625–70.

de Halleux, A., 'Personnalisme ou essentialisme trinitaire chez les Pères cappadociens?' *Revue théologique de Louvain*, 17 (1986): 143–4.

de Lubac, H., *Corpus Mysticum: The Eucharist and the Church in the Middle Ages* (Notre Dame, Ind.: University of Notre Dame Press, 2007).

de Régnon, T., *Études de théologie positive sur la Sainte Trinité*, 3 vols (Paris: Retaux, 1892–8).

de Satgé, J., *Mary and the Christian Gospel* (London: SPCK, 1976).

Del Colle, R., 'The Triune God' in C. E. Gunton (ed.), *The Cambridge Companion to Christian Doctrine* (Cambridge: Cambridge University Press, 1997), pp. 121–40.

Deleuze, G., 'Bergson's Conception of Difference', in J. Mullarkey (ed.), *The New Bergson* (Manchester and New York: Manchester University Press, 1999), pp. 42–65.

Denzinger, J., *Enchiridion Symbolorum*, 26th edn (Freiburg: Herder, 1947).

Derrida, J., *Spectres of Marx* (New York and London: Routledge, 1994).

Derrida, J., *On the Name* (Stanford, Calif.: Stanford University Press, 1995).

Derrida, J., *Points . . . Interviews 1974–1994* (Stanford, Calif.: Stanford University Press, 1995).

Derrida, J., *The Gift of Death* (Chicago, Ill.: University of Chicago Press, 1995).

Derrida, J., *The Politics of Friendship* (London and New York: Verso, 1997).

d'Eypernon, T., *Le Mystère primordial: la trinité dans sa vivante image* (Brussels and Paris: L'Éditions Universelle/Desclée de Brouwer, 1946).

DiNoia, J. A., *Knowing and Naming the Triune God: The Grammar of Trinitarian Confession*, in A. J. Kimel (ed.), *Speaking the Christian God: The Holy Trinity and the Challenge of Feminism* (Grand Rapids, Mich.: Eerdmans, 1992), pp. 162–87.

Dionysius of Rome, 'Letter to Dionysius of Alexandria', in J. Neuner and J. Dupuis (eds), *The Christian Faith in the Doctrinal Documents of the Catholic Church* (London: Collins, 1983).

Drobner, H. R. and C. Klock (eds), *Studien zu Gregor von Nyssa und der christlichen Spätantike* (Leiden: E. J. Brill, 1990).

Duke, O. J. and R. F. Streetman (eds), *Barth and Schleiermacher: Beyond the Impasse?* (Philadelphia, Pa.: Fortress Press, 1988).

Dunn, J. D. G., 'I Corinthians 15.45: Last Adam, Life-giving Spirit', in B. Lindars and S. S. Smalley (eds), *Christ and the Spirit in the New Testament* (Cambridge: Cambridge University Press, 1973), pp. 127–42.

Ecumenical Patriarchate, *Unto the Churches of Christ Everywhere*, Encyclical of the Ecumenical Patriarchate (1920).

Eusebius, *Praeparatio Evangelica*, MPG 21.

Faith and Order Commission, *The Nature and Mission of the Church*, Faith and Order Document No. 198 (Geneva: World Council of Churches, 2005).

Feenstra, R. J. and C. Plantinga Jr. (eds), *Trinity, Incarnation and Atone-*

ment: Philosophical and Theological Essays (Notre Dame, Ind.: University of Notre Dame Press, 1989).

Fermer, R. M., 'The Limits of Trinitarian Theology as a Methodological Paradigm', *Neue Zeitschrift für Systematische Theologie und Religionsphilosophie* 41 (2) (1999): 158–86.

Fiddes, P. S., *Participating in God: A Pastoral Doctrine of the Trinity* (London: Darton, Longman and Todd, 2000).

Ford, D. and D. W. Hardy, *Jubilate: Theology in Praise* (London: Darton, Longman and Todd, 1984).

Fortman, E. J., *The Triune God: A Historical Study of the Doctrine of the Trinity* (Philadelphia, Pa.: Westminster, 1972).

Foster, J., *The Immaterial Self: A Defence of the Cartesian Dualist Conception of the Mind* (London and New York: Routledge, 1991).

Foucault, M., *The Order of Things* (London: Tavistock Publications, 1970).

Foucault, M., *Discipline and Punish: The Birth of the Prison* (London: Allen Lane, 1977).

Fraigneau-Julien, B., 'Réflexion sur la signification religieuse du mystère de la Sainte Trinité', *Nouvelle Revue Theologique*, 87 (7) (1965): 673–87.

Gabriel, A. K., 'Pneumatological Perspectives for a Theology of Nature: The Holy Spirit in Relation to Ecology and Technology', *Journal of Pentecostal Theology*, 15 (2) (2007): 195–212.

Galot, J., *Who is Christ? A Theology of the Incarnation* (Rome: Gregorian University Press; Chicago, Ill.: Franciscan Herald Press, 1980).

Gibbon, E., *The History of the Decline and Fall of the Roman Empire* (London: J. M. Dent and Son Limited, Everyman edition, 1910).

Gilligan, C., *In a Different Voice* (Cambridge, Mass.: Harvard University Press, 1982).

Gorringe, T., *Love's Sign: Reflection on the Eucharist* (Madurai: Tamilnadu Theological Seminary, 1986).

Grabowski, J. S., 'Person: Substance and Relation', *Communio: International Catholic Review*, 22 (spring) (1995): 139–63.

Grant, S., *Sankaracarya's Concept of Relation* (Delhi: Motilal Banarsidass Publishers, 1999).

Gregory of Nazianzus, *Epistula*, MPG 37.

Gregory of Nazianzus, *Scholia*, MPG 36.

Gregory of Nazianzus, *The Fifth Theological Oration: On the Holy Spirit, Nicene and Post-Nicene Fathers*, ed. P. Schaff and H. Wace, Vol. VII, Second series (Peabody, Mass.: Hendrickson, 1994), pp. 318–28.

Gregory of Nyssa, *Adversus Arium et Sabellium*, MPG 45.

Gregory of Nyssa, *Contra Eunomium*, MPG 45.

Gregory of Nyssa, *To Ablabius, that there are not Three Gods* (*Ad Ablabium*), MPG 45.

Grenz, S. J., *The Social God and the Relational Self* (Louisville, Ky.: Westminster John Knox Press, 2001).

Gresham, J. L., 'The Social Model of the Trinity and Its Critics', *Scottish Journal of Theology*, 46 (3) (1993): 325–43.

Gresser, R., 'The Need for and the Use of Doxological Language in

Theology', *Quodlibet Journal*, 6 (1) 2004. Available online at <http://www.quodlibet.net>.

Grillmeier, A., *Christ in Christian Tradition*, I (London: Mowbray, 1975).

Gunton, C. E., *The One, the Three and the Many: God, Creation and the Culture of Modernity* (Cambridge: Cambridge University Press, 1993).

Gunton, C. E., *The Promise of Trinitarian Theology*, 2nd edn (London: T. & T. Clark, 1997).

Gunton, C. E. (ed.) *The Cambridge Companion to Christian Doctrine* (Cambridge: Cambridge University Press, 1997).

Hardy, D. W., 'The English Tradition of Interpretation and the Reception of Schleiermacher and Barth in England', in O. J. Duke and R. F. Streetman (eds), *Barth and Schleiermacher: Beyond the Impasse?* (Philadelphia, Pa.: Fortress Press, 1988), pp. 138–62.

Hardy, D. W., 'Created and Redeemed Sociality', in C. E. Gunton and D. W. Hardy, *On Being the Church: Essays on the Christian Community* (Edinburgh: T. & T. Clark, 1989), pp. 21–47.

Harnack, A., *What is Christianity?* (London: Williams and Norgate, 1901).

Harnack, A., *Lehrbuch in der Dogmengeschichte*, 4th edn (Freiburg: J. C. B. Mohr, 1909).

Hartshorne, C., *The Divine Relativity: A Social Conception of God* (New Haven, Conn.: Yale University Press, 1964).

Hegel, G. W. F., *Phenomenology of Geist (Spirit)* (Oxford: Oxford University Press, 1977).

Hemmerle, K., *Thesen zu einer trinitarischen Ontologie* (Freiburg: Johnannes Verlag Einsiedeln, 1992).

Heron, A. I. C., *The Holy Spirit* (Philadelphia, Pa.: Westminster John Knox Press, 1984).

Hick, J. (ed.), *The Myth of God Incarnate* (London: SCM Press, 1977).

Hilary, *De trinitate*, MPL 10.

Hill, W., *The Three-Personed God: The Trinity as a Mystery of Salvation* (Washington, DC: Catholic University of America Press, 1982).

Hodgson, L., *The Doctrine of the Trinity* (New York: Charles Scribner's Sons, 1944).

Illingworth, J. R., *Personality Human and Divine* (London and New York: Macmillan, 1894).

International Commission for Anglican–Orthodox Theological Dialogue, *The Church of the Triune God: The Cyprus Agreed Statement of the International Commission for Anglican–Orthodox Theological Dialogue 2006* (London: The Anglican Communion Office, 2006).

Inwagen, P. van, 'And Yet They Are Not Three Gods but One God', in T. V. Morris (ed.), *Philosophy and Christian Faith* (Notre Dame, Ind.: University of Notre Dame Press, 1988), pp. 241–78.

Irenaeus, *Adversus Haereses*, MPG 7.

Jasper, R. C. D and G. J. Cuming (eds), *Prayers of the Eucharist: Early and Reformed* (New York: Pueblo Publishing Company, 1987).

Jenkins, D., *The Glory of Man* (London: SCM Press, 1967).

Jenkins, D., *Living with Questions* (London: SCM Press, 1969).

Jenkins, D., *What is Man?* (London: SCM Press, 1970).

Jennings, T. W., Jr., *Beyond Theism* (Oxford: Oxford University Press, 1985).

Jenson, R. W., *The Triune Identity: God According to the Gospel* (Philadelphia, Pa.: Fortress Press, 1982).

Jenson, R. W., 'The Father, He . . .,' in A. J. Kimel (ed.), *Speaking the Christian God: The Holy Trinity and the Challenge of Feminism* (Grand Rapids, Mich.: Eerdmans, 1992), pp. 95–109.

Jenson, R. W., *Systematic Theology*, Vol. I (Oxford: Oxford University Press, 1997).

John of Damascus, *De fide orthodoxa*, MPG 94.

Johnson, E., *She Who Is: The Mystery of God in Feminist Theological Discourse* (New York: Crossroad, 1992).

Jüngel, E., *Gottes Sein ist in Werden* (Tübingen: J. C. B. Mohr (Paul Siebeck), 1986). Published in English as *The Doctrine of the Trinity: God's Being is in Becoming* (Edinburgh: Scottish Academic Press, 1976).

Jüngel, E., *God as the Mystery of the World: On the Foundation of the Theology of the Crucified One in the Dispute Between Theism and Atheism* (Edinburgh: T. & T. Clark, 1983).

Kant, I., *Critique of Pure Reason* (London: Macmillan, 1933).

Kasper, W., *The God of Jesus Christ* (London: SCM, 1984).

Kaufmann, G., *The Theological Imagination* (Philadelphia, Pa.: Westminster Press, 1981).

Kierkegaard, S., *Repetition* (1843), in *Kierkegaard's Writings*, Vol. VI: *'Fear and Trembling' and 'Repetition,'* ed. H. V. Hong and E. H. Hong (Princeton, NJ: Princeton University Press, 1983).

Kierkegaard, S., *Philosophical Fragments and Johannes Climacus*, ed. H. V. Hong and E. H. Hong (Princeton, NJ: Princeton University Press, 1985).

Kilby, K., 'Perichoresis and Projection: Problems with Social Doctrines of the Trinity', *New Blackfriars*, (October) (2000): 432–45.

Kimel, A. J. (ed.), *Speaking the Christian God: The Holy Trinity and the Challenge of Feminism* (Grand Rapids, Mich.: Eerdmans, 1992).

Kirk, G. S. and Raven, J. E., *The Presocratic Philosophers* (Cambridge: Cambridge University Press, 1960).

Krempel, L., *La Doctrine de la relation chez Saint Thomas* (Paris: Librairie Philosophique J. Vrin, 1952).

Küng, H., *Structures of the Church* (London, Burns & Oates, 1965).

Küng, H., *The Church* (London and Tunbridge Wells: Search Press, 1968).

LaCugna, C. M., 'The Relational God: Aquinas and Beyond', *Theological Studies*, 46 (4) (1985): 647–63.

LaCugna, C. M., *God for Us: The Trinity and the Christian Life* (New York: HarperCollins, 1991).

LaCugna, C. M., 'God in Communion with Us: the Trinity', in C. M. LaCugna (ed.), *Freeing Theology: The Essentials of Theology in Feminist Perspective* (New York: Harper Collins, 1993), pp. 83–114.

Lampe, G., *God as Spirit* (Oxford: Clarendon Press, 1977).

Lash, N., *Believing Three Ways in One God: A Reading of the Apostles' Creed* (London: SCM, 2002).

Lawrence, M., 'Theo-Ontology: Notes on the Implications of Zizoulas's Engagement With Heidegger', *Theandros* (Online Journal of Orthodox Christian Theology and Philosophy, 3 (2) (2005/2006). Available at

<http://www.theandros.com/zizheidegger.html> (Accessed 1 March 2008).

Lawson, H., *Reflexivity: The Post-Modern Predicament* (La Salle, Ill.: Open Court, 1985).

Le Mystère de l'église et de l'eucharistie à la lumière de mystère de la Sainte Trinité, Commission Mixte Catholique–Orthodoxe pour le Dialogue Theologique (1982) (Mesnil Saint-Loup: Éditions du Livre Ouvert, 1994).

Lienhard, J. T., E. G. Muller, and R. J. Teske (eds), *Collectanea Augustiniana, Augustine: Presbyter Factus Sum* (New York: Peter Lang, 1993).

Lindars, B. and S. S. Smalley (eds), *Christ and the Spirit in the New Testament* (Cambridge: Cambridge University Press, 1973).

Lindbeck, G., *The Nature of Doctrine: Religion and Theology in a Postliberal Age* (London: SPCK, 1984).

Lochet, L., 'Charité fraternelle et vie trinitaire', *Nouvelle Revue Theologique*, 78 (2) (1956): 113–34.

Locke, J., *An Essay Concerning Human Understanding*, Vol. 1. (London: Dent; New York: Dutton, 1972).

Lonergan, B., *The Way to Nicea: The Dialectical Development of Trinitarian Theology* (Philadelphia, Pa.: Westminster, 1976).

Lossky, V., *The Mystical Theology of the Eastern Church* (Cambridge and London: James Clarke & Co. Ltd, 1957).

Louth, A., 'Unity and Diversity in the Church of the Fourth Century', in Everett Ferguson (ed.), *Doctrinal Diversity: Recent Studies in Early Christianity: A Collection of Scholarly Essays*, Vol. IV (London: Garland, 1999), pp. 1–18.

Louth, A., 'The Ecclesiology of Saint Maximos the Confessor', *International Journal for the Study of the Christian Church*, 4 (2) (2004): 109–20.

Lumen Gentium (1964) in A. Flannery (ed.), *Vatican Council II: The Conciliar and Post Conciliar Documents* (Tenbury Wells: Fowler Wright Books, 1975), pp. 350–426. Available at <http://www.vatican.va/archive/hist-_councils/ii_vatican_council/documents/vat-ii_const_19641121_lumen-gentium_en.html> (accessed 11 March 2008).

Luther, M., *Lectures on the Psalms*, (*Dictata*, 1513–1516), *D. Martin Luthers Werke, Kritische Gesamtausgabe* (Weimar: Verlag Hermann Böhlausn Nochfolger, 1883–), 3.124.29.

McFadyen, A. I., *The Call to Personhood: A Christian Theory of the Individual in Social Relationships* (Cambridge: Cambridge University Press, 1990).

McGinn, B., *The Mystical Thought of Meister Eckhart: The Man from whom God Hid Nothing* (New York: The Crossroad Publishing Company, 2004).

Mackey, J., 'Are There Christian Alternatives to Trinitarian Thinking?', in J. M. Byrne (ed.), *The Christian Understanding of God Today* (Dublin: The Columba Press, 1993), pp. 66–75.

McKinney, R. (ed.), *Creation, Christ and Culture: Studies in Honour of T. F. Torrance* (Edinburgh: T. & T. Clark, 1976).

MacKinnon, D., 'The Relation of the Doctrines of the Incarnation and the

Trinity', in R. McKinney (ed.), *Creation, Christ and Culture: Studies in Honour of T. F. Torrance* (Edinburgh: T. & T. Clark, 1976).

Macmurray, J., *The Form of the Personal*, Vol. II: *Persons in Relation* (London: Faber and Faber, 1961).

McPartlan, P., *The Eucharist Makes the Church: Henri de Lubac and John Zizioulas in Dialogue* (Edinburgh: T. & T. Clark, 1993).

McPartlan, P., 'Eucharist and Church, Clergy and Laity: Catholic and Orthodox Perspectives', *International Journal for the Study of the Christian Church*, 2(1) (2002): 50–69.

Macquarrie, J., *The Principles of Christian Theology* (London: SCM Press, 1977).

Maddox, R. L., 'Wesleyan Theology and the Christian Feminist Critique', *Wesleyan Theological Journal*, 22 (1987): 101–11.

Marion, J.-L., *God without Being: Hors-Texte* (Chicago, Ill.: Chicago University Press, 1991).

Marion, J.-L., *Reduction and Givenness: Investigations of Husserl, Heidegger and Phenomenology* (Evanston, Ill.: Northwestern University Press, 1998).

Marion, J.-L., *Toward a Phenomenology of Givenness* (Stanford, Calif.: Stanford University Press, 2002).

Markus, R. A., *Saeculum: History and Society in the Theology of St. Augustine* (Cambridge: Cambridge University Press, 1988).

Maximos the Confessor, *Ambigua ad Ioannem*, MPG 91.

Maximos the Confessor, *Questiones ad Thalassium* 59, 202 B, *Corpus Christianorum, Series Graeca*, Vols. VII and XXII (Louvain: Brepols, 1980 and 1990).

Maximos the Confessor, *Capita Theol. et Oecon. Centuria*, I.1–4, MPG 90.

Melanchthon, P., *Loci communes rerum theologicarum seu hypotyposes theologicae* (Wittenberg and Basel, 1521).

Meredith, A., *The Cappadocians* (Crestwood, NY: St Vladimir's Seminary Press, 2000).

Metzer, P. L. (ed.), *Trinitarian Soundings in Systematic Theology* (London and New York: Continuum, 2005).

Metzler, N., 'The Trinity in Contemporary Theology: Questioning the Social Trinity', *Concordia Theological Quarterly*, 67 (3) (2003): 270–87.

Milbank, J., 'Theology without Substance: Christianity, Signs, Origins – Part 1', *Literature and Theology*, 2 (1) (1988): 1–17.

Milbank, J., 'Theology without Substance: Christianity, Signs, Origins – Part 2', *Literature and Theology*, 2 (2) (1988): 131–52.

Milbank, J., 'Can a Gift Be Given? Prolegomena to a Future Trinitarian Metaphysic', *Modern Theology*, 11 (1) (1995): 119–61.

Milbank, J. and C. Pickstock, *Truth in Aquinas* (London: Routledge, 2001).

Milbank, J., *Being Reconciled: Ontology and Pardon* (London: Routledge, 2003).

Molnar, P. D., 'The Function of the Immanent Trinity in the Theology of Karl Barth: Implications for Today', *Scottish Journal of Theology*, 42 (1989): 367–99.

Molnar, P. D., *Karl Barth and the Theology of the Lord's Supper: A Systematic Investigation* (New York: Peter Lang, 1996).

Moltmann, J., *The Crucified God: The Cross of Christ as the Foundation and Criticism of Christian Theology* (London: SCM Press, 1974).

Moltmann, J., *The Trinity and the Kingdom of God: The Doctrine of God* (London: SCM, 1981).

Morris, T. V. (ed.), *Philosophy and Christian Faith* (Notre Dame, Ind.: University of Notre Dame Press, 1988).

Mühlen, H., *Der Heilige Geist als Person* (Münster: Verlag Aschendorff, 1963).

Mullarkey, J. (ed.) *The New Bergson* (Manchester: Manchester University Press, 1999).

Neal, D., 'Out of the Uterus of the Father: A Study in Patriarchy and Symbolization of Christian Theology', *Feminist Theology*, 13, (September) (1996): 8–30.

Neuner, J. and Dupuis, J. (eds), *The Christian Faith, in the Doctrinal Documents of the Catholic Church* (London: Collins, 1983).

Newman, J. H., *The Arians of the Fourth Century* (1833) (Notre Dame, Ind.: University of Notre Dame Press, 2001).

Newman, J. H., *An Essay on the Development of Christian Doctrine* (Garden City, NY: Doubleday/Image, 1960), I.2.4.

Newton Clarke, W., *Christian Theology in Outline* (New York: C. Scribner's Sons, 1898).

Newton, I., *De Athanasio, & Antonio*, in *Theological Notebook*, 1684–1690.

Nichols, A., 'Wisdom from Above? The Sophiology of Father Sergius Bulgakov', *New Blackfriars*, 85 (1000) (2004): 598–613.

Nissiotis, N. A., 'The Importance of the Doctrine of the Trinity for Church Life and Theology', in A. J. Philippou (ed.), *The Orthodox Ethos* (Oxford: Holywell Press, 1964).

O'Donnell, J. J., *The Mystery of the Triune God* (London: Sheed and Ward, 1988).

One Lord, One Baptism, Commission on Faith and Order, Paper No. 29 (London: SCM, 1960).

Origen, *Contra Celsum*, MPG 11.

Origen, *De principiis*, MPG 11.

Origen, *In Johannem*, MPG 14.

Orphanos, M. A., 'The Procession of the Holy Spirit According to Certain Later Greek Fathers', in L. Vischer (ed.), *Spirit of God, Spirit of Christ, Ecumenical Reflections on the Filioque Controversy*, WCC Faith and Order Paper 103 (London and Geneva: World Council of Churches, 1981).

Otto, R., *The Idea of the Holy* (Oxford: Oxford University Press, 1977).

Ouellet, M., 'Trinity and Eucharist: A Covenantal Mystery', *International Catholic Review*, 27 (2) (2000): 262–83.

Paine, T., *The Age of Reason*, 1795.

Panneberg, W., *Systematic Theology*, Vol. I (Edinburgh: T. & T. Clark, 1991).

Pannenberg, W., 'Person' in H. F. V. Campenhausen, E. Dinkler, G. Gloege, K. E. Logstrup and K. Galling (eds), *Religion in Geschichte und Gegenwart*, 3rd edn (Tübingen: J. C. B. Mohr, 1957), pp. 230–5.

Pannenberg, W., *Jesus: God and Man* (London: SCM Press, 1958), pp. 34–5.

Parfit, D., *Reasons and Persons* (Oxford: Oxford University Press, 1984).

Pecknold, C. C., 'How Augustine Used the Trinity: Functionalism and the Development of Doctrine', *Anglican Theological Review*, (Winter) (2003): 127–42.

Pelikan, J., *Christianity and Classical Culture: The Metamorphosis of Natural Theology in the Christian Encounter with Hellenism* (New Haven, Conn.: Yale University Press, 1993).

Petavius, Dionysius, *Theologicorum dogmatum*, 6 volumes (Paris, 1644–50).

Philo of Alexandria, *De opificio mundi*, in *Philo*, Vol. I (London and New York: G. P. Putnam's Sons and Heinemann, 1929).

Philo of Alexandria, *De plantation*, in *Philo*, Vol. III (London and New York: G. P. Putnam's Sons and Heinemann, 1929).

Porter, L. B., 'On Keeping "Persons" in the Trinity: a Linguistic Approach to Trinitarian Thought', *Theological Studies*, 41 (3) (1980): 530–48.

Prestige, G. L., *God in Patristic Thought*, 2nd edn (London, SPCK, 1952).

Primavesi, A. and J. Henderson, *Our God Has No Favourites: A Liberation Theology of the Eucharist* (Tunbridge Wells: Burns & Oates; San Jose, Calif.: Resource Publications, 1989).

Pseudo-Dionysius, *The Divine Names*, MPG 3.

Rahner, K., *The Trinity* (London: Burns and Oates, 1970).

Rahner, K., *Foundations of Christian Faith: An Introduction to the Idea of Christianity* (London: Darton, Longman and Todd, 1978).

Ramsey, I. T., *Models for Divine Activity* (London: SCM Press, 1973).

Ratzinger, J., 'Zum Personverständnis in der Theologie', in *Dogma und Verkündigung* (Munich and Freiburg: Wewel, 1973), pp. 205–23.

Ratzinger, J., *Theologische Prinzipienlehre* (Munich: Erich Wewel, 1982).

Ratzinger, J., *Principles of Catholic Theology* (San Francisco, Calif.: Ignatius, 1987).

Ratzinger, J., 'Concerning the Notion of Person in Theology', *Communio: International Catholic Review*, 17 (autumn) (1990): 439–54.

Reynolds, P. L., 'Bullitio and the God beyond God: Meister Eckharts' Trinitarian Theology, Part I: The Inner Life of God', *New Blackfriars*, 70 (April) (1989): 169–81.

Reynolds, P. L., 'Bullitio and the God beyond God: Meister Eckharts' Trinitarian Theology, Part II: Distinctionless Godhead and Trinitarian God', *New Blackfriars*, 70 (May) (1989): 235–44.

Richard of St Victor, *De trinitate*, MPL 196.

Ritschl, A., *Justification and Reconciliation* (Edinburgh: T. & T. Clark, 1900).

Scheeben, M. J., *Handbuch der katholischen Dogmatik*, Vol. IV (Freiburg: Herder, 1948).

Schleiermacher, F., *The Christian Faith* (Edinburgh: T. & T. Clark, 1928).

Schmitz, K. L., 'The Geography of the Human Person', *Communio: International Catholic Review*, 13 (spring) (1986): 27–48.

Schwöbel, C., *God: Action and Revelation* (Kampen: Kok Pharos, 1992).

Schwöbel, C. (ed.), *Trinitarian Theology Today: Essays on Divine Being and Act* (Edinburgh: T. & T. Clark, 1995).

Schwöbel, C., *Gott in Beziehung: Studien zur Dogmatik*, Tübingen: Mohr Siebeck, 2002).

Schwöbel, C. and C. E. Gunton (eds), *Persons, Divine and Human: King's*

BIBLIOGRAPHY

College Essays in Theological Anthropology (Edinburgh: T. & T. Clark, 1991).

Sher Tinsley, B., 'Sozzini's Ghost: Pierre Bayle and Socinian Toleration', *Journal of the History of Ideas*, 57 (4) (1996): 609.

Shults, F. L., *Reforming Theological Anthropology: After the Philosophical Turn to Relationality* (Grand Rapids, Mich.: Eerdmans, 2003).

Smit, P.-B., 'The Bishop and His/Her Eucharistic Community: A Critique of Jean-Luc Marion's Eucharistic Hermeneutic', *Modern Theology*, 19 (1) (2003): 29–40.

Soloviev, V., *Lectures on Divine Humanity* (God Manhood), trans. Boris Jakim (Herndon, Va.: Lindisfarne Books, 1995).

Soloviev, V., 'Three Meetings', in *Poems of Sophia*, trans. Boris Jakim and Laury Magnus (Variable Press, 1996).

Sosckice, J. M., *Metaphor and Religious Language* (Oxford: Oxford University Press, 1985).

Stead, G. C., 'Why Not Three Gods? The Logic of Gregory of Nyssa's Trinitarian Doctrine', in H. R. Drobner and C. Klock (eds), *Studien zu Gregor von Nyssa und der christlichen Spätantike* (Leiden: E. J. Brill, 1990), pp. 149–63.

Stewart, M. Y. (ed.), *The Trinity: East/West Dialogue* (Dordrecht: Kluwer Academic Publishers, 2003).

Wood, S., 'Ecclesial Koinonia in Ecumenical Dialogues', *One in Christ*, 30 (2) (1994): 124–45.

Tanner, K., *Jesus, Humanity and the Trinity: A Brief Systematic Theology* (Edinburgh: T. & T. Clark, 2001).

Tanner, M., 'Opening Remarks', in T. F. Best, and G. Gassmann (eds), *On the Way to Fuller Koinonia*, Faith and Order Paper No. 166 (Geneva: WCC, 1994), pp. 5–6.

Taylor, C., *Sources of the Self: The Making of Modern Identity* (Cambridge, Mass.: Harvard University Press, 1989).

Tertullian, *Adversus Nationes*, MPL 2.

Tertullian, *Adversus Praxeam*, MPL 2.

Theophilus of Antioch, *Apologia ad Autolycum* (Oxford: Clarendon Press, 1970).

Thornton, L. S., 'The Christian Conception of God', in E. G. Selwyn (ed.), *Essays Catholic and Critical* (London: SPCK, 1926), pp. 123–50.

Tillard, J.-M. R., *Church of Churches: The Ecclesiology of Communion* (Collegeville, Va.: The Liturgical Press, 1992).

Tillich, P., *The Courage to Be* (London: Fontana, 1962).

Tomkins, O., *The Wholeness of the Church* (London: SCM, 1949).

Torrance, A. J., *Persons in Communion: Trinitarian Description and Human Participation* (Edinburgh: T. & T. Clark, 1996).

Torrance, T. F., 'The Christian Apprehension of God the Father', in A. F. Kimel (ed.), *Speaking the Christian God: The Holy Trinity and the Challenge of Feminism* (Grand Rapids, Mich.: Eerdmans, 1992), pp. 120–43.

Torrance, T. F., 'Toward an Ecumenical Consensus on the Trinity', in *Trinitarian Perspectives: Toward Doctrinal Agreement* (Edinburgh: T. & T. Clark, 1994), pp. 77–102.

Torrance, T. F., *Trinitarian Perspectives: Toward Doctrinal Agreement* (Edinburgh: T. & T. Clark, 1994).

Turcescu, L., 'Prosopon and Hypostasis in Basil of Caesarea's Against Eunomius and the Epistles', *Vigiliae Christianae*, 51 (4) (1997): 374–95.

Turcescu, L., ' "Person" Versus "Individual", and Other Modern Misreadings of Gregory of Nyssa', in S. Coakley (ed.), *Re-Thinking Gregory of Nyssa* (Malden, Mass. and Oxford: Blackwell, 2003), pp. 97–109.

Turcescu, L., *Gregory of Nyssa and the Concept of Divine Persons* (Oxford: Oxford University Press, 2005).

Volf, M., *After Our Likeness: The Church as the Image of the Trinity* (Grand Rapids, Mich.: Eerdmans, 1998).

Wace, H. and P. Schaff (eds), *St Basil: Letters and Selected Works, A Select Library of Nicene and Post-Nicene Fathers of the Christian Church* (Grand Rapids, Mich.: Eerdmans, 1996), Vol. VIII.

Wainwright, G., *Doxology: The Praise of God in Worship, Doctrine and Life* (London: Epworth Press, 1980).

Waterland, D., *Vindication of Christ's Divinity*, 1719, in *The Works*, ed. William Van Mildert, 3 vols (Oxford: The University Press, 1843), Vol. III, pp. 1–96.

Welch, C., 'Faith and Reason: In Relation to the Doctrine of the Trinity', *Journal of Bible and Religion*, 16 (1) (1948): 21–9.

Welch, C., *In This Name: The Doctrine of the Trinity in Contemporary Theology* (New York: Charles Scribner's Sons, 1952).

Whitehead, A. N., *Process and Reality: An Essay in Cosmology* (Cambridge: Cambridge University Press, 1929).

Whitehead, A. N., *The Adventure of Ideas* (New York: Free Press, 1967).

Wilder, A., 'Community of Persons in the Thought of Karol Wojtyla', *Angelicum*, 56 (1979): 211–44.

Wiles, M., *Working Papers in Doctrine* (London: SCM, 1976).

Wilks, J. G. F., 'The Trinitarian Ontology of John Zizioulas', *Vox Evangelica*, 25 (1995): 63–88.

Williams, R., 'The Paradoxes of Self-Knowledge in the *De Trinitate*', in J. T. Lienhard, E. G. Muller, and R. J. Teske (eds), *Collectanea Augustiniana, Augustine: Presbyter Factus Sum* (New York: Peter Lang, 1993), pp. 121–34.

Williams, R., *Sergii Bulgakov: Towards a Russian Political Theology* (Edinburgh: T. & T. Clark, 1999).

Williams, R., *On Christian Theology* (Malden, Mass. and Oxford: Blackwell, 2000).

Williams, R., 'Introduction', in J. H. Newman, *The Arians of the Fourth Century* (1833) (Notre Dame, Ind.: University of Notre Dame Press, 2001), pp. xix–xlvii.

Yannaras, C., *The Ontological Content of the Theological Notion of Person* (Athens: University of Salonika, 1970).

Zimmermann, J., *Recovering Theological Hermeneutics: An Incarnational–Trinitarian Theory of Interpretation* (Grand Rapids, Mich.: Baker Academic, 2004).

Zizioulas, J. D., 'Human Capacity and Human Incapacity: A Theological

Exploration of Personhood', *Scottish Journal of Theology*, 28, (1975): 401–48.

Zizioulas, J. D., *Being as Communion: Studies in Personhood and Church* (London: Darton, Longman and Todd, 1985).

Zizioulas, J. D., 'The Ontology of Personhood', in A. I. C. Heron (ed.), *The Forgotten Trinity. 3, a Selection of Papers Presented to the BCC Study Commission on Trinitarian Doctrine Today* (London: BCC/CCBI, 1991).

Zizioulas, J. D., 'On Being a Person: Towards an Ontology of Personhood', in C. Schwöbel and C. E. Gunton (eds), *Persons, Human and Divine* (Edinburgh: T. & T. Clark, 1991), pp. 33–46.

Zizioulas, J. D., 'Communion and Otherness', Orthodox Peace Fellowship, Occasional Paper, 191 (1994).

Zizioulas, J. D., *Communion and Otherness: Further Studies in Personhood and the Church*, ed. Paul McPartlan (London: T. & T. Clark, 2006).

INDEX

Aachen (Aix-la-Chapelle) 9, 43
Abba (Father) 13, 15, 92, 136
Abhishiktananda 21
Abrahamic faiths 3
Absolute (The) 23, 24, 25, 36, 63, 65,
  66, 70, 75, 97, 104, 105, 122, 165n.
  35
Absolute Ego 63
act (divine) 26, 63, 64, 67, 69, 102,
  105, 106, 109, 111, 116
action (divine) 54, 67, 76, 100–103,
  107, 110, 111, 136
activity see: energeia
activity (divine) 6, 25, 49, 54, 56, 63,
  64, 65, 73, 92, 96, 100–104, 108,
  111, 112, 117, 124, 132
actuality 64, 92,
actus purus 26, 112, 115
Adam 126
advaita 21
advocate (Paralcete) 11, 15
Afanassieff, Nicolas 136
agape 11
agennetos see: unbegotten
aitia see: cause
alterity 119, 120, 121, 122, 123, 124,
  125, 127, 128, 142
analogy 23, 34, 65, 85, 131
apophatic 5, 21, 50, 100, 109
Apostles' Creed 47
Apostolic Age 14, 15
Aquinas, Thomas 25, 44, 45, 58, 61,
  77, 88, 96, 104, 108, 115, 122, 145
arche (Paternal) 60, 61, 62, 68, 123
Arianism 6, 38, 39, 40, 46, 48, 49, 50
Aristotle 30, 73, 101, 139
Arius 27, 38, 40, 41, 46, 48, 50, 54,
Athanasian Creed 145, 146

Athanasius 7, 9, 16, 39, 40, 41, 56,
  59, 60, 72, 73, 74, 101, 146
Auer, Johann 62
Aufhebung 113, 122, 167
Augustine of Hippo 6, 7, 25, 29, 34,
  38, 43, 48, 49, 50, 58, 59, 60, 61,
  67, 76, 77, 81, 101, 123, 124, 136

Badiou, Alain 110, 141
Balasuriya, Tissa 138
baptism 2, 10, 13, 14, 18, 19, 112,
  131, 133, 134, 148
Barnes, Michel René 5, 152
Barth, Karl 3, 25, 42, 52, 57, 63, 67,
  68, 69, 79, 80, 81, 93, 97, 98, 99,
  100, 104, 105, 106, 110, 111, 116,
  122, 133, 137, 158n. 59, 164., 20,
  165n. 34
Basil of Caesarea 18, 29, 71, 73, 77,
  150
Bayle, Pierre 40
becoming 105, 111, 112, 113
begotten (gennetos) 60, 89
Behr, John 134, 135, 136, 137
Bergson, Henri 121
Bernard of Clairvaux 145
binitarian (-ism) 13, 14
Body of Christ 16, 18, 112, 129, 131,
  134, 135, 136, 137, 141, 142
Boethius 58
Boff, Leonardo 29, 31, 32, 76, 81,
  82, 131, 132, 133
boiling see: bullitio
Bonhoeffer, Dietrich 36
Bourassa, F. 66
Braaten, Carl E. 42
Bracken, Joseph 64, 65
breathed forth (spiratio) 60, 156n. 20